# Hierarchies at Home

*Hierarchies at Home* traces the experiences of Cuban domestic workers from the abolition of slavery through the 1959 revolution. Domestic service – childcare, cleaning, chauffeuring for private homes – was both ubiquitous and ignored as formal labor in Cuba, a phenomenon made possible because of who supposedly performed it. In the Cuban imaginary, domestic workers were almost always black women, and their supposed prevalence in domestic service perpetuated the myth of racial harmony. African-descended domestic workers were "like one of the family," just as enslaved Cubans had supposedly been part of the families who owned them before slavery's abolition. This fascinating work challenges this myth, revealing how domestic workers consistently rejected their invisibility throughout the twentieth century. By following a group marginalized by racialized and gendered assumptions, Anasa Hicks destabilizes traditional analyses of Cuban history, instead offering a continuous narrative that connects pre- and post-revolutionary Cuba.

ANASA HICKS is Assistant Professor of History at Florida State University. She specializes in Latin American and Caribbean history, focusing on twentieth-century Cuba, the Hispanic Caribbean, women and gender, and labor studies.

# Afro-Latin America

*Series editors*

George Reid Andrews, *University of Pittsburgh*
Alejandro de la Fuente, *Harvard University*

This series reflects the coming of age of the new, multidisciplinary field of Afro-Latin American Studies, which centers on the histories, cultures, and experiences of people of African descent in Latin America. The series aims to showcase scholarship produced by different disciplines, including history, political science, sociology, ethnomusicology, anthropology, religious studies, art, law, and cultural studies. It covers the full temporal span of the African Diaspora in Latin America, from the early colonial period to the present and includes continental Latin America, the Caribbean, and other key areas in the region where Africans and their descendants have made a significant impact.

*A full list of titles published in the series can be found at:*
www.cambridge.org/afro-latin-america

# Hierarchies at Home

## Domestic Service in Cuba from Abolition to Revolution

**ANASA HICKS**

*Florida State University*

CAMBRIDGE
UNIVERSITY PRESS

## CAMBRIDGE
### UNIVERSITY PRESS

Shaftesbury Road, Cambridge CB2 8EA, United Kingdom

One Liberty Plaza, 20th Floor, New York, NY 10006, USA

477 Williamstown Road, Port Melbourne, VIC 3207, Australia

314–321, 3rd Floor, Plot 3, Splendor Forum, Jasola District Centre, New Delhi – 110025, India

103 Penang Road, #05–06/07, Visioncrest Commercial, Singapore 238467

Cambridge University Press is part of Cambridge University Press & Assessment, a department of the University of Cambridge.

We share the University's mission to contribute to society through the pursuit of education, learning and research at the highest international levels of excellence.

www.cambridge.org
Information on this title: www.cambridge.org/9781009074513

DOI: 10.1017/9781009070577

First published 2022
First paperback edition 2024

*A catalogue record for this publication is available from the British Library*

*Library of Congress Cataloging-in-Publication data*
NAMES: Hicks, Anasa, 1989– author.
TITLE: Hierarchies at home : domestic service in Cuba from abolition to revolution / Anasa Hicks, Florida State University.
DESCRIPTION: Cambridge, United Kingdom ; New York, NY : Cambridge University Press, 2022. | Series: Afro-Latin America. | Includes bibliographical references and index.
IDENTIFIERS: LCCN 2021063039 (print) | LCCN 2021063040 (ebook) | ISBN 9781316513651 (hardback) | ISBN 9781009074513 (paperback) | ISBN 9781009070577 (epub)
SUBJECTS: LCSH: Household employees–Cuba–Social conditions. | Women, Black–Cuba–Social conditions. | Cuba–History–1895– | BISAC: HISTORY / Latin America / General
CLASSIFICATION: LCC HD8039.D52 C943 2022 (print) | LCC HD8039.D52 (ebook) | DDC 640/.46097291–DC23/eng/20220301
LC record available at https://lccn.loc.gov/2021063039
LC ebook record available at https://lccn.loc.gov/2021063040

ISBN    978-1-316-51365-1    Hardback
ISBN    978-1-009-07451-3    Paperback

*To my parents, Brenda Sherard Hicks and Roderick Hicks, for always asking the right questions*

# Contents

# Figures

# Tables

# Acknowledgments

Officially, this book is the result of six years of work on a doctoral dissertation and four years of revisions, and of the brilliance and support of so many people in New York City, Havana, Miami, Tallahassee, and Palo Alto, to name just a few places. Unofficially, this book is the result of a childhood filled with books that my parents gave me, books that vividly chronicled African-American history, books in which I was able to see myself. I have never questioned whether the stories of African-descended people are worth telling because from the beginning my family told me that they were. To them I am most grateful. My parents, to whom this book is dedicated, have made all of this possible. I thank them for the kind of faith it is possible only for parents to have in their children, and I thank my brother, Kai Hicks, for finding academia an absurd career choice but being proud of me anyway.

I am grateful to my advisers and mentors at New York University (NYU). Ada Ferrer is everything that I could ask for in this regard. Her feedback on my writing and on my career has been invaluable. I'm also grateful to Barbara Weinstein for all I've learned in the classes I've taken from her and the many conversations we've had. I would also like to thank the rest of NYU's history faculty – especially Sinclair Thomson, Jennifer Morgan, and Greg Grandin – and the professors who guided my path outside of NYU, including Lillian Guerra, Marial Iglesias Utset, Nara Milanich, and Premilla Nadasen.

I also want to thank my colleagues in the history department at Florida State University for their support and community as I transitioned from graduate school to my first academic job. Outside of the history department, I would like to thank John Ribó and Jeannine Murray-Román for our many fruitful conversations about this project. Additionally, I am so grateful for the friends I've made in Tallahassee, who are too many to name here, for making a city whose name I could once barely spell feel like home in a few short years.

Henry Heredia and the staff at Juan Marinello Institute in Havana have been arranging my travel to Cuba and sponsoring the visa I needed to do research since 2012. I thank Henry especially for his kindness and generosity. I'm grateful to the staff at the National Archives of Cuba in Havana, the Provincial Historical Archives of Santiago de Cuba, and the National Library for their support. For providing me with food and shelter, I thank Celia Rosa Soto, Rafael Pérez, Ignacio and Carmen Vargas, and Agnes Renault and Osvaldo. For their help with my dissertation, I want to thank María del Pilar Díaz Castañon, Maria del Carmen Barcia, Oilda Hevia Lanier, and Olga Portuondo. For their companionship and support during my research trips to Cuba, I thank Elizabeth Schwall, Alexander Sotelo Eastman, and Andy Martínez.

I am grateful to series editors Alejandro de la Fuente and George Reid Andrews and to the editorial staff at Cambridge University Press, in particular Cecelia Cancellaro, for bringing this book to fruition. Alejandro has been supportive of this project since its existence as a dissertation, and I am thrilled for it to have found a home in the Afro-Latin America series. I also thank the anonymous readers at Cambridge University Press, whose comments made this book immeasurably better.

I would like to thank the staff at the Cuban Heritage Collection (CHC) at the University of Miami for their consistent support of my research. The CHC was one of the first places I did research for this project, and access to their wonderful archives has been invaluable to the development of my dissertation. I would also like to thank the Florida Education Fund for their support as I completed this book.

I am grateful to the entirety of the cohort that entered NYU with me in 2011 – especially Alaina Morgan, Tony Andersson, Dominique Jean-Louis, Emma Otheguy, Tej Nagaraja, and Jeannette Estruth. I also want to thank Joan Flores-Villalobos and Rachel Nolan for their friendship and their comments on my work. There are also former graduate students (now professors) from NYU and elsewhere who were so generous with their advice: Greg Childs, Daniel Rodríguez, Michelle Chase, Jennifer Lambe, Mike Bustamante, Elena Schneider, Adriana Chira, Bonnie Lucero, and David Sartorius. Thank you.

I fell in love with Cuba in Chapel Hill, North Carolina, and for that I must thank Louis A. Pérez, Jr. He plucked me from his undergraduate course of more than fifty people and suggested that I might be interested in writing a thesis, in applying to graduate school, in academia. His critique of my writing was most often that my own voice was impossible to detect. I am endlessly grateful for the faith he had in me and in my perspective.

Finally, thank you to my husband, Eli Wilkins-Malloy, whose unwavering support of me and this project has materially affected him much more than it has the other people I've thanked. Our life together, wherever it is, brings me joy and comfort on a daily basis.

# Author's Note

Something that makes discussions of race in Cuba even more complicated than they inherently are is the decision one must make regarding terminology. Whenever possible, I use the terms that people chose to describe their own racial identities or the terms that appear in documents related to specific persons. However, when writing more generally I use the terms "black" and "African-descended" frequently and somewhat interchangeably. This decision is not faithful to a direct translation from Spanish, since *negra* (black) means and meant a quite different racial category than *parda, mulata,* or *mestiza* – to list some racial terms that implied mixed (as opposed to "pure") African descent. In part, I use "black" and "African-descended" for convenience; but it is also part of my argument in *Hierarchies at Home* that people of any amount of African descent were, regardless of skin tone, frequently grouped together by elites and by the government. This was particularly true as it related to domestic service. Thus, readers should not read the term "black" as *negra* in the Cuban sense – meaning a specific racial category connoting very dark skin and kinky hair, distinct from a person who would be described as *mulata* – but rather as an umbrella term to describe all people who would identify as being, in some measure, of African descent.

Recently it has become standard across English-language media to capitalize the "B" in "black." As a Black woman, I celebrate the evolution of style to reflect the dignity of Black Americans. However, I have chosen not to capitalize "black" in this book. I use the word as an umbrella term, already translating from Spanish to English, and realize that many people in this book who fall under the category of "black" might not themselves identify as "Black." I believe that to identify as "Black" has political connotations – ones with which I identify. I do not want to make that decision for my subjects, whose voices have already been so muted.

# Introduction

## The Violent Intimacy of Nation-Building, Race, and Gender Inside Cuban Households

Five or ten years after Cuba became independent from Spain, a young girl in Havana played a trick on a family maid. The girl and the maid, Cleta, fought constantly, and one day the girl devised a plan to avenge herself. Cleta was "blacker than a jetstone," and – seeing Cleta "so black, so black, wearing such a white, starched uniform" – it occurred to the girl to throw flour all over the maid. She knew that it was wrong even as she took the flour, but she couldn't resist the impulse to commit what she called "whiteicide." The girl executed her plan and threw the flour all over Cleta, who of course was furious and humiliated. Even as Cleta marched to the girl's father to tell him what his daughter had done, the girl followed behind her, cackling with mirth. The girl's father sent her to her room right away, and later her mother came in to explain why what she did was wrong. Her mother reproached her because Cleta loved them so much and had been so humiliated by having a face full of flour. When her mother said, "poor Cleta," the girl immediately had a change of heart. She felt horrible. She apologized to Cleta, who forgave her. (The girl's father still grounded her for two weeks.)[1]

We have this story not because of who Cleta was but because of who the girl tormenting her grew up to be: the famed anthropologist of Afro-Cuban life and folklore, Lydia Cabrera. Cabrera attributed her initial interest in Afro-Cuban religion and culture to the domestic staff of her childhood, and she often referenced her own nursemaid, Tula, with extreme affection. Despite her love for Tula, however,

---

[1] Undated Interview, Box 13, Folder 7, Lydia Cabrera Collection, Cuban Heritage Collection (CHC), University of Miami, 119.

Cabrera was obviously not immune to petty displays of power over her family's domestic staff when she was young. The redemption arc Cabrera gives herself reflects her mastery as a storyteller – just as quickly as we witness her youthful cruelty, we see her contrition – but the fact remains that Cabrera was compelled to shower her extremely dark-skinned maid in white flour to highlight just how far away she was from whiteness.

Cleta was older than Cabrera's father, the historian Raimundo Cabrera, who was born in 1852 in the western city of Güines. Cleta was also from Güines.[2] Thus, it is probable that Cleta was born enslaved and possible that she was enslaved by the Cabreras before they employed her. More than a story about a privileged young girl's mischief, this story is about legacies of enslavement and violence. In the 1960s, Cabrera herself would insist that domestic service had *benign* roots in Cuba's slave past, that enslaved domestics were beloved members of elite white families. But her own memory contradicts her. Cabrera's act of "whiteicide" against Cleta was a cruel prank, not the kind of brutal violence that was definitional to slavery. But Cleta, likely formerly enslaved, might have experienced that kind of violence as well. Would she have drawn a connection between attacks that left a scar and those that left her "white?"

There is no shortage of books on Cuba's independence struggles, and a plethora of studies inspired by and drawing on Cabrera's work has bolstered her well-deserved reputation as a pioneering intellectual. Cleta, however, lacks context in Cuban historiography. This victim of "whiteicide" – and other workers like her – were important not just to Cuban households but to Cuban identity in the twentieth century. *Hierarchies at Home: Domestic Service in Cuba from Abolition to Revolution* gives Cleta her due. For some sixty years, domestic service sustained Cuban households and sustained a façade of racial harmony in Cuba. In those same sixty years, domestic servants asserted their citizenship and their value as workers – actions that challenged the façade that their work upheld. In exploring the myth and the reality of domestic service in Cuba, *Hierarchies at Home* reveals that intimate relationships between domestics and their employers folded racialized and gendered hierarchies into *cubanidad* – the condition of being Cuban – throughout the twentieth century.

[2] Ibid.

## I.I DOMESTICS AND THE MYTH OF RACIAL HARMONY

Domestic servants – people I define broadly as those who were paid to sustain a private household through cooking, cleaning, childcare, and other tasks – were an integral part of the ideal Cuban family. Symbolically, domestic servants in post-emancipation Cuba were almost always women of African descent. The myth of domestic service being entirely performed by black women – perpetuated in legal documents, political discussions, newspapers, and magazines – was an essential component of the larger myth of Cuban racial harmony. For most of the twentieth century Cubans told themselves and the outside world that relations between African- and European-descended citizens were benign, even affectionate; and the performance of intimate labor for white Cubans by black Cubans bolstered that argument. Cubans presented evidence that for centuries the work that black Cuban women performed for white Cuban families tied the groups together into a happy family. Therefore, Cuban society itself was a happy family.[3] This image of the black domestic servant as "one of the family" naturalized racial hierarchies that flourished alongside ideas about racial harmony in twentieth-century Cuba.

Importantly, however, Cubans' racialized and gendered perception of who comprised the domestic servant workforce was frequently statistically incorrect. For example, until the 1940s most domestic workers were men who cooked, gardened, and acted as butlers and drivers in private homes.[4] The ranks of domestic workers in Cuba actually declined steadily in the first half of the twentieth century – from 23 percent of the working population in 1899 to just 3 percent by 1943. At their peak in that same year, black women only ever comprised 40 percent of the domestic service workforce.[5] African-descended women did not actually dominate in domestic service to the degree that sources about domestic service would

---

[3] "First, the family offered an indispensable figure for sanctioning social hierarchy within a putative organic unity of interests. Because the subordination of woman to man and child to adult were deemed natural facts, other forms of social hierarchy could be depicted in familial terms to guarantee social difference as a category of nature." McClintock, *Imperial Leather*, 45.

[4] United States War Department, *Report on the Census of Cuba, 1899*, 403–404; *Censo de la república de Cuba, 1907*, 508–510; *Census of the Republic of Cuba, 1919*, 380.

[5] This was in 1943. White women – native and foreign – comprised 35 percent of the workforce, with men comprising the remaining 25 percent. Junta Nacional del Censo, *República de Cuba, Censo de 1943*, 1112–1114.

have us believe; but their overrepresentation in such discourse betrays an important truth. The real and symbolic employment of African-descended women as servants in private homes was essential to maintain the gendered and racialized hierarchies that had defined the sugar plantations and urban streets of colonial Cuba. That the *real* domestic servants who cleaned, cooked, and cared for the vulnerable would increasingly challenge their labor conditions and those lurking hierarchies was, perhaps, an unforeseen obstacle to the maintenance of class stratifications.

To study domestic service in Cuba is to witness a process of racialization as it happened, or failed to. *Hierarchies at Home* illuminates and problematizes the trope of the black *doméstica* in Cuba. The trope is not unique to Cuba: The image of a nurturing black woman who cares for a white family pervades post-slavery societies in the Americas. However, the stereotype in Cuba never reached the level of popularity that it did in other post-slavery societies – in Cuba there were never any statues dedicated to the "black nanny," as there were in Brazil.[6] The stereotype of the black *doméstica* rests on shaky ground, made all the more so by the 1959 Revolution and its rejection of the racism and classism of republican Cuba. In the disparity between the racial idea of domestic service and the reality, we find the attempt at racializing the work a process often made invisible by its own success. Other historians of race in Cuba and Latin America have brilliantly examined the impact of racialized stereotypes on African-descended people; *Hierarchies at Home* traces the effort to create one such stereotype.

As domestic servants participated in protests and work stoppages, elites recoiled at their behavior and grew nostalgic for the servants of yesteryear. In the 1870s, conservatives longed for the enslaved domestics of the 1840s; in the 1940s, the same people longed for the *criadas* (maids) of the 1920s. In Santiago de Cuba in 2015, a white woman told me that her grandmother's servants' respect and decorum were a positive legacy of slavery. The expression of longing for a "simpler time" of abject obedience from servants was a safe way to long for a bright line separating black and white Cubans.[7] Such racialized nostalgia, of course, reveals the lie of the myth of racial harmony: African-descended Cubans never passively accepted their inferior status. The ubiquity of such nostalgia throughout the twentieth century clues us in to the reality that in terms of race and labor, there was never a "simpler time."

---

[6] See McElya, *Clinging to Mammy*; Seigel, *Uneven Encounters*.
[7] For a US example, see Wallace-Sanders, *Mammy*.

*Hierarchies at Home* highlights the violence of intimacy inherent to domestic service in Cuba. The physically and emotionally close relationships between employers and employees both masked and enabled physical and rhetorical violence against those employees. The insistence that "yesterday's servants" were like family suggested that, like family, no legal regulations should guide or control their treatment. Elites and conservatives in Cuba deployed the supposed intimacy of the domestic service relationship to argue against and obstruct labor protections for domestic workers. This book does not argue that such intimacy was not really there. The love that many Cubans felt for their domestics and that many domestics reciprocated is palpable and present throughout this book. Rather, *Hierarchies at Home* argues that, in the case of servants, love was often tinged with possession. Possession translated to consistent resistance to acknowledgment of domestic service as formal labor, which led to material conditions that made life difficult for many servants. The violence of intimacy had concrete consequences for domestic workers in Cuba.

## I.2 CUBAN LABOR, RACE, AND DOMESTIC SERVICE'S EXCLUSION

Throughout the twentieth century, domestic servants in Cuba strove for legislative protection and failed to achieve it. They unionized and received no recognition from the federal government. While many domestic servants were not black women, the gendered racialization of the work beyond its demographic reality allowed for domestics' exclusion from formal labor politics in Cuba. Domestic servants who were not black women – black, white, and East Asian men, and Spanish women – found their work and their bodies denigrated to match the disdain that many elites felt for black women. The work's association with African-descended women rendered it "informal" and "unskilled" labor, just as domestic service's association with women has done in many other parts of the world.[8]

In Cuba, the casting of domestic service as informal and unskilled was purposeful. Domestics' familial status reinforced Cuba's national

---

[8] Domestic service is not gendered female everywhere: In many parts of Africa, for example, domestic service is closely associated with men. See Pariser, "Masculinity and Organized Resistance in Domestic Service in Colonial Dar es Salaam, 1919–1961," 109–129; Hansen, "Household Work as a Man's Job," 18–23.

self-image as a racial democracy. If domestics became workers, with their labor acknowledged as skilled or valuable, what would become of the hierarchies so easily distilled into the image of a black maid with a white family? It mattered little that many domestic servants were Spanish immigrant women, and that many more were men. Domestic service's failure to receive legislative protection and domestics' failure to unionize was directly related to the perceived predominance of women of African descent in the field. The association of domestic service with African-descended women was rooted in the island's very recent past of plantation slavery.

While they rarely statistically dominated domestic service overall, the majority of working African-descended women in Cuba *were* domestic servants throughout the twentieth century. What we find if we excavate working black women's experiences is that far from happily serving as wet-nurses, handmaids and laundresses to white families throughout the twentieth century, domestic workers organized and made increasingly radical demands over that exact time period. Despite the intimate and supposedly quasi-familial nature of the work, domestics in Cuba understood their labor as *work* and agitated for formal protections. Even those servants who most closely resembled the demographic stereotypes imposed on all domestic workers were not compliant, submissive, or "part of the family."

Activism on behalf of and spearheaded by domestic servants grew slowly throughout the twentieth century, in tandem with labor activism in other fields. Unlike other workers, though, domestics never received the labor protections they sought. Reforms that emerged from a political revolution in 1933 excluded domestic workers even as they protested in sympathy with other laborers and organized among themselves. Although several groups called for the passage of protective laws for domestic workers at the 1940 Constitutional Convention, no mention was made of them in the constitution. And finally, after Fidel Castro and the 26th of July movement toppled Batista's presidency in January of 1959, the government chose to eradicate domestic service entirely rather than legislate and regulate it by opening schools to retrain domestics in occupations more appropriate to a society in the process of transcending class.

By declining to legislate on domestic service, the Cuban government ensured that much of its population of color and especially women of color would be subject to abuse and neglect by the very same people who claimed that the archetypal domestic service relationship was one of love and closeness. *Hierarchies at Home* elucidates how, among other strategies, the rhetorical use of intimacy kept black Cubans and immigrant men and women physically and legally vulnerable in a society that was supposed to be free of discrimination. In tracing domestic service over much of a century, *Hierarchies at Home* follows the efforts of some of Cuba's most marginalized citizens in their daily maneuvering to survive. It traces domestic workers' efforts not just to survive but to take advantage of Cuban citizenship. As it tells the story of domestic service in Cuba, it tells the story of Cuba itself. The relationship between servant and employer that defined domestic service was a synecdoche for race relations within the Cuban nation and therefore a primary site for the anxieties that Cubans felt about historical change.

## I.3 DOMESTIC SERVICE AND CHRONOLOGY: AN ALTERNATIVE TIMELINE OF THE CUBAN TWENTIETH CENTURY

The myth of the black female domestic servant in twentieth-century Cuba had foundations in the island's slave society past: Before slavery's abolition in 1886, enslaved people performed the reproductive labor necessary to keep sugar and coffee plantations functioning. In the late twentieth century, some Cubans could trace the genealogies of their families' domestic workers back to their ancestors' enslavement of African and African-descended captives.[9] The archetype of a beloved enslaved *nodriza* (wet-nurse) or *nana* (nanny) became particularly pervasive in the island's republican era. Images of happy plantation families comprised of masters and slaves underscored nostalgic longing for docile domestic servants in the twentieth century and helped the image of the black *doméstica* persist even when most domestic workers were men. A brief engagement with the colonial history of domestic service and slavery reveals that such longing was for a time that never existed. The disparity between the memory and reality of colonial slavery paralleled the disparity between the memory and reality of domestic service in the twentieth century.

Cuba was a slave society by the end of the eighteenth century, almost entirely dependent on the production of sugar by enslaved workers. As the enslaved population grew, Spanish colonial authorities attempted to

---

[9] Adriana Fernández-Silva told the story of her nanny, María de los Reyes, to StoryCorps in 2010. María de los Reyes was born to an enslaved domestic servant in Cuba. When slavery was abolished, María's mother stayed on with the family who had enslaved her, and, eventually, María de los Reyes became a nanny to the children of her mothers' charges. StoryCorps Historias Interview with Adriana Fernández-Silva, 2010, http://merrick .library.miami.edu/cdm/ref/collection/chc5246/id/294.

more explicitly control the kinds of labor enslaved people could perform. The 1789 Slave Code clarified that their primary vocation would be in field labor "and not the trades associated with sedentary life." Owners of domestic slaves were obliged to pay an additional tax of two pesos per month to the Spanish government.[10] Over the course of Cuba's transformation from a marginally relevant Spanish colony to a major source of income for Spain, "productive labor" took clear precedence over the reproductive and domestic labor that enslaved domestics performed.

In the nineteenth century, the ranks of domestics diversified: Free domestic service coexisted alongside enslaved domestic service. Free women of African descent worked as cooks, laundresses, and seamstresses. Men, too, advertised themselves as available to perform work as cooks, handservants, and house cleaners.[11] The island's Spanish governor forced soldiers to find other work when there was no military activity; thus, off-duty Spanish soldiers regularly worked as domestic servants.[12] Chinese "coolie" laborers, too, worked as domestics. Between 1848 and 1888 more than two million Chinese men traveled to the Americas to work on plantations, on railroads, and in mines.[13] Once their contracts were up, many Chinese became cooks in private homes. They had a reputation for being excellent chefs and skilled imitators of *criollo* cuisine.[14]

As independence movements gained traction in Cuba and became increasingly tied to abolitionist sentiment, Spain began to court the loyalty of enslaved people. The Spanish government passed the 1870 Moret Law, stipulating that children born to enslaved women after the law's passage were free, two years into an independence war that saw huge numbers of enslaved men and women flee their plantations to fight on the side of the rebels.[15] In February of 1880, Spain promulgated the Law of the Abolition of Slavery. For a period of eight years, former slaves would work for wages under their former owners as a way of slowly transitioning to freedom. Under the institution of the *Patronato, patrones* (patrons, or former owners) still had rights to the labor of their former slaves, but

[10] "Royal Decree and Instructional Circular for the Indies on the Regulation, Treatment and Work Regimen of Slaves," in *Voices of the Enslaved*, 49.

[11] Franklin, *Women and Slavery in Nineteenth-Century Colonial Cuba*, 132–133.

[12] Casanovas, *Bread, or Bullets!*, 62.     [13] López, *Chinese Cubans*, introduction.

[14] For examples of this stereotype, see Ripley, *From Flag to Flag*; Skelly, *I Remember Cuba*.

[15] Scott, *Slave Emancipation in Cuba*, 64. For a transnational database of "free womb" laws across the Americas, see Yesenia Barragán's Free Womb Project, https://thefreewombproject.com/.

they had slightly more responsibilities to the *patrocinados* (apprentices, formerly enslaved). *Patrones* had to feed, clothe, and medically care for *patrocinados* and their children. They also had to educate young *patrocinados*, and they had to pay former slaves over the age of eighteen a monthly stipend. Failure to fulfill those responsibilities could result in the premature freeing of *patrocinados*. So too could mutual agreement by *patrono* and *patrocinado* and the renunciation of a *patrocinado* by his or her *patrono*. The Spanish government abolished slavery completely just six years after the *Patronato* was introduced, not eight years as was originally planned.[16]

During the Ten Years' War (1868–1878), military leaders had been ambivalent about their cause's relationship to black liberation and racial equality, but the decade after that war's end had seen a decisive turn in the racial ideas of Cuba's most prominent *independentistas*. Cuba's last war for independence began nine years after abolition, in 1895. This new independence struggle was explicitly anti-racist, drawing on a "raceless" brotherhood among (male) Cubans who demanded sovereignty and were willing to pay in blood.[17] The war's brutality, and especially the plight of the *reconcentrados* – peasants rounded up from the countryside and placed in unsanitary and cramped camps on the outskirts of cities – captured the imagination of the American press and lent legitimacy to the US government's long-standing desire to take control of Cuba. In August of 1898, Cuba's struggle for independence ended strangely: Spain surrendered not to the Cuban rebels but to the US military, which had declared war on the European nation just three months prior. Cubans emerged from the war no longer colonial subjects, but not quite citizens either.

Cubans would have to grapple with their new status as a nation and the long legacy of slavery at the same time. Thirty years of war and attempts at gradual abolition had revealed the lie of docilely enslaved Africans; the dawn of a republic would coincide with the growing pains of a newly free labor system. The United States, functionally Cuba's new metropole, worried in particular about the "work ethic" of formerly enslaved women: A US consul reporting from the province of Cienfuegos in 1884 wrote that "in Cuba, as in the United States, the negro women on being freed are disposed to withdraw from field labor

---

[16] Scott, *Slave Emancipation in Cuba*.     [17] See Ferrer, *Insurgent Cuba*.

and devote themselves to household work."[18] All over the post-slavery Americas, formerly enslaved women withdrew from the labor expected of them. The rejection of bound service must have been felt most acutely in the case of domestics, whose job it was to care for their employers "like one of the family."[19] Late nineteenth-century ambivalence and concern about black women's work in particular echoed in the contradictory demographics and stereotypes of domestic servants in the first half of the twentieth century.

Throughout this book, readers will find noticeable disparities between census data and the discourse around domestic service: Most strikingly, almost none of the sources in this book discuss male domestic service. Men were a majority of domestic servants until the 1940s (and a stark majority in the depths of the Great Depression), and the group most associated with domestic service – black women – moved in and out of the work in the first half of the twentieth century, as did foreign-born white women. Additionally, in the first half of the twentieth century the ranks of servants in Cuba steadily declined. The chapters that follow will delve more deeply into these trends. But *Hierarchies at Home* will show that the numbers elucidated in Tables I.1 and I.2[20] were not tied to the social realities that Cubans themselves created. As the work became less demographically relevant to Cuban society, its cultural importance grew: Some of the most frenzied debates about domestic service occurred in the decade when the smallest-ever number of Cubans worked in the field. The myth of domestic service was absolutely essential to maintaining Cuba's racialized and gendered hierarchy. The raceless *cubanidad* the island publicly espoused and the racially stratified counter-*cubanidad* that domestic service upheld ran on parallel tracks, each ensuring the other's continued course over decades.

The Cuban nation that the heroes of the independence wars envisioned in 1898 looked very different from what conspirators fought for in the

---

[18] United States Consular Reports, *Labor in America, Asia, Africa, Australia, and Polynesia*, 253.

[19] Don Francisco Baguer, in his quest to retain Donata as a *patrocinada*, argued precisely that she had been raised from a young age as though she were "one of the family." "Demanda de D. Francisco Baguer contra una resolución de la Junta de Patronato de esta Provincia por la que se declara escenta del mismo en la patrocinada Donata," 5 diciembre 1882, Fondo Consejo de Adminstración, Legajo 88 Num. 8101, ANC.

[20] For both charts, see United States War Department, *Report on the Census of Cuba, 1899*; *Censo de la república de Cuba, 1907*; *Census of the Republic of Cuba, 1919*; *Censo de población, Estadísticas industrial y Agrícola de Cuba, 1931*; República de Cuba, *Informe General del Censo de 1943*.

TABLE I.I. *Composition of domestic service workforce, 1899–1943*

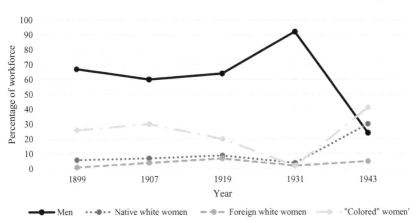

TABLE I.2. *Percentages of domestic workers within working populations, 1899–1943*

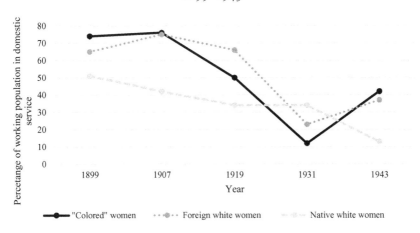

1933 uprising against Machado, which was again different from what rebels planned in 1959. But domestic service, perpetually necessary, cut across these distinctions. The ebb and flow in representation of various groups in the domestic service workforce, elucidated in Tables I.1 and I.2, suggest alternative dividing lines for twentieth-century Cuban history. *Hierarchies at Home*, while it is a twentieth-century story, reaches back to narratives from the nineteenth century and moves past 1959 to follow the trajectory of domestic workers. The book thinks across years typically used as points of division, finding continuities between eras of enslavement, rebellion, republicanism, and revolution.

## 1.4 DEFINING DOMESTICITY: A BRIEF REVIEW OF THE LITERATURE

The intimate nature of domestic service contributes to ambiguity about what domestic service *is*, who performs it, and what relationship those performing it have to the people for whom they work. Such ambiguity reinforces intimate ties between servants and employers, as they must negotiate to work out the terms of the labor. To investigate this relationship between ambiguity, intimacy, and power as fully as possible, *Hierarchies at Home* adopts an expansive definition of domestic service. In her political history of reproductive labor in the United States, Laura Briggs defines such labor as "the work necessary to the reproduction of human life – not only having and raising children but also feeding people, caring for the sick, the elderly, and those who cannot work; creating safety and shelter; building community and kin relationships; and attending to people's psychic and spiritual well-being."[21] *Hierarchies at Home*, then, defines domestic service as reproductive labor for pay, in private homes.

My definition of domestic service, drawn from an application of reproductive labor to the category, owes much to feminist political theorists, who have been writing about the topic for decades. However, the work of some feminist scholars who have developed this understanding of reproductive labor envisions an ideal world in which domestic service is obsolete. If the neoliberal world order – in which all people work increasingly long hours while pay stagnates – were transformed, the logic goes, then the performance of reproductive labor for money would become irrelevant.[22] Such a vision is not utopian for domestic worker activists.

[21] Briggs, *How All Politics Became Reproductive Politics*, 2.
[22] Kathi Weeks's formulation of work versus not-work, for example, puts reproductive labor squarely in the category of what ideally would be understood as not-work; and while Briggs devotes a chapter to domestic workers' relationship to wealthy Americans, she is critical of the need for paid domestic service at all. I understand that both of these are critiques of capitalism in its twenty-first-century iteration, but I maintain that both critiques ignore the fact that many domestic workers want labor protection, not the full dissolution of their work. See Weeks, *The Problem with Work*; Briggs, *How All Politics Became Reproductive Politics*.

Other scholars of paid and unpaid reproductive labor highlight the pitfalls of global compartmentalization of paid reproductive labor as "not-work" while lifting up the voices of domestic servants who want not the elimination of their labor field but respect for it as difficult and valuable.[23] So, while I employ an expansive definition of reproductive labor to categorize what domestics servants did in Cuba throughout the twentieth century, I also highlight that domestic servants in Cuba increasingly engaged in activism as workers throughout the same decade. They wanted their work recognized, not erased.

Increasingly after the 1970s, historians of Latin American women's labor showed that female workers in fields ranging from textiles to meatpacking to prostitution regularly organized and demanded rights for themselves. They exposed the often-false dichotomy between the public and private spheres as working women negotiated their professional and personal lives in ways that shaped the factory, the street, and the home.[24] Classic books about domestic service in Latin America – including the anthology *Muchachas No More: Household Workers in Latin America and the Caribbean* and the monograph *House and Street: The Domestic World of Servants and Masters in Nineteenth-Century Rio de Janeiro* – built on such pioneering work, carrying interventions about women's work into the field of domestic service. In private homes as in factories, "*muchachas*" across Latin America did advocate for themselves and organize when possible. Studies of enslaved domestic service also applied the questions of labor to a nineteenth-century context, joining together labor and slavery studies in new ways.

A special edition of the *Hispanic American Historical Review* (*HAHR*) in 2011 "historicize[d] the interplay between public and private in shaping Latin America's uneven and often ambivalent experience of commodifying reproductive labor."[25] Articles on paid reproductive labor in Chile, Mexico, and Argentina linked the history of reproductive labor with historiography on modernization, state formation, and family relationships in Latin America. *Hierarchies at Home* is indebted to this project of inserting the "problem" of reproductive labor into sociopolitical histories of Latin America. This book argues not only that

---

[23] Parreñas and Boris, *Intimate Labors*; Premilla Nadasen, *Household Workers Unite*.
[24] See Dias, trans. Ann Frost, *Power and Everyday Life*; French and James, eds. *The Gendered World of Latin American Women Workers*.
[25] Olcott, "Introduction," 2.

the history of domestic service in Cuba provides a narrative counter to the nationalist narrative of racial democracy but also that this counter-narrative made the myth of racial democracy possible. *Hierarchies at Home* also addresses lacunae that Jocelyn Olcott named in her introduction to the 2011 *HAHR*: race and sexual violence. Racial hierarchies are a primary concern of this book, and throughout I highlight intersections with and connections between domestic service, sex work, and sexual predation. The arguments I make about race and sex are what allow me to understand domestic service from the perspective of intimacy and power.

*Hierarchies at Home* is a history of a labor field whose centrality to the global economy increases daily. In the twenty-first century, women travel from their rural homes to urban centers, from impoverished nations like the Philippines to wealthy regions like western Europe, to clean, cook, and care for infants and elders. These migration flows demonstrate the profoundly essential nature of the work domestic servants have always done and continue to do. The abuse these women endure demonstrates that nations all over the world continue to decline to protect labor considered unskilled or informal. The book helps us understand how the work can be simultaneously so important *and* so denigrated. In its focus on Cuban domestic service in history, *Hierarchies at Home* calls attention to the need for careful analysis of the contemporary structural impediments to protection of domestic servants worldwide and offers a model for such studies.

In this book, the erasure of domestic servants from the field of labor is as much a methodological concern as a political one. It is a history of people never intended to be subjects of historical inquiry. No archive I visited had a collection dedicated to domestic service or domestic servants. Thus, this manuscript utilizes a wide array of often unlikely sources. Knowing that most working black women were domestics in the first half of the twentieth century, I searched for them in the archive, hoping that would lead me to evidence of domestic servants. I looked for documentation of labor unrest, hoping that someone would document the activities of servants. I looked in criminal records, wondering if I might find evidence of conflict between maids and employers. Sometimes my instincts were correct; more frequently, I was surprised by the sources I found that mentioned domestic workers. In searching for historical evidence of a field of labor considered so ubiquitous that it was invisible, I had to look everywhere. Thus, the archive I have created spans 100 years and includes criminal cases, doctors' advice on breastfeeding, letters written to CIA-backed counterrevolutionary organizations, and more.

The subaltern school of history has "read against the grain," excavating the stories of marginalized people from documents inherently hostile to their cause, to great effect. *Hierarchies at Home* "reads along the bias grain" to follow black female domestics. Reading along the bias grain entails challenging the hegemonic narrative of archival documents, seeking to center the subject of interest – in this case, the domestic worker – while interrogating the very composition of the archives that would obscure her and acknowledging the violence of that obscurity.[26] Along the bias grain, I find that discourses about black female servitude underpinned elite visions for Cuba's future at every point of its present. In examining the provenance of my sources as much as their content, we see that domestic service was central to questions of economy, foreign policy, crime, and politics in Cuba. Domestic workers appear in court cases, in lists of civic organizations, in condescending missives about appropriate behavior, in pleas for reform before constitutional committees. *Hierarchies at Home* employs legal, cultural, and social history sources to excavate their stories.

Throughout the book, I refer to my subjects as domestics, domestic servants, and domestic workers, and by their specific positions if I know them: maids, cooks, nannies, laundresses. In Spanish, these women were referred to as *criadas, sirvientas, trabajadoras domésticas*, and *domésticas* (maids, servants, domestic workers, and domestics). Sometimes, documents (especially court cases) are ambiguous about women's occupations. I lean into that ambiguity rather than banishing it from my analysis because of the ambiguity of working-class Cuban women's lives. Working-class women in Cuba moved in and out of different occupations, ones that often included domestic service. As Eileen Findlay found in the case of late-colonial Puerto Rico, poor women in the Spanish Caribbean did a great number of things to stay afloat financially, and I am inclined to be broad rather than narrow in my notion of who was a domestic.[27]

The field of labor history has much to gain, conceptually and theoretically, from letting domestic workers in: While neither the pre- nor the post-revolutionary Cuban state ever successfully regulated domestics' actions *as workers*, domestics in Cuba behaved like other workers.

---

[26] Fuentes, *Dispossessed Lives*, 7; see also Stoler, *Along the Archival Grain*.
[27] Findlay, *Imposing Decency*.

They negotiated for better conditions, quit bad jobs to find better ones, and acted in solidarity with people in other labor fields. But even as we add domestics to the category of workers, it's important to interrogate the standards by which we identify "workers" and the value that nations place on that category. The disassociation of domestic workers and "labor" allowed for what I call a counter-*cubanidad* to flourish on the island. *Hierarchies at Home* argues that domestics were indeed workers, but it also argues that the state's persistent refusal to identify them as such had implications far deeper than vacation days or protection from abuse. The existence of domestic service as an extra-labor category allowed racialized hierarchies to persist in a supposed racial democracy. Labor histories must contend with how inclusion or exclusion from the field of labor can shape entire societal structures.

## 1.5 BOOK OUTLINE

After slavery ended and Cuba became independent, domestic service remained vital to the stability of Cuba's social infrastructure. A new focus on health and medicine, partially driven by the US occupation of the island, contributed to concerns about the inner and outer workings of Cuban households. The new focus on hygiene collided with a much older behavioral standard of honor, a slippery term invoking race, gender, and sex – specifically female virginity.[28] Chapter 1 explores the juxtaposition of "modern" concerns like hygiene and ancient concerns of honor and proper behavior to highlight how domestic workers' physical bodies were subjects of scrutiny and avatars for early republican anxieties. Medical nationalists were convinced that Cuba, having become independent just when scientific knowledge was expanding worldwide, could become a standard-bearer for progressive public health policies.[29] But the government's focus on literal hygiene and the figurative hygiene of the new republic regularly resulted in a hostile fixation on working-class women's bodies and movements. Additionally, older standards of honor carried into the republican era with physical consequences for domestic servants. Public health magazines that warned against "mercenary" wet-nurses, for

---

[28] Often a family's honor was dependent on the preserved chastity of its women. Race affected honor: Elites automatically assumed that people of African descent had less honor than their white counterparts, but African-descended communities had their own internal standards of honor as well. See Stern, *The Secret History of Gender*; Johnson and Lipsett-Rivera, eds. *The Faces of Honor*; Twinam, *Public Lives, Private Secrets*.
[29] Rodríguez, "A Blessed Formula for Progress."

example, evoked hostility to and suspicion of domestic workers' physical bodies at the turn of the twentieth century.

Chapter 2 explores Afro-Cuban responses to stereotypes that connected blackness, dirtiness, and servitude. Using black newspapers and the legal petitions of black women in Santiago de Cuba, I examine the tension between "racial uplift" – the notion that African-descended people could prove their worthiness as citizens by behaving "respectably" – and the lived realities of many black Cuban women. Middle-class black Cubans were a likely cohort to take up the cause of domestic servants. But in the first two decades of the twentieth century, mostly they did not. With the exception of the radical *Partido Independiente de Color* (Independent Party of Color, or PIC), in their publications black Cubans focused on professional careers, education, marriage, and respectable sociability – *not* working-class concerns. As dozens of widowed and single domestic workers met with lawyers in Santiago de Cuba to seek compensation for their relatives' service in the independence war, magazines of various Afro-Cuban social clubs used photography to present images of black female innocence and propriety and published articles about ideal marital relationships. This chapter joins narratives of black political activism with the mundane activities of domestic servants both to elucidate the tension between different groups of African-descended people and to find points of intersection.

Chapter 3 pairs the expansion of liberal and religious solutions to working-class problems with increasing labor radicalism in Cuba. In the second decade of the twentieth century, the Catholic Church and the Cuban government created institutions to help domestic servants and to institutionalize education in domestic sciences for young women. A Spanish Catholic religious order that sought to help young domestics opened in Havana in 1918. Schools of the Home, run by the Cuban government, opened in the same year. However, the 1910s were also marked by phenomena that challenged these charity- and education-based initiatives: rapidly increasing Caribbean migration to Cuba, growing labor unrest, and the feminist movement. These contradictory trends all found expression in the experiences of and discourse surrounding domestic workers. This chapter also considers the politics of the archives and how domestic workers were written out of stories of labor resistance at the very moment such resistance occurred.

Chapter 4 delves into Cuban legal culture and its relationship to domestic service. Transcripts of Cuban law, the 1940 Constitution, the papers of corporate personnel in Cuba, personal speeches and papers of radical feminists, and labor publications all demonstrate that domestic workers *did* collectively organize. In response, government officials and journalists used discourses of intimacy and family to blunt that activism and to deprive domestic servants of rights afforded to other workers. Cuba's pre-1959 government passed just one law related to domestic service in 1938, and it was rescinded one week later after widespread opposition. The opposition to Decree 1754 insisted that a domestic worker was like "one of the family" – a notion with a long history in Cuba and in the history of domestic service globally. Chapter 4 shows that this depiction of service was deliberately used as a weapon to bludgeon the collective organizing of domestic servants. Unionization of domestics failed in Cuba, by traditional standards: The single union formed was unsuccessful in gaining legal protections for domestics. Domestic workers did not fail for lack of trying: They failed because more powerful forces worked against them. *Hierarchies at Home*, in juxtaposing labor history with reproductive history in its exploration of just how Cubans legislated (or failed to) on domestic service, expands historians' understanding of how the law affected people's daily lives.[30]

Chapter 5 examines the 1959 Cuban Revolution's relationship with domestic service, picking up in 1961 where Chapter 4 left off. Through the Federation of Cuban Women, the revolutionary government famously created training programs for domestic servants to learn tasks like typing, teaching, and taxi driving, thereby eliminating the supply of domestic workers on the island. The schools for domestics, along with rehabilitation programs for prostitutes and schools for *campesina* (farmer) women, were emblematic of revolutionary integration of the masses into its political project. The transformation of domestic service in the 1960s reflected Cubans' deepest fears and hopes about the revolutionary future, as documentaries about the schools as well as letters smuggled out of Cuba and to counterrevolutionary US organizations demonstrate. The revolution made women who worked as domestics prominent symbols of the transition from a class-based hierarchy to an egalitarian society; so too did the state regularly use domestic work as an idea or a trope that represented the bourgeois callousness of yesterday's Cuban elite. Ultimately, however, the elimination of service altogether was not as

---

[30] Jocelyn Olcott wrote that "just as including slavery studies under the rubric of labor history fostered fruitful reconsiderations in both places, placing reproductive-labor studies in dialogue with labor historians promises to generate a fuller understanding of the factors that animate historical experience." Olcott, "Introduction," 4.

radical a project as those that domestic workers themselves had undertaken in the 1930s and 1940s. Then, they had envisioned maximum work hours and guaranteed rest, established salaries and homes for when they lost their jobs and therefore their housing. Instead, they got the eradication of their work.

The final chapter (Chapter 6) of *Hierarchies at Home* explores memory and intimacy between the 1960s and 1980s. This chapter uses oral histories conducted in Havana and in Santiago de Cuba as well as literature and memoir to historicize the emotions that surrounded domestic service. The genuine intimacy between domestics and their employers is palpable in the sources used in this chapter. I argue not for the absence of intimacy between domestic workers and their employers throughout twentieth-century Cuba, but for its dangers. Physical and emotional closeness did the work of magnifying power differentials, not lessening them. Additionally, intimacy between domestic servants and their employers was inherently racialized. Scholars of Cuban culture and history used the trope of domestic service to prove that Cuba was and had always been a racially harmonious nation. An institution that had always distilled racial hierarchy in Cuba into its purest form was used to argue for a horizontal equality that never existed.

After she committed "whiteicide" against Cleta, the family maid, the young Lydia Cabrera was brought to tears by her mother's admonition that Cleta *loved* them. Lydia had used the tools of Cleta's trade against her, showering her with a common kitchen ingredient that Cleta might have used to feed Cabrera's family; but what made Lydia remorseful was Cleta's *love*. Cleta's emotional closeness to the Cabreras, not the realization that Lydia had wasted the time and resources of a household employee, induced Lydia's guilt. That is what *Hierarchies at Home* historicizes: the racialized expectation of intimacy between domestic and employee. The violence of that expected intimacy was definitional to the political and social history of domestic service in twentieth-century Cuba, a history untold until now.

# I

## Embodied Anxieties

### *Hygiene, Honor, and Domestic Service in Republican Cuba*

From the perspective of a housewife and her domestic staff, a day inside a well-appointed Cuban home in the first decade of the twentieth century might have looked something like this. In the morning, servants would clean the house from the inside out. That meant a daily cleaning of the floors with water and a mop, and a weekly cleaning of the walls with varnish or enamel. Spring water was the best for cleaning, although rainwater or well-water would do. Servants would also polish wood furniture regularly. After cleaning the house's interior, servants would make their way outside, to the grounds. The poorest homeowners could use coats of lime plaster or plaster of Paris to maintain their walls with paintbrushes or brooms. The *ama de casa* (mistress of the house) would supervise this cleaning.

A *niñera* or *manejadora* (nanny) supervised the children during the morning, overseeing their breakfast and making sure that they got to school, if there was no tutor. After supervising the morning housecleaning, the *ama de casa* would leave the house to shop. Once a week, a laundress would come with clean clothes or to do the laundry in an interior room. It was the *ama de casa*'s job to put the laundry away in its rightful place – clothes in closets, linens on tables and beds.

The housewife and her staff would also collaborate on meal planning. Buffet-style dinners were traditional, where people seated at the table served themselves from large platters. "The Russian service," in which servants stood behind seated guests to serve them food from platters, was also acceptable. In any kind of formal dinner, it was imperative that servants be sensitive to the slightest desires of the guests. In an informal setting – perhaps a dinner of just the family – men were tasked with serving the wine. It was considered inappropriate for children to dine with adults, which meant that *niñeras* and *manejadoras* would be occupied during that time as well. After dinner, guests would be ushered into a different room for coffee, liquor, and dessert.[1] The next day, the tasks would begin again.

Renée Méndez Capote, born into an upper-middle-class family in Havana in 1901, wrote bluntly that "the organization of domestic service in the Republic was based in slavery. The salaries were risible." She wrote that in all houses, without exception, domestics were expected to work from six in the morning until the "wee hours of the night," noting that in her home servants were allowed time off during the day and were done at eight o'clock. They were given one day off every fifteen days. However, married servants had to justify their desire to sleep away from her family's home two or three times per week.[2]

In 1899, over one-fifth of working Cubans were engaged in "domestic and personal service," which the census defined as that performed by "those whose contribution to society is in the form of personal services rather than of goods or of services upon goods." Only agricultural, fishery, and mining work (grouped as one category) was more common on the island. Over two-thirds of working women and almost one-fifth of working men were employed in domestic and personal service, but 67 percent of domestic workers were men. Seventy-five percent of working "colored" women were domestic workers – the census did not differentiate between native and foreign "colored" people, nor did it address whether "colored" might have included Chinese laborers.[3] Sixty-five percent of working foreign white women, mostly from Spain, were domestic servants. Many occupations existed under the umbrella of domestic service: Gardeners and florists, housekeepers and stewards, launderers and laundresses, and servants were all included. Servants could include handmaids, butlers, cooks, and chauffeurs.[4]

Advertisements for domestic workers and advertisements placed by domestics looking for work were vague and hinted at unspoken but universally understood standards of service. While they did identify what

---

[1] Ernestina, *El ama de casa*, 123–124.
[2] Méndez Capote, *Memorias de una cubanita que nació con el siglo*, 117–129.
[3] United States War Department, *Report on the Census of Cuba*, 510. For a history of "coolie" labor in Cuba, see López, *Chinese Cubans: A Transnational History*.
[4] United States War Department, *Report on the Census of Cuba*.

kind of domestic was needed – a handservant, nanny, cook, or chauffeur –
usually advertisements did not go into detail about the kind of work one
position or another entailed. A typical ad from 1901 read, "a middle-aged
Spanish maid is desired, for all home tasks and to sleep in the home."[5]
Often there was a warning that domestics who applied to various posts
should "know her obligation," likely a nod to the emotionally taxing
nature of domestic work: Knowing one's obligation connoted that one
would behave in a respectful and subservient manner. One advertisement
read in its entirety, "servant – one is solicited who knows her obligation."[6] Such ambiguous advertisements suggest that the day described at
this chapter's outset was not actually typical. Most people who employed
domestics did not employ a staff. They might have employed just one
maid "for all tasks." "Knowing her obligation" might have also implied
that the tasks of a single domestic might be many, and that she should not
object to any of them.

Even with so many African-descended women in the field, anti-black
racism was palpable; elites seemed to prefer Spanish women. In a footnote
to his 1898 travelogue of Cuba, the American author Richard Davey wrote,

> Since the abolition of slavery, some few Galegos have emigrated from Spain,
> mainly to seek employment in the houses of the wealthy. It may interest the reader
> to know that the peasantry of Galicia have for many ages supplied Spain and
> Portugal with their best domestic servants. They are an honest and frugal race,
> faithful to their employers, and excellent cooks to boot. They are much sought
> after in Cuba, where they obtain higher wages than they can in the Peninsula.[7]

Working-class Spaniards, apparently, were desirable in the old and
new worlds. Salaries, rarely listed in advertisements, revealed two things
when they did appear: first, that payment in cash and in kind was fairly
common and, second, that there was a severe racialized wage gap. An
advertisement from March 17, 1901, specifically requested a "young girl
of color" to help with cleaning and to take care of a child while living in-
house. Her salary would be four pesos monthly and clean clothes. Just
three days later another advertisement called for a Spanish maid to work
as a nanny: Her salary would be twelve pesos and clean clothes.[8] While
the second advertisement did not state whether the *criada peninsular*

---

[5] "Se desea una criada de mediana edad peninsular, para todos los quehaceres de la casa y
que duerma en la colocación." *Diario de la Marina*, March 2, 1901.
[6] "Sirviente – se solicita uno que sepa su obligación." *Diario de la Marina*, March 23, 1901.
[7] Davey, *Cuba Past and Present*, 17.
[8] *Diario de la Marina*, Solicitudes, March 17 and 20, 1901.

(Spanish maid) would live in the house, most nannies did at the time. The only discernible difference between the two advertisements is the race of the person requested.

Newspaper advertisements written by would-be domestics and would-be employers assumed that the specific tasks of domestic service would be apparent to anyone reading those words. "Knowing her obligation" is opaque to us but was probably not to a reader in 1901. This chapter clarifies another opaque and perpetually naturalized relationship: that of the domestic worker's physical body to the Cuban state. Two impulses that could have been at odds but actually reinforced each other gripped policymakers after Cuba's transition from colony to republic: hygiene and honor. Both North American policymakers and Cuban "medical nationalists" – doctors, scientists, and journalists – touted Cuba's potential to be the first nation founded with sound scientific knowledge of hygiene and its worth. But this modern hygiene movement did not dislodge colonial notions of honor. In fact, policymakers and actors in republican Cuba's legal system used the language of hygiene and modernity to perpetuate ancient standards of honor that had guided Latin America's social realm for centuries.

Domestic workers were at the center of consideration of hygiene in private homes – after all, they were the ones cleaning walls and floors and furniture. Domestics also cared for children, and Cuba suffered from an abysmally high infant mortality rate at the start of the twentieth century. Domestics' physical cleanliness and their capacity to clean and to nurture were foremost in concerns about hygiene; the demographic makeup of the domestic workforce in Cuba also made such workers important to hygienic considerations. Most working black and immigrant women were domestics. Daniel Rodríguez's work has shown how both groups' cleanliness and understanding of hygiene and science were regularly called into question by the new Cuban government.[9]

Honor and morality were inextricably linked to hygiene, and the moral comportment of domestic servants was an overarching concern of people who would employ them. Honor and its racialized standards continued to affect the lives of poor and non-white Cubans amid rapid social transformation. Ironically, domestics' physical proximity to their employers – people purported to have more honor than they did by virtue of their economic status – often endangered their honor. Physical intimacy

---

[9] Rodríguez, *The Right to Live in Health*.

allowed for physical and rhetorical violence against domestics, as it had when Cuba was a slave society. The work of domestic service sexualized, endangered, and turned mercenary the bodies of its laborers.

Drawing on the work of feminist scholars Elizabeth Grosz and Moira Gatens, historian Natalia Milanesio considers the body "a site of intervention or inscriptive surface 'on which laws, morality, values and power are inscribed.'" She considers, as well, Gatens's formulation of the "imaginary body" – an understanding of the physical body that favors the societal and social prioritization of certain body parts over others, for example, and a common use and practice of the body through educational, medical, and governmental institutions.[10] Both the body as inscriptive surface and the imaginary body are important in this chapter. Onto domestic workers' bodies policymakers and health officials wrote what they feared and hoped for in the new nation. Those same people deployed "imaginary bodies" to make both governmental and domestic recommendations for best hygienic practices. Using both the expanding hygiene movement and the still integral standard of honor as a framework, this chapter explores how Cuban nationalism was lived through the men and women expected to keep Cuba(ns) clean.

First, I explore the regulation of prostitution in Cuba – an occupation often associated with domestic service. The chapter then turns to the republican government's focus on breastfeeding – perhaps the most intimate bodily practice classified as domestic service. The chapter finally delves into several sexual assault cases involving domestic workers, paralleling those cases with earlier ones from the *Patronato* courts. The early republic's focus on hygiene distilled the personhoods of domestic servants into the hygienic sufficiency of their physical bodies, just as the institution of slavery had reduced enslaved men and women to their physical usefulness. Exploring the embodied experience of being a domestic worker in early republican Cuba reveals a physical connection between enslavement and freedom, something domestic workers in later decades would insist was their daily reality.

## 1.1 SEX WORK AND THE SOCIAL BODY

Sexual vulnerability had been definitional to enslavement. Domestic slaves, who lived in the homes of their masters, were particularly

---

[10] Milanesio, "Redefining Men's Sexuality," 466.

vulnerable to sexual coercion. After abolition, black women's bodies were legally their own, but sex work and domestic service overlapped regularly in republican Cuba, highlighting the continued vulnerability of African-descended women. The regular exchange of sex for money was a major concern of the US occupying forces in Cuba and the nation's nascent medical establishment. For them, sex work's popularity betrayed both a dangerous lack of concern for hygiene and questionable morality on the part of prostitutes and their customers. Very early twentieth-century analyses of prostitution and its roots would set the scene for the prolonged association between domestic and sex work in Cuba.

Sex work was legal but regulated in Cuba, and had been since the colonial era. Since 1840, prostitution had been regulated by a Special Hygiene Commission. In 1902, the secretary of the commission for the entire island, Ramón María Alfonso, found that 86 of 251 prostitutes he had interviewed – 34 percent – had previously worked as domestics. Domestics, especially maids and laundresses, were the most predominant of all professions among women who had become prostitutes.[11] Unsurprisingly, the occupation that attracted the highest numbers of prostitutes was also the occupation with the lowest wages. The lowest-paid female labor in Cuba was that of the handmaid: She made an average of thirty centavos daily as of 1903.[12]

The hygiene inspector of the city of Guantánamo, Dr. F. Sabas, had a cultural explanation for the prolonged existence of sex work. Young women whose lovers seduced and then abandoned them turned to prostitution when they had no other way to support themselves. This, he wrote in a 1902 report, was the "Haitian way," a practice imported over a century ago when French whites and their slaves fled the Haitian Revolution for eastern Cuba.[13] Sabas explained that women who turned to "the Haitian way" were too lazy to engage in domestic service when their lovers abandoned them.

We cannot know precisely what Sabas meant in calling the supposed practice "the Haitian way," but his invocation of Haiti reveals layers of racialized assumptions about the influence of the first independent

[11] Alfonso, *La prostitución en Cuba y especialmente en La Habana: memoria de la Comisión de Higiene Especial de la Isla de Cuba elevada al Secretario de Gobernación cumpliendo un precepto reglamentario*, 29.
[12] Alfonso, *Manumision Económica de la Mujer Cubana*.
[13] "Estado A. Sinopsis de informacion necesaria a la comission de Higiene Especial," 12 diciembre 1902, Fondo Gobierno Provincial, AHPSC. The population estimate for the city of Guantánamo is from the 1899 census.

Caribbean nation on Cuba, the most recent one. St. Domingue (as Haiti was known before it declared independence) had a long history of sexual relationships between white men and African women: Their couplings had created an entire class of people known as the *gens de coleur*, or people of color. *Gens de coleur* could not participate in St. Domingue's government, but they could and did acquire property. Many of the wealthiest residents of St. Domingue were *gens de coleur*, the result of cross-racial romantic or sexual relationships, and their upward mobility and increasing disdain for the racism of the colony contributed to the conflict that overtook St. Domingue in 1791.[14] As enslaved insurgents and militias of *gens de coleur* gained ground in the 1790s, many white coffee- and sugar-makers fled the territory for more stable colonies. They landed mostly in Cuba and New Orleans. Economically, St. Domingue's fall was Cuba's rise: The island replaced Haiti as the world's sugar supplier, drawing on the expertise that expat St. Dominguans brought with them as they fled. Apparently, they also brought sexual practices new to Cuba.

Of course, Cuba and every other American colony had a large population of mixed-race people. The prevalence of such a class was not unique to Haiti. Sabas seems to have come up with the concept of "the Haitian way" on his own, but, across the Americas, Haiti had become a watchword for instability, danger, and strangeness. In his report, Sabas imbued a tale as old as time – a young woman turning to sex work because her lover has left her – with a sinister analysis of Haitian culture. Cuba had just had its own supposedly anti-racist revolution, but Sabas's warning harkened back to the early nineteenth century in Cuba, when Spanish officials warned that the metropole was the only barrier to the island's sliding into Haitian-like chaos.

Thinly veiled warnings aside, Sabas's logic was tenuous. None of the thirty-two working prostitutes he had documented in his city (population around 7,000) were foreign. Nine were white, six were black, and seventeen were *mulata*, or mixed race. The Haitian migration to eastern Cuba and to Guantánamo especially was 100 years past. Despite these facts, which were inconvenient to his argument, his point was clear: Prostitution was foreign, and it was a racial problem. The institution was atavistic, not rooted in the reality of modern-day Cuba.

Alfonso drew a similar conclusion at a talk he gave at the Second National Congress of Charity and Correction in 1903. He attributed

---

[14] James, *The Black Jacobins*.

prostitution to the migration of women to Cuba from places such as the Canary Islands – Spain's island colony off the West African coast – insisting that no such vice had existed in Cuba before 1868 and the beginning of the Ten Years' War. Another contemporary scholar connected vice and the solicitation of prostitutes in Havana to Chinese immigrants, claiming that rates of venereal disease were highest in neighborhoods occupied by Chinese workers.[15] While most Chinese workers by this time worked on sugar plantations, Chinese men also regularly worked as cooks and gardeners in private homes. But the association between non-native *cubanidad* (Cubanness) and sex work that Sabas and Alfonso pushed was false. Even as he associated domestic service with foreignness, Alfonso reported that native white women comprised most of the population of sex workers in Cuba. For all his and others' hand-wringing about the importation of vice from African, French, or even Chinese culture, prostitution was a home-grown problem, borne, most agreed, from the abysmal wages that women earned.[16]

Whether they were deficient morally or just financially, sex workers had to be contained for the physical and moral health of other Cubans. In Havana, "zones of tolerance" – geographically constrained parts of the city in which brothels could function – existed from the nineteenth century until the 1960s. Officials made piecemeal attempts to separate sex workers from the general population in other cities: In November 1900, a representative of Santiago de Cuba's General Hospital wrote to the Civil Governor of Oriente Province, instructing him that the hospital could no longer offer beds to prostitutes sent there by the Special Hygiene Commission. In addition to a simple lack of sufficient resources, the letter explained, the superintendent of hospitals worried that the prostitutes would mix with other women in the unit, exporting their deficient moral values.[17]

Sex work evoked the unruliness of physical bodies.[18] No government could ever fully contain what its citizens did with their bodies, and the exchange of sex for money made that explicit. The desire to contain sex

---

[15] Sippial, *Prostitution, Modernity, and the Making of the Cuban Republic, 1840–1920*, chap. 4.

[16] Alfonso, *La prostitución en Cuba y especialmente en La Habana*, 22.

[17] Negociado de Sanidad, no. 181, 26 noviembre 1900, Fondo Gobierno Provincial, AHPSC.

[18] Sippial, *Prostitution, Modernity, and the Making of the Cuban Republic, 1840–1920*; Hynson, "Count, Capture, and Reeducate." See Chapter 6 for an extended discussion of sex work later in the twentieth century.

work and control sex workers was about more than the possible spread of
disease or the other kinds of crime that could flourish in brothels; it was
about the desire to subdue bodies that were deviant. In October of 1911,
a hygiene inspector – employed to regulate sex work in Cuba – arrested a
twenty-two-year-old woman and her mother in the city of Marianao on
the suspicion of such deviance. The inspector took the two women to the
local police precinct, called someone on the telephone, left the precinct,
and then returned – finally allowing them to leave because he could not
find a doctor (ostensibly to inspect them). The next month, the twenty-
two-year-old, Catalina Hernandez, complained about their poor treatment to the authorities. Catalina and her mother, Petrona, were *not*
prostitutes. They were laundresses. They were also migrants from
Puerto Rico.

The police identified the hygiene inspector who had detained Catalina
and Petrona as 19-year-old Alberto García. He suspected them of clan-
destinely practicing prostitution but had no evidence attesting to that fact;
they were guilty of little more than being black in public. Domestic
workers, especially cooks and washerwomen, *were* more likely to exist
in public than middle- or upper-class women who did not have to work or
who were married, which made them more vulnerable to accusations of a
deviant life. Had García successfully detained Catalina and Petrona until
a doctor arrived to inspect them, they probably would have been subject
to the kind of painful and invasive "inspections" that were typical of
policy around prostitution at the time.[19] García lost his job and was fined
200 pesos for illegally detaining Petrona and Catalina.[20] That he was
punished for his behavior is remarkable. But the offense had to be
extreme before anyone would be punished: García had literally pulled
two women off the street based on appearance alone.

García's overzealous accosting of Catalina and Petrona was at least
partially borne of his own inclinations, but it also reflected the zealousness
of regulators and enemies of sex work in the decades after independence.
In the sexual assault cases later in this chapter, we will see echoes of his
immediate assumption that the women must have been sex workers;
women of African descent were denied the assumption of sexual

---

[19] Findlay describes the horrific inspections that Puerto Rican prostitutes endured at the turn
   of the twentieth century in her book on race and sexuality in Puerto Rico. Under the guise
   of public safety, these physical inspections amounted to sexual abuse. Findlay, *Imposing
   Decency*, chap. 3.
[20] Juzgado de Instruccion de Mariano, Causa num. 189, 11 noviembre 1911, Audiencia de
   la Habana, ANC.

innocence that white women often received. The looming threat of an "inspection" points to the physical repercussions of the hygiene movement and a lingering fixation on honor. From a "health" perspective, it was important that women engaged in sex work be inspected. From an honor perspective, women walking about freely were suspicious. From the perspective of domestic workers, the focus on public hygiene likely looked like a new gloss on an old form of control.

### 1.2 BREASTFEEDING AFTER SLAVERY: WET-NURSES IN EARLY REPUBLICAN CUBA

Sex work was an explicitly bodily practice, one that Cuban officials simultaneously regulated and resented. In its bodily nature it closely paralleled a form of domestic service that, like sex work, had deep roots in the island's slave history: wet-nursing. Wet-nurses had been an integral part of the Cuban slave plantation; after abolition, *nodrizas* (wet-nurses) became symbolic of racial harmony and the affection of black Cubans for their white superiors.[21] Breastfeeding someone else's baby was an act of radical intimacy, and no other kind of domestic labor so encompassed the trust that needed to exist between *empleada* (employee) and *dueña* (mistress) to ensure the health and safety of the Cuban household. Anxieties over wet-nursing emerged in the context of a new focus on hygiene, both during the US occupation and after. The health of babies was essential to the nation's hygiene and modernity. Who was feeding them?

The question was not unique to Cuba nor even to the Americas. Wet-nursing is an ancient practice, and anxieties about wet-nursing are as old as the work itself. Concerns about breastfeeding and wet-nursing were often tied to rapidly changing political situations in the Americas. In late eighteenth-century Peru, for example, elites began to fear the encroaching authority of enslaved *nodrizas* in their households, as the Bourbon reforms called Creole (white Peruvian-born) political rights into question.[22] As Brazil hurtled toward the twentieth century, the end of slavery, *and* the end of its status as a Portuguese colony all at the same time, nationalists there grew suspicious of the influence of wet-nurses, too.[23] Cuban circumstances paralleled those of Peru in the eighteenth century and Brazil at the turn of the twentieth. Cuba had moved much closer to a

[21] For a Brazilian example, see Seigel, *Uneven Encounters*, especially chap. 6.
[22] Premo, "'Misunderstood Love,'" 231–261.
[23] Otovo, *Progressive Mothers, Better Babies*.

more (nominally) racially equitable society than ever, one reliant on free labor. What would childrearing look like in this new era?

*La Higiene*, a magazine published in Havana for "the interests of health and scientific knowledge," frequently discussed the importance of choosing the right wet-nurse, if one was to be chosen at all. *La Higiene* was the brainchild of Dr. Manuel Delfín Zamora, a prominent doctor and hygienist. He edited and directed the magazine from 1891–1895 and from 1900–1907. *La Higiene*'s main concern was child health. Delfín, who himself wrote many of the articles, opined frequently on optimal diets, clothing, and environments for children. His magazine concerned itself with poor children in Cuba and with the state of the government's public hospitals. Directed at women and published three times monthly, *La Higiene* relentlessly urged women to take seriously the physical health and wellbeing of their children. Wet-nursing comprised a large portion of this concern. Delfín regularly published articles about what nursing women should consume to provide optimal nutrition to their babies (yes to root vegetables, no to excessive caffeine and alcohol).[24] Although Delfín believed that mothers should breastfeed their children themselves, he accepted the fact that middle- and upper-class white women simply did not do so.

"Not everyone who has given birth and had a baby at her breast is qualified to be a wet-nurse," admonished *La Higiene* in 1901. Women could lack abundant breast milk, have insufficiently nutritious breast milk, have transmissible diseases, or have defective breasts. According to *La Higiene*, these were possibilities for all women and probabilities for "mercenary" wet-nurses, as the magazine regularly referred to women who were paid to nurse infants. To prevent against the calamity of hiring a deficient wet-nurse, Delfín and a partner, Dr. Cuervo, established a center for wet-nurses in the heart of Havana. Families hiring from their center would know that these women had been examined and approved to breastfeed by two doctors. When the announcement of the center ran in *La Higiene*'s November 1901 edition, the center already had thirty wet-nurses registered, although many more women than that had applied and been rejected.[25] There's no evidence that this wet-nursing center lasted very long, but by 1913 inspection of wet-nurses had been institutionalized in the city of Havana by the new Children's Hygiene Service. All wet-nurses in Havana had to be registered and

---

[24] Delfín, "Alimento y lactancia," *La Higiene*, 513.
[25] Delfín, "Reconocimiento de nodrizas," *La Higiene*, 826.

undergo regular medical evaluations, including offering samples of their own breastmilk for inspection.[26]

Contemporary assumptions about African-descended women were quietly hostile to the notion that black women could be good wet-nurses. A 1902 *La Higiene* article described the ideal wet-nurse: She was between twenty and thirty years old, with a robust constitution, without symptoms of any acquired or inherited disease. Ideally, she was at once "docile and tranquil" and "active and intelligent," so that she could "jealously and tactfully" care for her charge.[27] Health experts rarely attributed these characteristics to women of African descent, even if they were mothers themselves. Before the abolition of slavery many observers of Cuban society had assumed that black women were incapable of maternal affection. When Cuba's "Free Womb Law" passed in 1870, one foreign observer claimed that the law had transformed the "Negro nursery" on slave plantations. Whereas before, enslaved women were supposedly loath to care for their offspring, since they too would become slaves, now those nurseries were places of affection and care.[28] Because of the Moret Law, the foreigner argued, black women could love their children.

His surprise stemmed from his assumption of black female neglect of their offspring, a deeply rooted and commonly held racist understanding of black maternity. European preoccupation with the "monstrosity" of African women, who according to various sources could suckle over their shoulders and felt no pain during childbirth, dates back to the sixteenth century. As the trade in enslaved people across the Atlantic world expanded in the seventeenth century, a distinction between the reproductive labor of European and African women emerged: European women's reproductive labor took place solely in the domestic sphere, but African women's reproduction was part of the extractive capitalist economy. Their bodies created labor, not babies.[29] The comfortable relationship between African-descended women's reproductive labor and economic extraction rang as true in nineteenth-century Cuba as it did in early-modern England.

After abolition, women of African descent could no longer fit so neatly into the extractive economy. They became less desirable as wet-nurses and domestics than they had been when their labor was forced.

---

[26] Rodríguez, "A Blessed Formula for Progress."

[27] Rothschild, "*El amamantamiento. Elección de una nodriza*," 1044–1045.

[28] Gallenga, *The Pearl of the Antilles*, 123–124.

[29] Morgan, "'Some Could Suckle over Their Shoulder,'" 188.

Advertisements for wet-nurses were as racialized as the ads for other
kinds of domestic service in Cuba, especially at the very beginning of
the twentieth century. Families who placed ads for wet-nurses frequently
specified their desire for a Spanish nurse, and women who advertised
themselves for jobs as wet-nurses almost always mentioned their Spanish
heritage or their recent arrival from that country.[30] While during slavery
it might have been understood that wet-nurses would be of African
descent, after emancipation and independence their presence in white
homes was more suspect.

Potential wet-nurses faced intense pressures. In advertisements for wet-
nurses from Havana's long-running daily *Diario de la Marina*, most
families requested a woman who had given birth between one and four
months previously. The phrase *"leche entera"* appeared in almost all of
the advertisements from *Diario de la Marina* in 1901. The only clue that
*leche entera* was not the only option was a single advertisement claiming
that the family would accept a wet-nurse at *leche entera* or *media leche*.
Literally, these phrases mean "whole milk" and "half milk"; in practice,
*"leche entera"* connoted a willingness to nurse the recently born child
exclusively, as opposed to nursing both the client's child and the nurse's
own offspring. This would have been a painful choice: In Chile doctors
railed against mercenary wet-nursing precisely because it could lead to the
malnourishment and death of the nurses' own children.[31]

Advertisements also regularly requested that potential wet-nurses bring
their own babies to be inspected by the family who might hire them,
ostensibly to verify that the nurse's milk was sufficient to raise a healthy
baby. Women who placed advertisements to be hired also offered to bring
their babies along for viewing. In advertisements for enslaved wet-nurses,
the potential nurses' children were frequently not mentioned at all, which
suggested that the child would not accompany his mother. While pre-
abolition Cuban society held white mothers in high esteem, they saw
black mothers as breeders, merely fulfilling a "biological function" within
their designated role as laborers.[32] In the twentieth century women who
offered to bring their babies along to be inspected were making clear that
they had children of their own, but the situation was not necessarily
better. Beyond their own bodies being subject to inspection and scrutiny,

---

[30] *Diario de la Marina*, advertisements, March 1901 and 1916.
[31] Milanich, *Children of Fate*, 37–38; Franklin, *Women and Slavery in Nineteenth-Century Colonial Cuba*.
[32] Franklin, *Women and Slavery in Nineteenth-Century Colonial Cuba*, 146.

wet-nurses regularly had to subject their offspring to the same treatment. Did anyone involved see the irony in a family verifying that a wet-nurse was capable by the appearance of her own baby – a baby whose health would surely decline if his mother was hired *a leche entera*? Wet-nurses' bodies, especially black women's bodies, were available for extraction; that the extraction might cause them emotional pain was of secondary importance to the needs of the middle class.

As in the rest of Latin America, wet-nursing gradually declined as the twentieth century continued. While there were an equal number of solicitations and offers for wet-nursing in *Diario de la Marina* ads in 1901, by 1916 the numbers were lopsided. Far more women were offering their services as *nodrizas* than families were asking for them, which might have been wage-related: While mention of salary was even rarer for wet-nursing advertisements than it was for other kinds of service, elsewhere in Latin America wet-nursing was more lucrative than other kinds of domestic service.[33] The differential between demand for and supply of wet-nurses was even more extreme by 1928. As late as 1937, however, apparently wet-nursing did still happen: *Diario de Cuba*, Santiago's daily, ran an article in April of that year with advice on how to monitor one's *nodriza*.[34]

Wet-nursing was a particularly important example of how domestic servants' physical and moral behavior could come under strict surveillance since common intelligence at the time was that both of these components of character could directly affect a baby's health and well-being. Scrutiny of wet-nurses' health and character began in the nineteenth century, when owners of African-descended women put them up for sale and extolled their virtues as wet-nurses.[35] It continued into the twentieth century, as is seen through advertisements. And at least in Havana, scrutiny of wet-nurses was institutionalized through the Child Hygiene Service. As Cuba moved farther away from slavery, negative scrutiny of wet-nursing increased. Black female maternity, separated from coercive labor, was seen as a threat.

Cross-racial wet-nursing was common and symbolically very important across slave societies in the Americas. In the United States, enslaved black women nursed their white masters' children; African-descended

[33] Milanich, *Children of Fate.*
[34] "Los Madres Deben Tener Mucho Cuidado Con los Niños en el Período de Lactancia," *Diario de Cuba*, April 11, 1937.
[35] Franklin, *Women and Slavery in Nineteenth-Century Colonial Cuba.*

women did the same in Brazil.[36] Later on in the twentieth century, elite Cubans would deploy the black *nodriza* as a symbol of racial harmony, pointing out that many members of the island's wealthiest families had been raised at the breast of a black wet-nurse. Along with the milk they'd suckled, they had supposedly imbibed affection and respect for Cuba's African-descended population. Thus, eventually cross-racial wet-nursing became a metaphor for Cuba's multiracial democracy. But this close examination of standards and fears about wet-nursing reveals that when it was common, public health officials treated black wet-nurses with suspicion and contempt. And the job itself endangered black families by forcing nursing mothers to sell their milk away from their own children. What was supposedly salubrious and fortifying for the Cuban nation was emotionally and physically difficult labor.

In early twentieth-century Brazil, too, wet-nurses were referred to as "mercenary." But the medical establishment in Brazil expanded massively in the twentieth century. Particularly in the Northeast, medical professionals came to understand black domestic workers – or *mãe pretas* – as mothers in their own right, not just caregivers to other people's children. Poor women in Bahia took advantage of health clinics and medical initiatives for their babies in massive numbers beginning in the 1920s.[37] While Cuban doctors organized and made public health strides before 1959, there was no comparative expansion of access *or* shift in perception in Cuba before 1959.[38] Brazil had a booming industrial and agricultural sector, and therefore money to spend on public health; Cuba's economy remained tied primarily to the sugar economy. Thus, while hostility toward domestic workers and wet-nurses in Brazil waned somewhat as their roles as mothers were considered, the same thing did not happen in Cuba. Economic and societal fragility would not allow for it.

While in the early 1900s, medical nationalists like Delfín and other doctors believed Spanish colonialism was to blame for appalling health outcomes for the poor in Cuba, by the 1920s they had begun to blame the poor themselves. Havana's infant mortality rate was high around 1908 because of poor nutrition, so these men flooded Cuban media and Havana's neighborhood with helpful information about how to properly feed infants (with breastmilk). By the 1920s, however, when

[36] West and Knight, "Mothers' Milk"; Marko, "A Wet Nurse, Her Masters, a Folkhealer, a Pediatrician, and Two Babies."
[37] Otovo, *Progressive Mothers, Better Babies.*
[38] Rodríguez, *The Right to Live in Health*; Urban, "The Sick Republic."

mortality rates had not dropped, doctors and intellectuals concluded that it was not benign ignorance but resistance to science that endangered infants and Cuban health more generally: "The stubbornly high death rate was an indictment of a Cuban people that was not up to the task of hygienic citizenship."[39] In the minds of these intellectuals, "mercenary" wet-nurses were one symptom of a larger disease – the refusal of the poor (a category including domestics) to bend to the will of those who, supposedly, knew better. The hostility toward these "mercenaries" was yet another expression of the tension between the desire for political, economic, and medical "progress" in Cuba and the reality of a profoundly racialized social hierarchy.

## 1.3 SEXUAL DANGER AND DOMESTICS' BODIES

The conflict over "who knew better" when it came to physical and moral propriety had the most devastating consequences for women who were sexually assaulted. In February of 1901, the thirty-one-year-old *moreno* (black) tailor Martín Hipólito Travieso reported a crime, telling Havana police officers that his twenty-two-year-old sister, *morena* Cecilia Piedrahita, had been raped by her boyfriend the night prior. After a stroll with twenty-six-year-old chauffeur Santiago Peñalver, Cecilia told Martín, Santiago had told her that if she did not "satisfy his desires" he would choke her to death. For his part, Santiago claimed that he had indeed taken Cecilia's virginity but that she had invited him to do so after a walk with her and several other young women.

In court documents, Cecilia was alternately listed as a washerwoman, a cook, and unemployed.[40] The listing of Cecilia as "unemployed" in one court document likely signified that she did not work "outside of the home," a common dichotomy in early twentieth-century Cuban court documents. Inside people's homes, however, she washed and cooked. It may have been her status as a domestic worker that kept Cecilia from going to the police herself. Cecilia might have felt that the police would be more amenable to hearing out a respectable, married, and gainfully employed man rather than a single domestic servant who had, by her own admission, been out in public with another man. Cecilia's stroll with Santiago and several other young women, whom we can assume were

---

[39] Rodríguez, "A Blessed Formula for Progress," 229.
[40] "Violación de Cecilia Piedrahita por el Moreno Santiago Peñalver y Alarcón," 20 febrero 1901, Legajo 544 Num. 19, Audiencia de la Habana, ANC.

also members of the working class, suggests a less restrictive social life than young upper-class Cuban women would have enjoyed. This less restrictive social life could be dangerous: Outside the (supposedly) protective sphere of adults who controlled their behavior, domestic servants had few people to vouch for their respectability and for their rights to protection.

When the police asked Cecilia why she agreed to stay with Santiago alone in the hallway outside her apartment, she responded that she assumed he just wanted to kiss and fondle her, not to have sex with her. She stayed quiet as Santiago raped her, not wanting to disturb her neighbors with her screams. The rape was only discovered the next day when her sister, Candita, noticed a stain on the hallway couch and asked Cecilia what had happened.[41] A doctor inspected Cecilia for evidence of rape and found no physical suggestion of violence. Santiago was freed based on a lack of evidence, and Cecilia and her sister received citations for lying to the police.

Cecilia had her siblings, but she lived in Havana without parents or a husband. She went out socially with her boyfriend and other friends. She welcomed some sexual activity with her boyfriend but had clear sexual boundaries that she tried to enforce. We don't know whether she had to be convinced to speak with Havana police officers, but when she did speak, she was startlingly frank. Cecilia violated many of the gendered norms of sexual respectability in early republican Cuba. Her story, tragic by definition, offers a rare vivid portrait of a self-possessed young woman. Other cases like Cecilia's similarly present valuable glimpses of womanhood or girlhood in Havana. From pages that document their vulnerability emerge suggestions of tangible lives, of women whom we might imagine meeting.

The notations of physicality in these assault records ground the stories in physical space, inviting a visceral understanding of how the violence of an honor-based society lived inside vulnerable young women's bodies. In their testimonies, we hear how they fought back against or tried to negotiate with the violence, both immediate and structural. Blood on a hallway couch, adolescent wrists gripped by a grown man's hands, a tryst in a half-built house: These details are tiny echoes of the intimate violence that young women like Cecilia and other women I'll document must have faced regularly. Strides in modernization in early twentieth-century Cuba

---

[41] "Violación de Cecilia Piedrahita por el Moreno Santiago Peñalver y Alarcón," 20 febrero 1901, Legajo 544 Num. 19, Audiencia de la Habana, ANC.

did little to loosen associations between blackness, poverty, and physical and mental inferiority. The same notions of "honor" that undergirded discussions of breastfeeding and prostitution, and slipped into more modern notions of hygiene, endangered the physical safety of female domestic workers and often stripped them of any justice the court might have offered.

Celia Alfonso y Díaz was eight years old when she entered Cuba's asylum system in 1900, an orphan of the wars for independence. She lived at an American Red Cross orphanage in Güines, a small town about thirty-one miles southeast of Havana, for seven years. (Güines was also the birthplace of Raimundo Cabrera and Cleta – Lydia Cabrera's father and her domestic from the Introduction.) The Red Cross had opened the orphanage when it arrived in Cuba in October 1898 to help *reconcentrados* and soldiers toward the end of the war for independence. In 1907, a woman named María Teresa Toscano hired Celia to work as a domestic in her home in Guanabacoa, about twenty-six miles from the orphanage in Güines. Celia might have been trained for exactly this kind of work. At a similar orphanage in Madruga, just thirteen miles from her own orphanage in Güines, girls took sewing and dressmaking classes. Celia might have been enrolled in similar classes and trained in the domestic arts.[42] But just one year later, at sixteen, Celia found herself pregnant and at the center of a statutory rape case.

Señora Toscano testified that Celia had been complaining of fatigue and dizziness in late October of 1907, so she took her to the doctor. The doctor told Toscano that Celia was pregnant. Confused and disturbed, Toscano tried to return Celia to the asylum, but the secretary of the orphanage convinced her to keep and care for Celia. However, Toscano said, Celia became uncooperative and truculent, refusing to talk to Toscano about the pregnancy or about anything else. By mid-December she had returned Celia to the asylum. Despite all evidence, Toscano avowed that Celia could not have gotten pregnant while employed at her home – she rarely left the home, and when she did, it was in the company of Toscano's small daughter, whom Celia cared for.

Celia was more forthcoming with one of the nuns at the asylum than she had been with Toscano. She testified that indeed, she'd had "amorous relations" with Ricardo Daumil, a carpenter building a house across the street from where she lived with Toscano. Celia testified that Daumil had

---

[42] Red Cross, *La Cruz Roja en Cuba*, 27–29.

deceived her, promising her marriage in exchange for sex. He was charged with statutory rape on March 28, 1908. Ricardo Daumil was difficult to find: By April 22, he was still on the lam, and by the end of June 1908 the Havana police had given up on finding him. But by a stroke of luck, Daumil was apprehended and imprisoned on August 17, where he awaited his trial.[43]

For all that trouble, he was found innocent of any wrongdoing because the court could not verify whether he had actually deceived Celia. There is no record of what happened to Celia or to her baby after the trial. Celia was black and Ricardo was *mestizo*. While the court document outlining the case in March of 1908 noted that the Red Cross knew nothing about Celia's parentage or relatives, Celia told nuns at her asylum exactly who her parents were. Her father was José Alfonso of Güines, and her mother was María Díaz of Havana: She did not know where they were, but she certainly knew them as her parents. It raises the question why the Red Cross did not have this information. Did they not ask, or not care? It was all too easy a narrative to believe that a young black girl had no parents, no lineage to go back to. Perhaps it was too easy to believe, as well, that a young black domestic worker would agree to sex with full knowledge of the possible consequences.[44]

Celia's attempt to chart her own path shines through the archival narration of her plight. Having been moved from an orphanage to the home of a stranger, Celia stole moments for herself with a young man across the street. She secured a promise of marriage from him; if he had fulfilled that promise, Celia would have been set up for the kind of familial stability she had not known for some time. A married woman could not be moved around like a chess piece, as Celia had. Her plan failed, and her lover left her alone and pregnant. Still, Celia was choosy about who to trust. Toscano was clearly not trustworthy, but the nuns at the asylum where she'd grown up were. The choices the sixteen-year-old made did not work out in the way she'd surely hoped, but her deliberation troubles a simple narration of victimization or naivete.

Celia was born in the same year that José Martí formed the Cuban Revolutionary Party while exiled in New York City. Somehow, she lost her parents in Cuba's violent and chaotic transition from a Spanish colony to an American neocolony. She was raised in one of the most

[43] "Causa formada por Estupro a virtud de querella del Ministerio Fiscal, 25 May 1908," Audiencia de la Habana, Legajo 459 Num. 2, ANC.
[44] Ibid.

visible examples of that neocolonialism – a Red Cross asylum – and then turned loose into a *new-born Cuba*, as one American writer termed the island just a year before Celia became a ward of the Red Cross.[45] The Red Cross raised her to work and to be a good girl. In becoming pregnant, she failed to live up to these standards, and the court's decision reflected the suspicion and hostility that her employer clearly felt toward her. Institutions reflective of Cuba's transformation – the Red Cross, the republican courts – combined with the ancient standard of "honor" to categorize, in the end, Celia's story as one not of victimization but of descent into vice.

Seven years later, little had changed. Teresa Sánchez Castaño washed clothes for people in her Guanabacoa home, and she often sent her daughter, thirteen-year-old Regla María Sánchez, to deliver clean clothes to her clients. One of her clients was a mestizo man named Enrique Guerrero y Ruíz. In June of 1914, Regla and her cousin, twelve-year-old Elena Bentancourt y Sánchez, went to Guerrero's apartment to deliver the clothes Regla's mother had washed. According to Elena and Regla, after they'd given Guerrero his clothes and were standing in the doorway, waiting for payment, Guerrero grabbed Regla by the arm, slammed the door shut, threw her on his bed, and raped her.

Guerrero told Regla that if she told anyone, she and her cousin would be sent to prison. The prosecution recommended that for his crime Guerrero receive fourteen years in prison and a fine of $2,000, and that he take financial responsibility for any offspring who might result from his attack on Regla. Speaking on Guerrero's behalf, his lawyer denied the story wholesale. Guerrero maintained that the transaction was unremarkable: Regla and Elena had dropped off his clean laundry, he had paid the girls, and they had promptly left.

Guerrero's lawyer attempted to cast doubt on the teenager's good reputation – Regla María's teacher reported to the police that the girl behaved well in class and made a very good impression – and her narration of what, exactly, had happened that day at Guerrero's solar.[46] In a list of questions that he submitted to the Audiencia, he asked Teresa whether she had ever had an inkling that Guerrero was "in love with" her daughter, how it was possible that she did not notice anything wrong with Elena or Regla on the day in question, and precisely what symptoms

[45] Matthews, *The New-Born Cuba.*
[46] "Violación de la menor Regla María Sánchez," Audiencia de la Habana, Legajo 492 Num. 4, ANC.

Regla displayed that made Teresa think she had been deflowered. He asked Regla herself with what, precisely, Guerrero covered her mouth if his hands were busy closing the door, why she did not scream for help when Guerrero removed his hands from her mouth to close the door, and Guerrero's precise actions as he raped her. The lawyer had sixteen questions for Regla, most of which asked her to explain in minute detail why, if she was truly raped, she did not "resist" at every possible second. The implication, of course, was that if she *had been* deflowered, she had consented. His strategy worked: Guerrero was acquitted on all charges. The prosecution appealed, stating that Regla's delay in reporting the attack was not due to its not having happened but instead to her fear, but the Court denied the appeal, upholding Guerrero's innocence.[47]

Both Celia and Regla found themselves in dangerous sexual situations because of financial need, but the Cuban courts failed to recognize their claims as legitimate, at least partially because of their class positions and lack of clear ties to a traditional family. Although the image of a landed Cuban family with generations of domestic workers remaining in their service is a popular one, stories like Celia's and Regla's are representative of a more piecemeal and less stable kind of domestic work, one that could lead to precarious circumstances. These girls were not like "one of the family" for the people who employed them. When Celia became pregnant, her employer literally gave her back to the orphanage from which she'd hired her. Far from being ensconced in a nurturing environment, Regla was raped by one of her mother's clients. Just as the notion of family played a large role in the struggles between *patrones* and *patrocinados* as Cuban slavery gradually ended, family – or lack thereof – played a huge role in the safety and wellbeing of young women like Celia, Regla, and Cecilia. Regla and Cecilia found what little support they had in their biological families – the people related to them by blood, not by employment ties.

Standards of honor and hygiene in Cuba had brought young women like the three described here in for suspicion about their dedication to the project of modernity and cleanliness. Such standards flourished across the globe in postcolonial and post-emancipation contexts. In the United States, black women's supposedly deviant sexuality was connected to their reluctance to work on terms untransformed by their freedom from slavery.[48] Indonesia's transition from Dutch colony to independent

---

[47] Ibid.    [48] Hunter, *To 'Joy My Freedom*; Glymph, *Out of the House of Bondage*.

nation caused profound anxiety about Indonesian domestic servants' influence in white homes.[49] Cuba was no different, and on the island the stereotypes shaped by the hygiene movement made domestic workers vulnerable to a double violence: the violation of their bodies and the indifference of the court system.

The sexual violence that Cecilia, Celia, and Regla María faced mirrored the experiences of enslaved domestics before full abolition. During Cuba's slow end to slavery, *Patronato* court records betrayed both the myth of a functioning plantation family and the truth of dangers of the physical closeness inherent to domestic service. They also revealed that enslaved women were more than willing to challenge their owners and push the legal limits in demanding their freedom. In January of 1882 in Santiago de Cuba, a *patrocinada* called Feliciana made a legally dubious demand of the *Patronato*: She asked to be freed on the grounds of abuse. Feliciana was the *patrocinada* of Don Manuel Martínez, but she was actually under the authority of his son, Don Fernando. Feliciana complained that Don Fernando's wife had beaten her in the face with a stick as punishment for a reason that she did not specify. An expert witness verified that Feliciana had "light marks" at the bridge and base of her nose, another at an angle with her right eye that appeared to be scarring, and another on her cheek. The witness suggested that the marks on her nose and her eye had been produced by a "hard object," and that the mark on her cheek must have been produced by a hand or another material "with an uneven surface." There were even more scars on her neck.[50]

Physical violence was actually not a legal ground for freedom under the *Patronato*.[51] Thus, Feliciana was gambling by basing her claim for freedom on violence. She might have believed her case was egregious enough that either the authorities would take pity or her *patrón* would relent: Rebecca Scott speculated that enslaved people might have used claims of *sevicia* (excessive violence) to improve their circumstances, betting that their *patrones* might free them or treat them better if they were threatened with court cases.[52] But if Feliciana was betting that her *patrón* would be cowed, she was mistaken. Martínez denied all claims against his family. According to him, Feliciana had cut her foot on a bottle days previously when she was on the street Pozo del Rey. When

---

[49] Stoler, *Carnal Knowledge and Imperial Power.*
[50] "Libro de Actos, Año 1882," AHPSC, 108–109.
[51] Scott, *Slave Emancipation in Cuba,* 145.  [52] Ibid., 145.

she entered his house, Martínez said, she had lost so much blood that she fainted and hit her head on a wooden box, causing the marks on her face. Three of Martínez's associates, who were supposedly in the house at the same time, confirmed the story. The Santiago *Patronato* dismissed Feliciana's case.[53]

A month later, a woman named Jacinta appeared before the Santiago *Patronato* three times. The first time, she accused her *patrono* of prohibiting her from depositing money into the account through which she could buy her freedom, of refusing to let her find work outside his authority (ostensibly to contribute to her purchasing her own freedom), *and* of physically abusing her: A small scar on the back of her head was evidence of his brutality.[54] Her *patrono*, Don Leonardo Calderón, denied all allegations. In fact, he insisted that he had wanted Jacinta out of his house and had encouraged her to make deposits in her account.[55] The *Patronato* decided to continue investigating Jacinta's injuries and had her transferred to the hospital.

Jacinta was back before the *Patronato* just three days later. After she had appeared in court on February 6, Calderón had beaten her with a stick as punishment for her petition. The *Patronato* referred the case to a judge, who finally resolved it on February 22. That hearing revealed that Jacinta's three small sons, one of whom was still breastfeeding, were at the root of the conflict between her and Calderón. Calderón claimed that he was happy for Jacinta to look for work and even happy for her to take her sons with her. He merely told her that if she did take her sons with her, he would *not* compensate her for their expenses. Calderón's neighbors insisted that he had never beaten Jacinta. Her case against Calderón was dismissed.[56]

A domestic servant was any *patrocinada* who could demonstrate to the *Patronato* that she had worked in any capacity outside field labor for a period of four consecutive months.[57] Feliciana was likely a domestic in the city of Santiago de Cuba: She allegedly entered her *patrono*'s house after returning from outside. Generally, enslaved people working in the

---

[53] "Libro de Actos, Año 1882," Archivos Históricos Provinciales Santiago de Cuba, AHPSC, 108–109.

[54] Ibid., 139–140.

[55] The *Patronato* stipulated that the payments required of *patrones* could be placed with a local junta. It seems here that Jacinta was blocked from her legal right to do so. Scott, *Slave Emancipation in Cuba*, 130.

[56] "Libro de Actos, Año 1882," AHPSC, 139–140.

[57] Ortiz, *Los negros esclavos*, appendix; Cowling, *Conceiving Freedom*, 134.

fields lived in their own quarters and would not have had cause to enter their master's house. Jacinta's case, too, reveals a physically and emotionally intimate relationship with her *patrono*. His insistence that he wanted her "out of his house" and his attachment to her three sons – whether for financial reasons or otherwise – betrays her status as a domestic *patrocinada*.

These are just two cases of hundreds across Cuba for the duration of the *Patronato*, from 1880 to 1886. Combined, they prove little. But the uncomfortably detailed descriptions of Jacinta's and Feliciana's injuries, almost undoubtedly perpetrated by their *patrones*, evoke the dangers of living with one's former enslavers. These women's pursuit of their freedom before the end of their contracts demonstrated a defiance of the institution that enslaved them and promised to set them free, gradually. In claiming *sevicia*, although it was not a violation of the terms of the *Patronato*, Jacinta and Feliciana both went outside of the bounds of the institution, implying that the *Patronato*'s terms were not good enough. In doing so, they joined the chorus of African-descended people in Cuba who dismantled the institution of slavery through their words and their actions.

These five stories of physical and sexual violence – and the measures the survivors took to assert their own version of what happened – are not stories from "inside the circle," as Saidiya Hartman termed her analysis of black American women's transgressions at the turn of the century.[58] Based on court documents, they are decidedly outside the circle of the lived reality all five women (girls) shared, and I am unwilling to speculate about what happened inside their heads. But in highlighting the choice that Celia made to believe Ricardo when he promised marriage, in lingering on Cecilia's desire for *some* but not *any* sexual activity with Santiago, in pointing out that Feliciana made her claim despite *sevicia* not being grounds for freedom, I hope I have created a more well-rounded image of both the physical dangers of domestic service at the turn of the century *and* the ways individual girls and women tried to combat them.

## 1.4 HYGIENIC AND DOMESTIC IDEALS

For policymakers and elite Cubans, sex workers were obviously deviant. Wet-nurses had to be watched closely, and girls who worked as maids

---

[58] Hartman, *Wayward Lives*.

were prone to lying about rape. The question remained: What were *good* servants like? How did they exist in their bodies?

Filomena and Máximo were two servants who knew their place. They were a married couple from Guanabacoa who worked in the home of Doctor X, a medical doctor in Havana. Doctor X regularly talked to his servants about medical and political issues while they served him breakfast or lunch. Filomena, a white middle-aged woman, was the perfect student for the doctor: curious, health-obsessed, and uneducated. Doctor X explained to Filomena, a hypochondriac, the importance of breastfeeding for infants, the problem of tuberculosis, and the epidemic of *muermo* (glanders), a disease that killed horses, which spread around Havana at the turn of the twentieth century. Filomena could be funny: When the doctor told her, for example, that *muermo* affected *"la raza equina"* (the equine species), she asked if that was the same as *"la raza china"* (the Chinese race).[59] Máximo, Filomena's husband, was a veteran of the war for independence. He asked fewer scientific questions of the doctor and was more likely to discuss the politics of the countryside with him.

One typical morning in Doctor X's house, Filomena announced that she wanted to emigrate because she was horrified by all of the upheaval surrounding the new constitution and the controversy of the Platt Amendment. The doctor patiently explained to her that while democracy could be chaotic, it was the best form of government. As they were talking, Máximo entered the doctor's house with his head covered in blood. A public meeting about the Platt Amendment that he attended had become violent, and people had thrown rocks, one of which had hit him. He had managed to clean the wound, which the doctor told him was a good thing to do, since it could have gotten infected and given him tetanus. The doctor explained the difference between tetanus that infants contract and tetanus caused by contact with contaminated objects. "Oh! Liberty!" Filomena exclaimed. "Not liberty; rocks," the doctor responded drily.[60]

In contrast, María Antonia was a bad servant. She cooked for Doña Ramona and Don Matías, who were new parents to the two-year-old Nenito. They loved him, but they had no experience with babies and received a lot of advice from their neighbors and relatives. María Antonia was a prolific bad-advice giver. Her suggestions often made Nenito ill. For example, María Antonia told Doña Ramona that if she wanted to stay

---

[59] Delfín, "Mañanas científicas," *La Higiene*, 20 febrero 1901, 499–500.
[60] Delfín, "Mañanas científicas," *La Higiene*, 30 mayo 1901, 619–620.

pretty, she should not breastfeed Nenito; instead, she should give him cow's or goat's milk. Later, she incorrectly instructed Don Matías on how to bathe Nenito, which resulted in the boy getting chills. Utterly lacking in formal expertise, María Antonia, who had been born in Africa, thought it appropriate to offer advice on childrearing.

Filomena and Máximo were ideals of good domestic servants. They were good people, ingenuous country folk who loved Cuba with all their hearts and who listened to authority with enthusiasm. They had very little in common with María Antonia, the African cook whose bad advice constantly endangered poor Nenito. Filomena, Máximo, and María Antonia really only had one thing in common, aside from their jobs: None of them were actual people. They were all characters created by Dr. Manuel Delfín, used in two serials in his health magazine *La Higiene*. The best body for domestic servants to have, perhaps, was one that only existed on the pages of a magazine.

Filomena and Máximo appeared in a recurring series called "*Mañanas científicas*" ("Scientific Mornings"), which Delfín used to expound upon the medical and political topics of the day. María Antonia appeared in "'Poor Nenito!' (The Story of Many Children)," intended as a warning against unverified childrearing advice. Considered individually, both serials have obvious morals. But juxtaposing the three domestic servants that Delfín created as archetypes highlights what being a good servant and a bad servant entailed in the eyes of professional Cubans.

Unlike María Antonia, Filomena knew the limits of her authority. In one episode of "*Mañanas científicas*," three women came in succession to see the doctor, and Filomena had to turn them away because he was ill. Each of the women offered Filomena herself money to consult about their babies' illnesses, but she turned each of them down because she "knew nothing about medicine." This was in 1907, when Filomena had been working for the doctor for more than ten years; ostensibly, she had picked up some simple advice that she could have passed on, but she refused. After the women left, she said to herself, "Had I been a curer, I would have made eight or ten pesos ... but I also would have killed three or four babies."[61]

Filomena and Máximo were white in the illustrations of "*Mañanas científicas*." María Antonia was explicitly black and African. She consistently relied on instinct rather than verifiable medical knowledge, which in

---

[61] Delfín, "*Mañanas científicas*," *La Higiene*, 10 junio 1907, 351.

"Poor Nenito!" always adversely affected Nenito. There were constant snide references to María Antonia's "*de nación*" heritage and a suggestion of the kind of African-based medical knowledge that Delfín despised and mistrusted. In contrast, Dr. X's white servants, even if their rural medical knowledge differed from his recommendations, were always willing to accept his authority as a doctor. It was not exactly María Antonia's blackness that made her suspect but rather her willingness to prioritize her own knowledge, rooted in African medical traditions as opposed to Western science. Ironically, scholars later in the twentieth century would point to these African-centric medical and religious traditions as the most uniquely Cuban part of the national culture.[62]

Delfín's juxtaposition of the appropriately deferent servants and María Antonia's unwillingness to cede to Western medical knowledge was a microcosm of the growing intellectual movement in Cuba (and elsewhere) that favored Western medical science and represented "the growing hegemony of science as the anodyne to social ills."[63] Stories of *brujería* (witchcraft) flooded Cuban newspapers in the early twentieth century. The most famous case was that of the little girl Zoila, a two-year-old whose body was found on a farm in Güines in 1904. Several black men and women were found guilty of sacrificing the young girl to increase the potency of their spells.[64] María Antonia, Delfín's fictional African servant, was nowhere near a *bruja* (witch). Her suggestions were well-intended for Nenito, even if they ultimately endangered him. But both stereotypes – the dangerous *bruja* and the meddlesome *doméstica* – were rooted in "racial discourses premised on the primitivism and inherent criminality of people of African descent."[65] María Antonia was excessively confident in her own authority, whereas Filomena and Máximo bowed to Dr. X's instructions. Discourse like Delfín's promoted the notion that the María Antonias of Cuba needed to be shown the right way.

In 1907, just 16 percent of working Cubans were domestics, down 7 percent from 1899.[66] Fewer people were electing to become domestic servants, and those who *were* electing to become domestics were more likely to be black women than had been the case in 1899. Black women comprised 26 percent of the domestic service workforce in 1899, but

[62] Lydia Cabrera Collection, CHC.    [63] Bronfman, *Measures of Equality*, 52.
[64] Ibid., chap. 2.    [65] Ibid., 64.
[66] United States War Department, *Report on the Census of Cuba*, 403–404; *Censo de la república de Cuba*, 1907, 508.

29 percent in 1907.[67] With fewer domestics altogether and the ones left more likely to be black women, Delfín's warnings about the María Antonias of the world were well-timed for his audience. But María Antonia was not real. Neither were Filomena or Máximo. The ideal domestic servant, it seemed, did not exist. But real ones did, and they would continue to exercise and demand control over their bodies and their lives.

## 1.5 CONCLUSION

Catalina and Petrona, the women detained in Marianao, were laundresses, not sex workers. But their status as laundresses came with stigma too: Most people in Havana collected rainwater for washing their homes and clothing, and that standing water could lead to mosquitos breeding. City health officials enacted harsh regulations in 1901.[68] These regulations most likely acutely affected laundresses' work and the public's perception of it. Republican Cuba's focus on "hygiene," literally and figuratively, seeped into all aspects of Cuban life, like the water that health officials insisted be drained regularly. Frequently, concerns about hygiene and modernity closely resembled racialized standards of honor.

This chapter has explored how domestic servants fared in the first years of the twentieth century. Societal holdovers from the slave/colonial era – like honor – and standards locking into place with the new republic era – like hygiene – intersected to cast a hostile sheen on domestic servants' morality. Hostility toward domestic servants was not just rhetorical but physical. In associations with prostitution, disdain toward "mercenary" *nodrizas*, and court cases that cast skepticism on young women's innocence, domestic workers literally embodied the social anxieties of a new nation.

In its exploration of the physical bodies of domestic servants, this chapter has also illuminated some demographic aspects of the work and Cuban understanding of the island's place in the Americas. Puerto Rico, Spain, China, and Haiti have all figured into this conversation about domestic service in Cuba. While migration to the island would spike in the 1910s and 1920s, it's clear that from the dawn of the Cuban republic domestic service was work deeply connected to migrant communities on

---

[67] United States War Department, *Report on the Census of Cuba*, 403–405; *Censo de la república de Cuba, 1907*, 508–510.
[68] Rodríguez, "A Blessed Formula for Progress."

the island. The suspicion and hostility toward domestic workers and the suspicion and hostility toward non-Cuban migrants fed on each other.

Petrona and Catalina's experience also offers insight into the topic of Chapter 2. We would not know about what happened to them if Catalina had not complained to the police. Unlike Cecilia, Celia, and Regla María, Catalina and her mother received some semblance of justice. But all four women were notable for their willingness to talk to legal authorities. Chapter 2 examines the responses of black Cubans to the hostility and suspicion they faced in the decades after independence. Cubans of African descent presented themselves to mainstream Cuban society differently depending on their class backgrounds. Domestic workers comprised a large portion of Cuba's black population, but that did not necessarily lead to corresponding acknowledgment of their work.

# 2

# Of Domestic (and Other) Offices

## Black Cubans' Claims after Independence

The Rebel Army symbolized Cuban nationalism in the second half of the nineteenth century, and the men who fought for Cuban independence embodied nationalist fervor and pride. Quintín Bandera was one such man. He had participated in insurgent rebellions since the 1850s and had accompanied the two most famous generals of the last war for independence – Antonio Maceo and Máximo Gómez – during the invasion of the western end of the island. Unlike many famous soldiers (including Maceo), Bandera survived the war, achieving the rank of general before it ended. But Bandera was black and dark-skinned, and his position as a war hero faltered in the aftermath of the war and during the US occupation.[1]

The occupying US government denied Bandera full compensation for his military participation, and he struggled to find work. He worked for a while as a garbage collector and later was offered a job as the face of Crusellas – a Cuban laundry soap company. The company approached Bandera because "his condition as a dark-skinned man won him sympathy among the black and white washerwomen across the capital, and they commercially exploited his status as General of the War of Independence."[2] African-descended Cubans had participated in and frequently led the independence struggle. But after victory the government moved to deprive Afro-Cubans of such dignity.[3] A man like Bandera was

---

[1] Ferrer, "Rustic Men, Civilized Nation."    [2] Padrón Valdés, *Quintín Bandera*, 7–8.
[3] Ada Ferrer documented how, in the last year of the war for independence, the Rebel Army began replacing black and mixed-race leaders with white, educated officers. After the United States occupied the island, black veterans were routinely humiliated and denigrated by American and white Cuban solders. Ferrer, *Insurgent Cuba*, chap. 6: Lucero, *Revolutionary Masculinity and Racial Inequality*.

relegated to selling soap to laundresses, who were supposed to sympathize with him as a fellow Afro-Cuban.

Those laundresses themselves might have been freedwomen. While their contributions to ending slavery and to Cuban independence never reached the notoriety of Bandera's contributions, they too played a role in these world-historical events. But just as Bandera found himself pandering to their labor, laundresses, maids, and nannies found their labor denigrated and their morality and hygiene – both literal and figurative – called into question. Crusellas's advertisements featuring Banderas distilled two strains of white Cuban nationalism in the early twentieth century: racism against dark-skinned Cuban men and hypervigilance of the bodies of black women.

This chapter switches our focus to ask, not what was behind the decisions of hygienists and policymakers, but what were the responses of men and women like Bandera and the laundresses to whom he sold soap. In the decades after Cuban independence, how did Cubans of African descent lay claim to their rights as respectable Cuban citizens? Other scholars have traced the intellectual history of black Cubans before 1933, demonstrating that they demanded inclusion in the nascent vision of nationalism that white Cubans espoused.[4] Here, I further interrogate the written contributions of African-descended Cubans to investigate where working-class and poor black Cubans, especially domestic workers, fit into their vision of inclusion.

A short answer to that question is: They did not. Mostly, the class of black Cubans with the resources and platforms to make their politics known did not expend that privilege on the concerns of working-class and poor black Cubans. Instead, especially through the 1920s, black intellectuals pushed back against depictions of black Cubans as only worthy of domestic service or manual labor.[5] In many ways, the black intelligentsia in Cuba erased a large part of the black experience. To claim respectable citizenship, they eschewed discussions of the work that most black women did to survive. A political party that integrated working-class black concerns and demands for fair treatment and respectability did emerge: With its radical positions on racial equality, national sovereignty, and labor, the PIC showed black *and* white Cubans that the "black vote" was more than just a passive mass to be bribed or sweet-talked. But the

---

[4] Pappademos, *Envisioning Cuba*; Guridy, *Forging Diaspora*; de la Fuente, *A Nation for All.*

[5] Pappademos, *Envisioning Cuba*, introduction.

violent end of the PIC suggested to many that such radical and unapologetically anti-racist activism was the wrong approach, and other black media sources turned their lens inward. Respectable citizenship could instead be predicated on traditional gender roles and family structures.

In an ideal nuclear family, the patriarch provided for his wife and children, who as a result did not have to work at all. Although this was far from reality for most Cubans of African descent, it was the fantasy that both black liberals and black radicals at the time envisioned. Both groups envisioned domestic work as women's work, and indeed domestic service was more feminized among black Cubans than in the overall population. While, in 1907, 60 percent of all domestic workers were men, 23 percent were men of color and 30 percent were women of color – a clear majority. Seventy-six percent of working women of color were domestics, while just 15 percent of working men of color were.[6] Black men of influence in these first couple of decades of the twentieth century wanted to protect domestics, whom they understood to be female, not by pressing their labor claims but by hopefully taking them out of the workforce altogether.

This chapter contributes to an intellectual history of the black Cuban "aspiring classes," a term historian Michele Mitchell coined to refer to upwardly mobile African Americans after the US Civil War.[7] In his study of cultural exchanges between black North Americans and black Cubans, historian Frank Guridy pointed out the dearth of literature on the black Cuban aspiring classes, noting that "the historical experiences of Afro-Cubans who do not fit into the categories of slaves, patriots, musicians, workers, communists or *santeros* … have generally been overlooked."[8] Of course, this book *is* concerned primarily with workers, specifically domestic workers. But in the early twentieth century, while most working black women were domestics, they were not the people who wrote black *cubanidad* into being. Thus, I respond to Guridy's call by looking at how the aspiring classes dealt with – or did not deal with – their poorer counterparts. Black Cuban journalists and activists shaped an image of African-descended Cubans to rebut racist stereotypes about their race, but what effect did discourses of Cuban blackness that erased working-class concerns have on black working-class people, especially domestics? And did the erasure contribute to a more radical turn among domestics and other workers later in the twentieth century?

---

[6] *Censo de la república de Cuba, 1907*, 508–510.     [7] Mitchell, *Righteous Propagation*.
[8] Guridy, *Forging Diaspora*, 13.

Legal documents that domestic workers had drafted by lawyers in Santiago de Cuba offer access to the social world of these women and what they sought from the Cuban government. Afro-Cuban magazines offer access to the intellectual milieu of middle-class black Cubans. Novels depicting the plight of servants offer access to how artists thought about race in early republican Cuba. But none of these sources allow us to say with confidence that we *know* what it was like to be a black domestic worker in the decade after emancipation.[9] In this chapter, for example, there is no whole figure of the black male domestic worker, although we know from census data that he existed. If the black *female* domestic worker was not of political interest to the aspiring classes in the early twentieth century, the black *male* domestic worker was of even less interest: At least domestic service was (stereotyped to be) women's work. There was no space in the political imaginary for men to claim rights based on such feminized labor, and so they do not appear in the archives. This erasure, too, is part of the story of domestic service and blackness in Cuba.

The erasure of poor and working-class Afro-Cubans from Cuban history, and labor histories specifically, inspired this book. In discussions of race in Cuba in the twentieth century, domestic workers have only ever appeared parenthetically, mentioned briefly in discussions of class divisions within black Cuban communities or as examples of the dangers of poverty. Especially before the late 1930s, domestic workers themselves wrote little of their experiences and struggles. Aspiring-class black Cubans had a vested interest in eliding the problems that domestics faced, but domestic workers resisted that elision. The elision and the resistance comprise this chapter.

## 2.1 *DE OFICIOS DOMÉSTICOS*, LEGAL DOCUMENTS, AND BLACK WOMEN'S VOICES

Over the thirty-year struggle for Cuban independence from Spain, soldiers of color insisted upon their worthiness as Cubans. They based their demands for respect and inclusion on the brotherhood of war.[10] After the war ended, veterans of color held fast to their demands and,

---

[9] Marisa Fuentes confronted a similar problem in her study of enslaved women in Barbados: "There were none of the voices I sought to document; no whole figures emerged that I could trace beyond a momentary mention." Fuentes, 144.
[10] Ferrer, *Insurgent Cuba*.

along with liberals in the new government, managed to obtain some measure of representation in Cuba's nascent democracy – they received the vote. Receiving what was owed them from years of military service, though, was more difficult. A mobilization in 1902 spearheaded by the Veterans and Societies of Color "challenged the newly elected administration on racially exclusive government hiring policies."[11] On a journey throughout Cuba at the end of 1903, the republic's first president, Tomás Estrada Palma, promised that all soldiers would be fully compensated for their military service, even if the government had to issue paper money or liquidate bonds – a campaign trip that suggests the government's payment of veterans was unsatisfactory.[12] The August Rebellion of 1906, in which opposition to Estrada Palma's possibly fraudulent second election armed itself, found support among black men who had supported Estrada Palma's rival in the first election. Their grievance that his administration had done little for African-descended men, especially veterans, remained as true in 1906 as it had been four years earlier.[13] And it was not just men, not just veterans, who were demanding their due. Women participated in the independence war effort too, sometimes as domestic workers. As non-soldiers, they were not eligible for the same kinds of compensation as veterans; however, in the first years of the new century and Cuba's independence, they asserted their eligibility as contributors to the independence movement.

On November 13, 1905, Mercedes Sánchez Aldana found herself before the lawyer Rogelio Bernal y Ferrer in Santiago. She was single, from Sagua la Grande but living in the city of Guantánamo at the time. In Guantánamo on October 5 of 1904, Sánchez had been legally recognized as the only inheritor of Celestino Sánchez Aldana, in her capacity as his natural mother.[14] Celestino had been a soldier in the Liberating Army during Cuba's last war for independence. When he died, she received half of his owed wages, which ended up being 570 pesos. In Santiago in 1905, Señora Sánchez was before Bernal y Ferrer to confer special power on two men to represent her in Santiago's courts, to help her access the second half of her inheritance.

---

[11] Pappademos, *Envisioning Cuba*, 65.
[12] Letter from H. G. Squires to Mr. Hay, October 17, 1903, in Papers Relating to the Foreign Relations of the United States, With the Annual Message of the President Transmitted to Congress, December 7, 1903, Letter 339, US Office of the Historian.
[13] Pappademos, *Envisioning Cuba*, chap. 1.
[14] Sons and daughters were referred to as "natural" or "legitimate"; the term "natural" here suggests that Celestino Sánchez was born out of wedlock.

On January 17, 1906, Rosa Estiven, a native of Cobre, appeared before the same attorney. Estiven appeared to confer special power on the businessman Leonardo Beatón to seek the inheritance of her natural son, Leoncio Estiven. Estiven's son had been a captain in the since-dissolved Liberating Army and had served directly under the famous general Antonio Maceo. On May 12 a widow named Adelaida Aciego enlisted the help of Leonardo Beatón to obtain the inheritance of Hilario Hechavarría, a soldier in the Liberating Army who was her legitimate spouse. Sánchez, Estiven, and Aciego were all listed as *de oficios domésticos* – of domestic offices, or domestic workers.[15] Just as their counterparts had faithfully shown up decades before at *Patronato* courts across the island, domestics in the new republic showed up too. After emancipation, journalists and government officials mocked and decried black women's rejection of field and domestic work and their prioritization of their family lives; however, in the first decade of the twentieth century, freedwomen and their descendants used those familial relationships to assert their citizenship and advocate for their rights as Cubans.

No longer needing to petition for their freedom, these domestic servants petitioned for funds that would sustain them. Although some men and women approached lawyers in groups, most of the almost seventy cases perused in Santiago were single women, hiring a lawyer alone. So many went to the same lawyer that an oral network of domestic servants telling their friends and relatives is certainly possible. However, just as women pursued their freedom via the *Patronato* by themselves, these women in Santiago de Cuba went to lawyers as individuals to make their claims.

Between 1905 and 1906 domestic workers appeared before the lawyer and notary public Rogelio Bernal y Ferrer in Santiago de Cuba to request inheritances from their brothers, sons, fathers, and lovers – almost all of whom had participated in the last war for independence, which ended in 1898. They requested amounts ranging from 280 to 1,962 pesos.[16] While

---

[15] "Poder Especial. La Señora Mercedes Sánchez Aldana a los Señores Faustino Quirch y Benigno Diago," 13 noviembre 1905; "Poder Especial, para reclamar haberes del Ejército Libertador. La Señora Adelaida Aciego, al Señor Leonardo Beaton," 12 mayo 1906, Rogelio Bernal y Ferrer Papers, Fondo Protocolos Notariales, AHPSC.

[16] "Poder Especial. La Señora Luciana Olivero, a los Señores Leonardo Beaton y Narciso Regüeiferos," 15 noviembre 1905; "Poder especial para cobrar haberes del Ejército Libertador. Las Señoras Antonia Rodriguez, Francisca Esteves y Dolores Dominguez, a los Señores Leonardo Beatón y Alejandro Herrera y Correoso," 24 abril 1906, Rogelio Bernal y Ferrer Papers, Fondo Protocolos Notariales, AHPSC.

many women were from Santiago, some were from other parts of the East, including Sagua la Grande, Bayamo, Caney, and Mayari Abajo. Some still lived outside Santiago but had traveled to the city ostensibly for the purpose of setting down these legal documents. The most common by far was called *poder especial* (special power), which conferred authority on a third party to represent people in court to claim the inheritances of their relatives. Santiago was the provincial capital, so to seek inheritance or to seek recognition as the legal inheritor of someone, it was necessary to travel to the city's courts. Bernal y Ferrer signed the documents conferring special power onto a woman's chosen representatives and certified that he found the applicant "in complete enjoyment of her civil rights and processed with the legal capacity to bestow this mandate."[17]

By the turn of the twentieth century, military service was an established path to respectable citizenship, especially for African-descended people in the Americas; although women usually were not formally in the military, they benefited from their male relatives' participation.[18] African American widows of the US Civil War pursued pensions from the federal government for decades after the reconciliation of the North and South, transforming their claims as time passed to ensure that they would be paid.[19] Cubans embarked on a similar path in the twentieth century: In 1903, 1906, 1911, and 1924, various veterans' organizations emerged and retreated, always making the regular payment of pensions a key part of their platform.[20] The timely and complete payment of veterans' salaries and pensions was a volatile political issue into the 1940s in Cuba. Especially in the decade after independence, with the economy in disarray, the salaries of fallen soldiers could have been life-sustaining to their families. Domestic service remained poorly paid work: One heartbreaking letter sent to the Beneficence Office in Santiago in 1908, in which a chronically ill man asked the government to take over care of his children, revealed that his wife made eight pesos monthly working as a maid.[21]

The women in these documents led independent lives. They were used to acting independently of male authority figures, even if they needed to

---

[17] "Poder Especial para reclamar haberes del Ejercito Libertador. La Señora Rosa Estiven al Señor Leonardo Beatón." 16 January 1906, Rogelio Bernal y Ferrer Papers, Fondo Protocolos Notariales, AHPSC.

[18] Beattie, *The Tribute of Blood.*     [19] Brimmer, "Black Women's Politics," 857.

[20] Hewitt, "Republican Ideas and the Reality of Patronage."

[21] "Negociado Beneficencia, Num. 332 (1908): Pablo A. Morote, interesa se le recojan en el Asilo de Beneficencia dos hijos menores que se encuentran enfermos y de desamparados." Fondo "Beneficencia," Legajo 172 Num. 40, AHPSC.

hire men to represent them in court. Mercedes Sánchez Aldana, for
example, was single but had a son who had been old enough to fight in
the war. She had at some point moved from one city to another, and she
had traveled to Santiago for legal reasons. The document never mentions
a potential male caretaker. Like many other women represented in similar
documents, Señora Sánchez had to do for herself. In Oriente province,
61 percent of employed women worked in domestic or personal service in
1907, and 77 percent of those women were unmarried.[22] Women like
Sánchez and Rosa Estiven grounded their respectability in their sons'
sacrifice for the independence project. Both were natural mothers –
unmarried – but that did not matter. What mattered was what they had
given up, and what they deserved.

The documents do not mention race, only the provenance of the
applicants and the men on whom they conferred special power. But there
are clues that the racial makeup of the women listed as de *oficios
domésticos* overlaps with the racial makeup of domestic workers at this
time. In 1907, people of color comprised about 30 percent of the population of Cuba, but just over half of domestic workers in Cuba were people
of color – a category that included African-descended and Asian men,
women, and children. Fully three-quarters of working women of color in
Cuba were domestic servants in 1907. Of the 6,700 women in Santiago
province who worked as servants or laundresses in that year, 81 percent
were of color.[23] Adelaida Aciego, for example, lived in Santiago but was a
native of Africa. She was an adult who almost certainly arrived in Cuba
before slavery was abolished in 1886, and so it is probable that she herself
was enslaved. Another clue is the phrase "*sin otro apellido*" (without
another surname) – while in the Latin American tradition free Cubans
had two surnames, many enslaved people only had the name of their
masters. Captive Africans who married each other and had children only
had one name to pass on to their children. Luciana Olivero, applying for
the inheritance of her brother in 1905, and María Barbara Mariño,
applying for the military pension of her recently deceased husband in
1940, also were both listed as "*sin otro apellido*." This does not *definitely*
mean that these women were of African descent, but it is probable.[24]

---

[22] *Censo de la república de Cuba*, 1907, 523–525.      [23] Ibid., 548.
[24] "Poder Especial. La Señora Luciana Olivero, a los Señores Leonardo Beaton y Narciso
   Regüeiferos," 15 noviembre 1905," Rogelio Bernal y Ferrer Papers, Fondo Protocolos
   Notariales, AHPSC. On the topic of naming and race in Cuba, see Zeuske, "Hidden
   Markers, Open Secrets."

The racial makeup of women applying for compensation had not just demographic but political implications. Rosa Estiven was sure to note in her application for representation that her son served under the famed general Antonio Maceo, who emerged as a leader of the independence movement after the Ten Years' War ended in 1878, famously rejecting Spain's peace treaty with more moderate members of the Liberation Army. He led the "Little War" from 1879–1880, and, when war broke out again in 1895, he was arguably the most famous general in the renewed Liberation Army. Known as the "Bronze Titan," Maceo's name remains synonymous with courage, revolution, and unmatched skill today.[25]

But a more apt parallel for Rosa Estiven is Maceo's mother, Mariana Grajales Cuello. Grajales, who lost nine of her thirteen sons in Cuba's struggle for independence, famously said that she only wished that she had more sons to give to the independence movement. It was through Grajales's sacrifices that Cuba became free. Throughout the twentieth century her reputation grew, and her life took on a mythical, saintly quality. In 1957, the mayor of Havana declared her the "mother of Cuba."[26] Like Grajales, Mercedes Sánchez, and countless other black women, Estiven had given up her son for Cuban independence. She deserved her son's inheritance because she was his mother, but she deserved Cuba's respect because she had given birth to a son who had carried out the orders of a national hero – arguably the man who most exemplified Cuba's anti-racist independence movement. The evidence of their sacrifice in these legal documents is a powerful testament to their own assurance of their contribution, despite their (supposedly) less-than-dignified occupation.

A second common type of document written up by Santiago lawyers was a retainer document – far less specific than the special power cases that named representatives to carry out specific actions. *Poder para pleitos*, or power for legal action, named people to carry out a long list of actions on the part of the applicant, but only in the event that they were needed:

Which gives and confers ample, sufficient and generous power, as much as by rights is required and necessary to Señor Doctor Rosendo Mauricio Ramón Carbonell y García, lawyer and resident of this neighborhood, so that he represents the person, rights and actions of the one whose matter is concerned, continues as follows:

---

[25] Ferrer, *Insurgent Cuba*.    [26] Stubbs, "Social and Political Motherhood of Cuba," 296.

First: so that he arrive in the name of the grantor and represent her as plaintiff, defendant ... or in whatever other legal capacity, before Courts, Hearings, Supreme Tribunals, Offices, and Authorities of all classes, in issues of trade, civilians of voluntary or contentious jurisdiction, trials declared to be of major or minor quantity, oral or special, of divisions of property and similar incidents of all types, of divorces, executives, mortgages, of bidding, bankruptcy, executors or those who have not made a will, suspensions of pay, debt relief, or pauses; files ad-perpetuam, of possessory pension and of territory; adjudications of goods, retractions, injunctions, provisional foodstuffs, of eviction for any cause, of arbitrators, of trials in default, criminals, correctionals, administrative, gubernatorial, contentious administrative and others that are necessary.[27]

This specific document guaranteed these benefits to a Jamaica native named Cathem Richards, who was "dedicated to the labors of her sex," but in January 1905 Celestina Furcas applied for the same kind of representation, as did Concepción Sánchez y Jiménez in July of 1906, and Regina Montiel and Antonia Cala y Boneau in January of 1907. While I recorded the three listed above between 1905 and 1907, there were none between 1907 and 1926. I recorded twenty-one documents in the files of various attorneys in Santiago de Cuba between 1926 and 1949.[28]

Today, many might associate such documents with wealthy people, who can afford lawyers on retainer for any legal situation that might come up. But in these cases, these women put representatives on retainer specifically *because* they were financially and/or socially vulnerable. Many of the hypothetical instances in which a lawyer would act listed in the document are situations that might acutely affect someone with an unregulated job: eviction, the suspension of pay, or dismissal. The Cuban imaginary associated domestic service with vulnerability and social marginalization, and in reality domestic workers *were* vulnerable and marginalized. But these documents – both the special power and the power for legal action – suggest that domestic workers were not passive about their social subordination. They took action to access material goods when they needed them, and they took *preemptive* action by identifying people who would help them in the case of a crisis.

These legal documents illuminate how women *de oficios domésticos* understood the new Cuban nation and their place in it. Their filing of legal documents at all demonstrates their faith in the laws that would guide Cuba. The specific reasons for their filings reflect that they believed

---

[27] "Poder para pleitos," 17 abril 1933, Juan F. Castellini y Vinet papers, Fondo Protocolos Notariales, AHPSC.
[28] Fondo Protocolos Notariales, AHPSC.

they were an integral and worthy part of the Cuban citizenry. But even as these women knew their own worth as citizens – people worthy of pensions and compensation – they were aware that mainstream (white) Cuban society disagreed. These women knew both that they were worthy of legal protection and that they *needed* legal protection. One response to the hostility toward domestic workers and black women described in Chapter 1 was this: simply to demand what was owed.

Other groups had other ways of resolving problems and ways around making claims on the government, for in early twentieth-century Cuba engaging the state was not necessarily the best way to resolve anything. For Spanish immigrants, there were the many Spanish mutual aid groups founded in the colonial era, many of which had low-cost healthcare and hospitals for members.[29] In the novel *La gallega* (*The Girl from Galicia*), the protagonist Llorca seeks help from a Galician immigrant organization when her employer's son rapes her.[30] There were the *casas de beneficencia*, one of which the chronically ill man wrote to for help with his children; there were the *sociedades de color,* which might have prevailed upon their networks to offer help. For diverse reasons, these avenues might not have been available to black domestic workers. Black Cubans could not have patronized Spanish mutual aid societies, and working and healthy people might have been turned away from the *casas de beneficencia*, as they might have from *sociedades* like Club Atenas. African-descended Cubans had few options outside of the state apparatus. These women who engaged the services of lawyers in Santiago were behaving proactively and prophylactically to challenges they knew they might face with little support from any community outside the ones they formed themselves.

## 2.2 BLACK MEDIA AND STATE VIOLENCE

It was amidst political chaos that women *de oficios domésticos* were demanding what was owed them. In 1906, Liberal Party members took up weapons against the Moderate Party, spurring the first US intervention since 1898.[31] Black participation in the Liberal party uprising had been high, and black politicians used that participation to gain access to more power in the existing political system in the 1908 elections. But many voting black Cubans felt their concerns were ignored by both parties.

[29] Rodríguez, "A Blessed Formula for Progress."   [30] Masdeu, *La Gallega*, 1927.
[31] Pappademos, *Envisioning Cuba*, 53.

In 1907, thirty men founded the Camagüey Directorate of Citizens of Color and wrote a manifesto pointing to blacks' meager share of public resources.[32] In 1908, a bit further east, black men formed another group: the *Agrupación Independiente de Color*, or Independent Association of Color. Created by African-descended independence-war veterans who felt that their voices were not being heard in the larger political sphere in Cuba, the party challenged the Liberal Party's traditional hold on the black Cuban vote.[33]

Shortly after its founding, the *Agrupación Independiente de Color* changed its name to the *Partido Independiente de Color*, or PIC. Much of the PIC's platform had to do with protecting black veterans and allowing them access to work, but a significant portion of their platform addressed broader concerns. The PIC demanded free education through the university level in Cuba, an eight-hour work day, distribution of national lands to Cubans, and the prioritization of Cuban workers over foreign workers. The PIC also demanded an end to the death penalty and judicial reform.[34] In 1908 the party launched a publication called *Previsión* (*Foresight*). Literary scholar Alexander Sotelo Eastman's pioneering work on the PIC and *Previsión* suggests that the newspaper was widely read throughout Cuba *and* throughout the African diaspora – the paper had subscriptions in every major city in Cuba and in Mexico, Puerto Rico, Hawaii, and the United States.[35]

It was not only through new political groups that black Cubans sought deeper participation in Cuba's democracy. Elite and aspiring-elite Cubans of color attempted to make themselves exemplars of respectability and civility. The black professional class was miniscule at the beginning of the twentieth century; the 1907 census cited just one black lawyer in all of Cuba and two black doctors. But it was precisely in response to the precarity and small size of the black professional class that they so stringently embraced the principles of racial uplift or racial progress that "emphasized cultural refinement, intellectual development, and moral reform."[36] They formed intellectual and cultural societies like Club Atenas and *La Unión Fraternal* in Havana, *La Bella Unión* and *El Gran Maceo* in Santa Clara, and *La Victoria* and *El Progreso* in Camagüey.[37] Many of these organizations also had corresponding

---

[32] Ibid., 56.  [33] Pérez, Jr., *Cuba: Between Reform and Revolution*, 166.
[34] Sotelo Eastman, "The Neglected Narratives of Cuba's Partido Independiente de Color."
[35] Ibid.  [36] Brunson, "Constructing Afro-Cuban Womanhood," 32.  [37] Ibid., 35.

publications that published articles, columns, and photographs celebrating racial progress and uplift.

The relationship between such cultural organizations and domestic servants is murky. In his 1959 collection of essays, lawyer and activist Juan René Bentancourt was highly critical of the nature of societies of color. He briefly explained that, after the independence wars in Cuba, segregation continued, and black Cubans saw the need to band together:

> But upon joining together, how did the black do it? Did he transplant or invoke his tribal African institutions? No. Did he create a sui generis organization, or at least one adequate for his necessities? No. How did he proceed then, the black, in creating his organizations? He created them in the image of the ones established by the dominant class.[38]

Betancourt went on to note that instead of fighting for racial equality, many black societies limited their struggle to, among other frivolous causes, "demanding certain luxurious dress codes to be able to attend their parties – causing many of them to reject girls who worked as domestic servants."[39] As far as actual membership, women could only join organizations like Club Atenas as associates of their husbands or male family members, and they had to be "respectable" – Frank Guridy confirms Bentancourt's accusation that domestic servants were regularly barred from participating in the activities of such associations.[40]

In contrast, the PIC's politics were explicitly aligned with the intersection of labor, race, and gender. In 1910, the novelist Policarpo Mira wrote into *Previsión* to announce that all proceeds from his forthcoming book tour would go to the PIC. The novel was *El camino: cuentecillo "especialimente para la familia de color"* (*The Path: A Short Story "Especially for the Family of Color"*). *El camino* features a young black woman named María Gilda. She works as an apprentice in a white couple's home, completing a maid's tasks while also learning to read and write, until Doctor Leopoldo, her boss, rapes her. The white family and her own father accuse her of being a seductress, and María Gilda flees and searches for a job as a domestic worker.

But María Gilda has a hero in her brother Lázaro, who identifies the problem not in his sister's (actually unimpeachable) behavior but in the patriarchal white power structure that limits black families' prospects. He dreams of an island-wide educational program that would fund the

---

[38] Bentancourt, "Las Sociedades Negras," *El Negro: Ciudadano del futuro*, 1959.
[39] Ibid.    [40] Guridy, *Forging Diaspora*.

education of poor black children. Eventually, with his help, María Gilda breaks free of domestic service and opens a clothing store – but not before Lázaro convinces their father to take action against María Gilda's rapist. In the story's climax, María Gilda's father kills Doctor Leopoldo in a duel.[41]

Mira eventually became the secretary of the regional PIC committee in Guanabacoa, just across the bay from Havana. His novel evoked the structural problems that the PIC identified within Cuba and embodied them in a young black woman forced into domestic service via sexual violence. While some historians have argued that the PIC was too narrow in its focus on black veterans to have gained a significant following among black Cubans between 1908 and 1912, Sotelo Eastman argues that the PIC's platform was expansive and inclusive – and that black Cubans *did* respond.[42] While groups like Club Atenas were declining membership to domestic workers, an active PIC member was distributing a novel that distilled black Cuba's problems into the body of one.

In 1910 – the same year that Mira pledged that his book tour proceeds would go to the PIC – the Morúa Law, which prohibited the formation of political parties based on racial difference, rendered the party illegal. In 1912, fearful that the Morúa Law would block the party from participating in the upcoming national elections, party leaders called for armed protest. President José Miguel Gómez's government responded brutally in eastern Cuba. White militias, encouraged by media coverage of "black barbarians," murdered between 3,000 and 6,000 black men, women, and children that summer in eastern Cuba.[43]

The viciousness of the response to the PIC was astonishing, but so too was the mainstream Cuban press's insistence on framing the conflict as one between barbarism (the PIC) and civilization (established political parties). The media's portrayal of PIC members as animalistic black men bent on destroying civilized Cuban culture helped enable the massacre.[44] At the same time, members of the government of Santiago de Cuba corresponded among themselves about the ways to best help and protect *white* Cubans in eastern Cuba, who had been displaced by the conflict. Private citizens donated money to come to the aid of white Cubans

---

[41] Sotelo Eastman, "The Neglected Narratives of Cuba's Partido Independiente de Color."
[42] Ibid.
[43] See, for example, Helg, *Our Rightful Share*; Bronfman, *Measures of Equality*; and de la Fuente, *A Nation for All*.
[44] Bronfman, *Measures of Equality*, 85–86.

supposedly made vulnerable by the armed conflict.[45] While people of African descent were being publicly lynched, the government fretted about how to protect white people, who really were not in danger at all.

Jesus Masdeu's 1920 novel *La raza triste* ended with the 1912 massacre, narrating how the fear of black barbarism penetrated the historically patriotic town of Bayamo. The novel's protagonist was a young mixed-race doctor named Miguel, optimistic at the novel's outset about his prospects in an independent Cuba but sick and imprisoned by the end. Throughout the novel – a harsh satirical take on the hypocrisy of Cuban race relations after independence – Miguel encounters the realities of domestic service twice. A poor black woman known as La Larga (the Long One) has three daughters, one of whom is a servant at the home of Don Pancho. Don Pancho is widely known to rape and then pay off the young girls he hires as servants, and this is precisely what happens to La Larga's daughter. Miguel attempts to create a mutual aid group to help the residents of the slum where La Larga lives with her daughters, but the group is panned as racist (anti-white).[46]

Later, Miguel hears of a woman named Norberta who routinely hires maids, works them to the bone for just under a month, and then fires them before the month's end so that she does not owe them their wages. When he confronts her, the police arrive to arrest him. Miguel tries political organizing to help the victim of a predatory employer; then he tries intrapersonal confrontation.[47] Neither is a successful counterweight to the white power structure in Bayamo.

If neither radical political organizing nor patriarchal defense was the answer to anti-black racism in Cuba, what could the aspiring classes do? The Camagüey-based Afro-Cuban magazine *Albores* (*Dawns*) might have been the answer. In a 1916 issue, *Albores* published two interviews about the nature of marital relationships between men and women. Inocencia Silveira – the daughter of a poet and student of pharmacy – answered questions on behalf of the fairer sex, and Mariano Castillo y del Pozo – director of a noodle factory in Camagüey – answered for men. The magazine asked searching personal questions: Who of your female friends is the most virtuous? What obligations does a woman have to her husband? What should marriage be rooted in: the inflexibility of a legal document, or mutual affection and the reciprocal recognition of merits and virtues?[48]

---

[45] *Fondo Partido Independiente de Color*, AHPSC.   [46] Masdeu, *La raza triste*.
[47] Ibid.   [48] *Albores*, Año 3, Número 35, 30 abril 1916.

It might seem like a far cry from demanding penal reform or creating industrial schools, but intimate and marital relationships were serious topics of conversation across the African diaspora. Choice of sexual partners and marital status were and had been important markers of status and class for African-descended Cubans; sexual behavior was as personal as it was political.[49] Painted with a broad brush as sexually voracious quasi-animals, aspiring-class black Cubans took care to highlight the legitimacy and morality of their romantic relationships when they could. Women of the aspiring class took care not to end up in situations like Celia's, the girl from the Red Cross orphanage who found herself pregnant and alone in 1907 (see Chapter 1). Both the content and the existence of the questions signaled to *Albores*'s readers that proper sexual behavior was of the utmost importance to maintain the respectability of the culture. The message was especially acute because of the legacy of sexual violence that had defined slavery for African-descended women and the stereotypes about their sexual appetites that continued to stalk them post-emancipation.[50]

*Albores* discussed more traditionally political topics as well, but it never approached the radicalism of the PIC's platform. Instead of indicting mainstream Cuban society for its ills, *Albores*'s focus mostly turned inward. One column lamented the closing of a local social organization but critiqued it for only accepting light-skinned black Cubans.[51] A beauty pageant, touted in May 1916, was canceled in September because the upcoming presidential elections (between conservative Mario García Menocal and liberal Alfredo Zayas y Alfonso) were too important for distractions.[52] But the beauty pageants, interviews about ideal marriages, *and* the discussion of unity amongst Afro-Cuban people of different skin tones and presidential politics were all political. Through its assertions of ideal womanhood, *Albores* made the case for ideal black Cuban behavior.

In the issues of *Albores* that I perused, labor rarely emerged as a topic of discussion. Domestic service never did. Black Cubans who aspired to the professional class distanced themselves from the images they must have known white Cubans clung to. They rejected imagery of members of their race as only maids, laundresses, chauffeurs, and gardeners, and filled

---

[49] Stolcke, *Marriage, Class and Color in 19th-Century Cuba*.
[50] For discussions of the topic in the North American context, see Mitchell, *Righteous Propogation*; Hartman, *Wayward Lives, Beautiful Experiments*.
[51] *Albores*, 15 junio 1916.      [52] *Albores*, 30 septiembre 1916.

the pages of their own magazines with their young women at debutante balls and their families all dressed in white and looking into the cameras: literal pictures of respectability. Elite Cubans of color formed social clubs and intellectual societies. They were doctors, lawyers, journalists, and politicians. They were wives. Domestic workers – encompassing so many tropes of servility, sexuality, and poverty – exemplified that which they wanted to escape.

The 1912 massacre had a suffocating effect on race-based activism in Cuba for decades afterward. *Albores*'s focus on the behavior and morals of African-descended Cubans, as opposed to the PIC's focus on structural impediments to black access to wages and education, suggests that for a time the black elite in Cuba concluded that an inward focus was a safer and better strategy than the PIC's radicalism. Michele Mitchell drew a similar conclusion from her study of late-nineteenth-century African American views on sexuality: After Reconstruction and the implementation of Jim Crow policies across the United States, black communities turned inward. Black Cubans turned inward, too, but often their conversations left out the most vulnerable among them.

For women in the ranks of the black Cuban aspiring classes, sheltering oneself inside a nuclear family was optimal. Race-based political activism had proven toxic. Work was no path to freedom: Cuban women of African descent were locked out of most well-paying professional jobs – leaving those who did work to labor as domestics; collective labor activism spearheaded by domestic servants was decades away. And while petitions to the state for compensation showed the steady insistence of working-class women that they were worthy members of the Cuban citizenry, we do not know the results of these petitions. Even novels suggested that black women's best bet was to be born into a family that could protect them – and that was not always enough. The optimal black nuclear family also demanded that men have jobs that would provide, meaning they would not perform domestic service. That this optimal nuclear family was an ideal mattered little to the people writing it into being. It mattered little that most working black women *were* domestics, that 15 percent of black men were, too, and that women like Cecelia Piehadrita were raped even though she did have a respectable married brother to protect her. The aspiring classes kept their eyes on that ideal and declined, at least publicly, to look at what was before them.

Some fifteen years after the 1912 massacre, the novelist Gerardo del Valle continued this tradition of determinedly looking to an ideal instead of reckoning with reality. In a section of the Havana newspaper *Diario de la Marina* called "*Ideales de una raza*" ("Ideals of a Race"), del Valle pontificated on black women's problems in Cuba. His essay managed to be both celebratory of and deeply hostile toward black women, refuting some of the worst claims against them by endorsing some of the other worst claims. Del Valle began by citing two "transcendental" characteristics of the black Cuban woman: her maternal love and her patriotism. According to him, rates of infanticide or child abandonment among black women were extremely low; black women were far more likely to raise "six, eight, or ten" children in a slum than abandon any one of them. Black women used the only resources they had – laundering or cooking – sacrificing their own ambitions so that their children could attend school and obtain a professional job: "Only [the black woman] knows the sacrifices it takes to achieve the beautiful spectacle of daily school attendance!"[53]

And according to del Valle, school attendance was paramount: "No social class has more need than the black woman to overcome the dark jungle of ignorance in which it has been immersed." Black women *needed* normal (teaching) schools, which produced caring and affectionate teachers, to drown out the "idolatrous beliefs" to which they were so vulnerable. Del Valle insisted that most black women were naïve and simple, too willing to engage in backward beliefs that held them down. The only solution was education.[54]

Within the month, a response appeared. Catalina Pozo y Gato, a doctor and writer, acknowledged the "sad truths" del Valle had laid out in his column. But her response chided del Valle for his focus on the supposed cultural deficiencies of black Cuban women and subsequent neglect of the structural obstacles that blocked black women's path to success. Pozo y Gato argued that black and white women were educated in Cuba at similar rates, but, whereas white women found jobs that reflected their education, black women were unable to: "I know cases of women of my race with painstaking education, languages, diplomas, titles, etc. working as domestics after having exhausted themselves pursuing a modest government position." Black women were locked out of retail positions and dignified jobs at factories and workshops. For Pozo y Gato, it was a stain on Cuba's national identity: "The racial prejudice eats away at Cuban nationality, nullifies its efforts, sterilizes its sacrifices and makes life bitter." At the beginning of November, del Valle had suggested

---

[53] del Valle, "La negra cubana," *Diario de la Marina*, 2 noviembre 1930.    [54] Ibid.

that while black Cuban women possessed more than sufficient patriotism, education was needed to make them worthy Cuban citizens. At the month's end, Pozo y Gato insisted that black Cuban women *were* worthy; it was Cuba's racism that made the nation itself unworthy of respect.[55]

By 1930, a pendulum shift in conversations about labor and gender and race had emerged, contemporaneous with a generational shift in Cuba's population. Five months before del Valle's and Pozo y Gato's editorial exchange, a society had emerged that presaged one aspect of domestic service's future in Cuba. The *Sociedad de Sirvientas* (Society of [Female] Servants), formed in June of 1930 in the heart of Havana, stated as its goals "the protection and mutual aid of its associates and their betterment, from a moral and intellectual point of view." For the fee of one peso a month, a member could expect guidance with job placements and "coverage of the most urgent necessities."[56] This type of society, which would proliferate in the 1940s and 1950s, indicated heightened awareness of domestic servants' needs. This society in particular openly associated the work with women, as Pozo y Gato did and activists would in later decades.

While sympathetic to female members of his race, del Valle went in for many of the same stereotypes that we saw in Chapter 1, calling on black women to become educated in order to rise above their supposedly inherent atavism. Pozo y Gato pivoted the blame from black Cuban culture to Cuban society itself, pointing out that lack of access to "good jobs" landed many black women in slums and as domestics against their will. While both were still mired in aspirational and respectability politics, Pozo y Gato challenged del Valle to consider that black women themselves were not the problem. In 1930, her argument already overlapped with those of more radical thinkers than herself or del Valle. These radical thinkers' voices would find full expression as Cuba hurtled toward revolution.

## 2.3 CONCLUSION

Many domestic workers have emerged in this chapter. There are the domestic workers to whom Quintín Bandera sold laundry soap, ostensibly charmed by his recognizable face and name. There are the domestics

---

[55] Pozo y Gato, "La mujer negra y la cultura," *Diario de la Marina*, 30 noviembre 1930.
[56] "Sociedad de Siriventas," 2 junio 1930, Fondo Registro de Asociaciones, Legajo 323 Exp. 9456, ANC.

who dutifully showed up at the law offices of Bernal y Ferrer in Santiago de Cuba, some having traveled many miles to demand what the state owed them. There is María Gilda, the vulnerable heroine of Mira's novel; there is La Larga's daughter, the victim in Masdeu's *La raza triste*. There are the friends of Catalina Pozo y Gato, reduced to domestic service despite having earned higher education. Most elusive are the domestic workers who lurk in the negative space of this chapter: the ones who do not emerge in magazines like *Albores*, the ones denied membership to Club Atenas, the men who appear in the census and nowhere else.

Only the women who appeared before the lawyers in Santiago de Cuba – and the nameless men and women who comprised the census data – are historically tangible. Archival documents place them in time and space. Other domestics are more ideas than men or women, made reference to (or ignored) but only there on the page; there is no evidence that domestic workers had any part in creating these images of themselves. Much historical writing happens this way: We gather all the references we can to the topic that interests us, combining them to gain a lens into that thing or group of people. But this methodology works best when output *by* that group of people – domestics, in this case – matches the references to them made by outsiders. For example, historians of José Martí can counterbalance all that has been written about him with the massive intellectual output of the man himself. But in the case of domestics, most of what we have is what other people said about them. The sources are lopsided.

It's important to highlight this lopsided nature of the sources because of the conclusions we draw from them. From manuals on breastfeeding, sexual assault cases, novels, newspaper articles, and more, the first third of this book has pointed out the ways in which domestic workers were vilified and victimized, cast as recalcitrant children or morally corrupt Jezebels. When I then point out that three-quarters of black women were domestic workers by the first decade of the twentieth century, the slippage between perceptions and reality becomes potentially dangerous. Perceptions of domestics were hostile, most black women were domestics, and many references to them assumed blackness; but real black women did not inhabit those stereotypes. We must keep in mind that domestic workers were real women (and men), existing in physical space – certainly affected by *but not living inside* the stereotypes that abounded about them. The sources I've drawn on that refer to domestic workers are valuable and important because they demonstrate how people thought about them and when they did not think about them. But even as we approach domestics' vulnerability, we must picture those *real* women, sitting inside lawyers' offices, waiting to sign their names with a signature or an X.

In the first three decades of the twentieth century, domestic workers – usually coded as black women– faced hostile stereotypes about their labor, their bodies, and their morality. Our insight into their responses to such hostility is limited by the limitations of the archive itself, but it yields this: Women of color subtly and steadily asserted their personhood in early republican Cuba. From the *Patronato* courts to lawyers' offices in Santiago, women who made their living as domestic servants expected the Spanish (and then Cuban) government to treat them justly. Domestic workers could not rely on middle-class African-descended Cubans to advocate for them; the vibrant black press ignored the work, instead celebrating the intellectual and domestic achievements of black Cuban women. Elite and aspiring-class black women in twentieth-century Cuba wanted to distance themselves from associations with service.

But Pozo y Gato's 1930 column presaged a transformation that was beginning even before she responded to del Valle. Black women's legal and political activities began to coalesce into what we now recognize as activism in the second decade of the twentieth century. As the republic became established – and then almost collapsed – the cultural touchstones of labor, activism, and charity also solidified, often all meeting in conversations around domestic service.

# 3

## Stopping "Creole Bolshevism"

### *Liberal Correctives to Increasing Labor Radicalism*

The Cuban economy collapsed in the mid-1920s when the price of sugar began to drop, a symptom of the global Great Depression that hit the United States a few years later. The government attempted to respond to the crisis by decreasing Cuban exports, but that only spurred sugar exports elsewhere and worsened the situation at home. Dissatisfaction with the island's political leaders grew. Gerardo Machado had been democratically elected as president in 1924, running on promises of reform and anti-corruption, but had become more dictatorial as his presidency continued. In 1928, Machado secured a second six-year presidential term through coercion, intimidation, and bribery of his political allies and rivals.

Dismay at Machado's brutal authoritarian tactics brought together Cubans from across political and economic spectra. The anti-Machado movement comprised workers, university students, feminists, and Cubans of all classes. Anti-Machado militants engaged in violence, and *machadistas* (Machado supporters) engaged right back. Bombings and shootings in broad daylight became commonplace in Havana. In September, the United States relayed to Machado that they could no longer support him, and the Cuban military intimated that they could no longer protect him. Machado and his inner circle promptly fled the island, and the university professor and doctor Ramon Grau San Martín took over.[1]

In the same month that Grau took over Cuba's governance, someone knocked on the door of an American couple living in Havana. James

---

[1] Pérez, Jr., *Cuba: Between Reform and Revolution*, 190–210.

Doyle Phillips wrote for the *New York Times* and lived with his wife Ruby. The person at their door asked for their servant, John. They invited John to a meeting for servants' rights; John agreed and attended. Ruby Hart Phillips attributed his eagerness to his nationality: "John, being a Jamaican, is quite keen on looking out for his personal rights." Ultimately, John chose not to join the servants' union even though those present at the meeting agreed to force *every* servant in Havana to join, even if they had to "break a few heads." John told James and Ruby that the people present at the meeting were "riffraff," the kind of people with whom he preferred not to associate. The Phillipses found their servant's snobbery hilarious.[2]

They might have been more relieved than amused at John's snobbery if they had been outside Havana. Grau's Government of 100 days quickly established a Ministry of Labor, decreed a minimum wage for sugarcane workers, and codified an eight-hour workday. But for many workers, these policies were too little, too late. Mill occupations, in which workers took over sugar mills, often holding captive and humiliating their managers, became commonplace. At the Miranda mill, 40 miles north of Santiago de Cuba, 3,000 members of a union struck from September 22 to October 5 of 1933. The domestic servants swore their loyalty to the strikers.[3] At the Báguanos mill, outside the eastern city of Holguín, sugar workers persuaded domestic servants to quit along with them. On the domestics' behalf, these workers, most of whom were Jamaican, demanded the following: a thirty-dollar monthly salary, free meals, and an eight-hour work day. They also demanded that servants perform one job only, specifying that "a servant is a cook or a washer but she will not work at both."[4]

The *Unión Doméstica* (Domestics' Union) of Camagüey formed in the same month that a recruiter knocked on the Phillipses' door, and domestics struck at the Miranda mill. The Union welcomed "cooks, washerwomen, nannies and handservants," with the goal of providing instruction and facilitating their development as workers.[5] This Camagüey group was presided over by two women – María Rosa Agüero and María Navarro. Agüero was an important name in Camagüey: In the nineteenth century two different men with the surname

[2] Hart Phillips, *Cuban Sideshow*, 147.     [3] Carr, "Mill Occupations and Soviets," 148.
[4] Carr, 154.
[5] Reglamento, "La Unión Doméstica," 6 October 1933, Fondo Registro de Asociaciones, Legajo 1 Num. 7, AHPSC.

fought for Cuban independence. Francisco Agüero is now a street in the city, and the city holds a monument to Joaquin de Agüero.[6] While the *Unión Doméstica* claimed to be apolitical, the date of its creation belies that claim. Camagüeyan domestic workers might not have been as ready to strike as their counterparts at sugar mills had been, but the fact of their joining such a group was itself transformative.

How had Cuba gotten to this point – where Machado had to be rushed out of the capitol building protected by guards, in fear for his life? Where servants were striking, demanding limits on their job descriptions, and joining domestics' cooperatives? It was not a straightforward line from the isolation and deprivation that many domestics experienced in the first two decades of republican Cuba to the radicalism that marked the mid-1930s, and it would not be a straightforward line afterwards, either. But for a brief moment, it seemed that Cuban domestic workers were poised to ride the cresting wave of change battering traditional Cuban politics.

Briefly, radicalism won out against liberal change. This chapter explores these dueling impulses in Cuba in the fifteen or so years before the 1933 Revolution. The struggle between liberal change and radical transformation was as palpable in transforming ideas about domestic service as it was in high-level political turmoil. While religious and secular organizations took up the cause of educating and uplifting domestics in the second decade of the twentieth century, domestic servants – offered classes and charity in place of stable work hours or salary guarantees – struck and occupied mills. They participated in solidarity strikes, flouting any notion of political docility. Before 1910, Cuban domestic servants had certainly advocated for themselves in criminal courts and with civil suits demanding compensation. But after 1910 their activism began to coalesce into collective action, based on their identity as workers. Their visibility as labor activists increased in the 1920s and 1930s as Cuban politics became more volatile, culminating in the 1933 Revolution.

Domestic servants comprised fewer people than they ever had before in Cuba: Between 1907 and 1919 the number of wage-earners in Cuba who worked in domestic or personal service decreased by 4 percent.[7] In 1907, 66 percent of wage-earning women in Cuba worked as domestics; in

1919, just under half of wage-earning women did.[8] Cuban men still comprised most domestic servants –Jamaican John was one of many – and this time period yields more documentary evidence of their presence than any other. Then another group entered the field: French and British Caribbean migrants. But, as Cuban politics became increasingly chaotic and the economy became more precarious, it became increasingly urgent to tie domestic service to womanhood and domestic interiors – and to deny its worth as labor.

It was no coincidence that domestics' participation in national politics and an increasingly vocal feminist movement coincided with a conservative and charity-minded approach to helping working women, and it was no coincidence, either, that new laws passed in the early and mid-1930s ignored domestic workers. The emotional logic of domestic service helps explain these contradictory phenomena. This emotional logic had to do with race relations in Cuba, dictating that racial interactions between Cubans of African and European descent be harmonious, affectionate, and familial. Nowhere was this clearer, supposedly, than in the close relationships between ostensibly black domestics and their ostensibly white employers. Militant domestic workers threatened the emotional logic of domestic service, which scaffolded the entire structure of Cuban race relations and was therefore far too important to let go. As this chapter moves back and forth between strikes and Catholic orders, between mill occupations and Schools of the Home, we will see how a smaller, more diverse, and more militant cohort of domestic servants threatened the supposed stability of Cuban households.

### 3.1 CHARITY OR SOLIDARITY: DUELING STRATEGIES FOR DOMESTICS' SURVIVAL

Strategies for finding domestics and for finding work as a domestic changed little during the first twenty years of the republic. In the 1910s, advertisements in *Diario de la Marina* continued to solicit women to work as maids, cooks, nannies, and wet-nurses. As they had in the early 1900s, the advertisements regularly failed to explicitly detail the kind of work expected. One advertisement called for a maid "without pretensions," while another called for a maid "who had served in well-known houses." Words like *fina* (refined) and phrases like "knowing her obligation" were

---

[8] Olmstead, *Cuba*, 626.

common in solicitations for domestic help. Although people posted in separate sections for distinct kinds of domestic work, a blurring of roles was common too. Advertisements for cooks often replicated this advertisement: "A cook is solicited to help with household chores."[9]

As they had back in 1901, domestic workers highlighted their racial background if it worked to their advantage. Spanish-born handmaids, cooks, and nannies routinely began their copy with reference to their foreignness. *Criolla* women had to indicate their respectability in other ways. One advertisement with no Spanish heritage to present read: "A young, serious and formal girl desires a placement as a handmaid or a nanny in a house of morality." Interest in a "house of morality" echoed across sections and racial distinctions, appearing in dozens of placement advertisements written by female domestic workers in one month in 1916 alone.

Insistence on working in a moral house was a response to the kinds of sexual danger domestic servants regularly faced – danger that, given the long legacy of sexual abuse of enslaved women, was heightened for African-descended domestics.[10] And while we cannot know for sure whether advertisements with no reference to Spanish birth were written by African-descended women, it is likely. Did black women feel the need to include more references to their character to compensate for their race?[11]

The danger that domestics might confront in seeking work was no secret. In 1914, one Father Cirilio Villegas organized a kind of mutual aid society that would benefit both "recently arrived" domestic servants and their *amas* (mistresses) within the Sacred Heart church in Havana. Nuns at Sacred Heart would teach the girls the nuances of domestic service in the capitol, and the society would offer protection and aid when the maids found themselves ill or unemployed. Employers or potential domestics who wanted to participate could leave their names at the church, which was located in the oldest part of Havana on Tejadillo street. Combining religiosity, honorable behavior, and material education, this project was typical of early overtures to domestic workers. The *Diario de la Marina* was "excited by the zeal of the mistresses and servants, so that they are united by love; the *amas* will have honorable servants, and the servants a sure door to spiritual and material salvation."[12]

---

[9] *Diario de la Marina*, "Solicitudes" y "Se Ofrecen," marzo 1916.    [10] See Chapter 1.
[11] *Diario de la Marina*, "Solicitudes" y "Se Ofrecen," marzo 1916.
[12] "Crónicas religiosas," *Diario de la Marina*, 20 noviembre 1914.

The Catholic Church might have been the first institution in Cuba to extend aid to domestic workers. The Church lacked the political influence in Cuba that it enjoyed in other Latin American countries, but upper-class Cubans especially still attended Mass regularly throughout the twentieth century. Poorer Cubans observed Catholic rites as well, even if they syncretized saints with Yoruba traditions in *santería*, Cuba's African-derived religion. It made sense that the Church would become involved in domestic service. What other institution had a stalwart following of the extremely wealthy – those who would employ domestic servants – and the extremely poor, who might turn to it for work?[13] Throughout the twentieth century, the Catholic Church ran dozens of free schools for boys and girls across the island, as well as night schools for female workers.[14]

Just one Catholic order, however, was wholly dedicated to domestic service. In 1876, a Spanish woman named Vicenta María López y Vicuña founded the religious order María Inmaculada, dedicated to young women who worked as domestic servants. In her youth, López y Vicuña had been inspired by the charity work of her aunt and uncle. Her aunt helped at a house in Madrid for young girls who had moved to the city in search of industrial jobs and were left penniless and "vulnerable to sin."[15] The Religiosas de María Inmaculada founded houses in 1912 in Buenos Aires and in 1913 in Santiago de Chile and Mexico. By 1915, however, the Mexican Revolution was in full swing. Fearing for the safety and future works of the sisters in Mexico, the heads of the order in Spain decided to send the sisters to Cuba to open a house in Havana. The goal of the community in Havana was to "educate, instruct, freely house and place young women dedicated to domestic service in houses with recognized honor."[16] Just as the Catholic Church's traditions were rooted in a centuries-old history spanning colonial and republican governments, the notion of honor bled into the Religiosas' understanding of their job regarding young women. The people who had inspired López y Vicuña – canonized in 1975 as a saint – wanted to prevent girls from falling into lives of "vice." For Catholic institutions like María Inmaculada and the

---

[13] In Chile, domestic workers and the Catholic Church formed alliances as well. See Hutchison, "Shifting Solidarities."

[14] Secretariado Económico Social de la Junta Nacional de Acción Católica Cubana, *Primer Catálogo de las obras sociales catolicas de Cuba*, 28.

[15] Guasch, *Religiosas de María Inmaculada al servicio de la Iglesia y la juventud en Cuba*, 14.

[16] Ibid., 20.

Church of the Sacred Heart in Havana helping domestic servants was an avenue to save the souls and the innocence of young girls.

But which young girls? The majority of young women María Inmaculada served were recently arrived Spanish immigrants.[17] The Sacred Heart Church on Tejadillo street also hinted at the Spanish heritage of the young women they wanted to help with the phrase "recently arrived." Over 400,000 Spanish immigrants arrived in Cuba between 1903 and 1916, and some Cubans argued that they pushed black women out of domestic service positions that they had previously enjoyed.[18] Between 1899 and 1919 foreign white women's share of domestic service had risen steadily: In 1899 they comprised just about 1 percent of domestic workers in Cuba, while by 1919 they were 7 percent.[19] Black women had comprised 26 percent of domestic workers in 1899, 30 percent in 1907, and 19 percent in 1919.[20] Thus, while foreign white women never seriously competed with black women for domestic service jobs, it might have felt that way in cities like Havana between 1907 and 1919, especially as these Spanish-oriented aid programs for domestics popped up.

Aside from men, African-descended women would have – or should have – been the main benefactors of any organization that sought to ameliorate the circumstances of domestic workers, but the media at the time rendered them invisible.[21] Photographic evidence in the one book published on the order is the only acknowledgment of black domestic workers' involvement in María Inmaculada.[22] Policymakers in early twentieth-century Cuba, discussed in Chapter 1, had been openly hostile to African-descended women's behavior. The gentle guidance that Sacred Heart and María Inmaculada offered might only have been so because its founders envisioned the young women they would help as white.

But gentle guidance was insufficient to quiet the building storm in Cuba. Strikes plagued Cuba constantly during the second decade of the twentieth century.[23] Economic conditions during and after World War

---

[17] Ibid., 90.
[18] *Informe de la compañera Edith Buchaca en la reunión nacional de mujeres, celebrada el 17 de junio de 1948*, Instituto de Historia.
[19] United States War Department, *Report on the Census of Cuba, 1899*, 404–405; Republic of Cuba, *Census of the Republic of Cuba, 1919*, 626–627.
[20] United States War Department, *Report on the Census of Cuba, 1899*, 404–406; United States War Department, *Censo de la república de Cuba, 1907*, 508–510; Republic of Cuba, *Census of the Republic of Cuba, 1919*, 626–628.
[21] Republic of Cuba, *Census of the Republic of Cuba, 1919*, 626–628.
[22] Guasch, *Religiosas de María Inmaculada*, 88–89.
[23] Pérez, Jr., *Cuba: Between Reform and Revolution*, 182.

I were abysmal for workers, as European nations canceled Cuban tobacco imports and the cost of living increased due to the supposed "war boom." Poor conditions led to increased militancy: Workers in various fields struck frequently in 1917 and 1918, and a general strike spread across the island in late 1918, alarming both Cuban and US officials.[24] Having started with railroad workers, the strike spread to other industries – mining, agriculture, buses, and public taxis, and even restaurants. Even after railroad workers and corporations resolved their dispute, sympathy strikes popped up across the island, making daily life difficult for the middle classes. In December of 1918, the General Manager of the Cuban Railway Company, G. A. Morson, wrote to his superiors in London:

> Such a complete tie-up of business has never been experienced in Cuba before. All stores, hotels, restaurants and eating houses were completely closed and it was very difficult, and for many impossible, to get anything to eat or drink. *Even the cooks and servants in many private homes refused to work.* [emphasis mine][25]

This was the only reference to domestic workers in the correspondence about this strike in US State Department records. Yet, Morson's aside suggests a wealth of possibilities. His implicit suggestion that domestics were not workers who could participate in strikes, rather merely servants who capriciously "refused to work," continued a long tradition of denying domestics the political consciousness to resist or agitate on their own behalf.[26] It was not coincidental that Cuban domestics were refusing to work during a general strike; they were *striking*. Morson's erasure of the domestics' political consciousness fit neatly into elites' studied refusal to acknowledge the labor orientation of domestic workers. Perhaps their absence from the records of these strikes is not evidence that they were not involved.

Second, despite his separation of "cooks and servants" from participants in the strike, it is clear that domestic workers were, in fact, "refusing to work" in sympathy with railway workers, just like most other laborers at the time. Perhaps domestics regularly participated in strikes across the

---

[24] Ibid., 181.
[25] G. A. Morson to W. J. Maslen, Esq., "Labor Troubles," December 19, 1918, RG 59, 837.504/94, National Archives, Roll 58.
[26] His bemusement at the idea that servants would "refuse to work" echoed Tera Hunter's analysis of domestic worker resistance in postbellum Atlanta. One of the most effective tools at those women's disposal was quitting their jobs, especially at inconvenient times for their employers. Southern white women ceaselessly complained about their maids quitting just before parties or dinners, ignorant of how much their mistresses needed them. Of course, these domestics were perfectly aware of how much they were inconveniencing their employers; that is why they did it. Hunter, *To 'Joy My Freedom*.

island. Railroads were essential to Cuba's sugar economy and had been since the island was a Spanish colony. Railroad employees enjoyed among the highest salaries on the island, and any economic turmoil that affected railroad employees' wages likely had a severe impact on the entire household. Were some striking domestic workers the wives, partners, sisters, or mothers of men employed by these railroad companies who knew their households could not subsist on domestics' wages alone? As it was elsewhere, striking might have been as much about considerations of family income as pure political solidarity.[27]

And were these striking domestics possibly men themselves? The 1919 census reported that 64 percent of domestic workers were men; this was up 4 percentage points from 1907. Advertisements in *Diario de la Marina* were separated by gender: *criadas y criados* (female and male servants), *cocineras y cocineros* (female and male cooks).[28] Men's increased entry into the domestic service workforce was likely related to the economic depression of 1917–1918 and the dearth of industrial and agricultural jobs pushing men back into a job many had left over the previous nineteen years. Morson's description of cooks and servants did not specify their genders, so it is possible that he was referring to at least some male cooks and servants.

Men comprised the majority of domestic workers in Cuba until the 1940s, but references to male domestic work are close to impossible to find in Cuban archives, and there's little research on male domestic workers in Latin America. In their analysis of domestic service in contemporary India, Raka Ray and Seemin Qayum refer to the paradigm of "failed patriarchy" to make sense of the stories male domestic servants tell about their lives. Despite men comprising the majority of domestic servants in India up through the twenty-first century, male servants in Kolkata see their occupation as a failure of their own masculinity. Cuban men, too, might have seen their domestic work as a failure: If they saw themselves that way, then so too might have other Cubans, causing them to elide their presence in the field.

As Michel-Rolph Trouillot wrote, "Sources are … instances of inclusion, the other face of which is, of course, what is excluded."[29] If domestic service was naturally less visible than other types of labor because of its execution inside homes, then elites' refusal to accept their political consciousness made the work doubly invisible. How many people saw

[27] Lindsey, "Domesticity and Difference."
[28] *Diario de la Marina*, "Solicitudes" y "Se ofrecen," marzo 1916.
[29] Trouillot, *Silencing the Past*, 48.

domestic workers striking – or heard about it, in the homes of their friends – across the island and refused to understand it as political? Cuban domestics' participation in an unprecedented labor strike was reduced to a "refusal to work" – a formulation that connoted laziness rather than political activism. These striking cooks' and servants' thoughts are unknowable, but Morson's dismissal of them is fallible. We cannot assume that domestic workers did not participate in workers' collective action just because no one mentions them. We can, however, note that domestic worker activism was erased even as it was happening.

In the face of such labor-related turmoil, the overtures of Catholic institutions to domestics might have seemed anachronistic to some, but they persisted. In August of 1919, María Inmaculada opened a school to train domestic workers. Young women who worked as servants could learn reading, basic math, calligraphy, embroidery, drawing, musical theory, and piano. The sisters of María Inmaculada helped these young women find placements with some of the wealthiest families in Havana. In 1920, the order inaugurated a boarding school where girls who did not live with the families they served could sleep. The sisters also visited the girls at the homes where they worked, to make sure that the señoras were treating them well, giving them days off, and taking care of them if they were ill. María Inmaculada and Father Villegas seemed intent on protecting girls' honor and pairing them with "good families." But the strikes of 1917 and 1918 show that women and girls (and probably men and boys) who worked outside of those Catholic institutions – which would have been most of them – developed their own, more radical strategies to protect themselves and their families.

## 3.2 CUBAN FEMINISM AND THE PROBLEM (OR SOLUTION) OF DOMESTICS

Another movement took off in Cuba as workers struck, one of which threatened to bolster or dismantle the entire national project, depending on whom you asked: one of Latin America's most vocal and successful feminist movements. Almost as soon as Cuba became independent, feminists began demanding suffrage. Beginning around 1912, women across the island formed organizations to advocate for their interests and legal and social protection.[30] Cuban feminists were nationalists who drew on notions of inherent differences between the sexes to argue

---

[30] Pagés, *En busca de un espacio.*

that their work could complement men's. They took advantage of Cuba's governmental instability to make legal inroads into their most dearly held issues: female suffrage, ensuring "respectable" jobs for women, eliminating lesser charges for men who murdered their wives due to adultery.[31]

Cuban feminists won such victories as the 1917 ratification of women's right to inherit and the 1918 legalization of no-fault divorce. In 1923, the first National Women's Congress convened in Havana. Though most women attending called for moderate legal change, building on the momentum of the earlier victories, some radical feminists called for more expansive social transformation. At the 1925 Second National Women's Congress, Ofelia Domínguez Navarro walked out in protest of the suppression of her campaign to legally recognize children born out of wedlock. This split was representative of Cuban feminism's trajectory before 1959: Mainstream Cuban feminists would continue to work with the national government to gain important but incremental legal advantages for Cuban women.[32] Radical feminists like Domínguez would continue to advocate on behalf of women, but they would do so under the umbrella of radical politics, not feminism.

Regardless of internal splits, the early feminist movement in Cuba threatened the status quo. Feminism encouraged women to leave their homes for the proverbial street, whether they demanded moderate or radical change; the women doing the demanding were among the first female lawyers, doctors, and journalists in Cuba. Thanks in large part to feminist activists, female workforce participation expanded by more than 50 percent between 1899 and 1919, and at the same time increased educational opportunities caused female illiteracy to decline by 20 percent.[33] These advances for women coincided with a decline in domestic work in Cuba: While 67 percent of working women were domestic servants in 1907, just 46 percent were in 1919. The second most popular field for working women in 1907 and in 1919 was "manufacturing and mechanical industries," defined as the work of transforming "the raw material furnished by the extractive industries into new forms or combinations."[34] In 1907, 21 percent of working women were involved in such pursuits; by 1919, that number had shot up by 11 percent. Work aside from domestic service was an increasingly realistic possibility for many Cuban women.

---

[31] Stoner, *From the House to the Streets*.     [32] Ibid., chap. 2.

[33] Pérez, Jr., *Cuba: Between Reform and Revolution*, 180.

[34] United States War Department, *Censo de la república de Cuba, 1907*; Republic of Cuba, *Census of the Republic of Cuba, 1919*.

Working women of the middle and upper classes employed servants to perform the domestic labor that they no longer could, but anti-feminists insisted that women endangered their homes when they left them to servants. Household management was serious work, insisted public health officials, writers, and advice-givers: The home was the foundation of the still-new Cuban nation. Subtly, many Cubans suggested that it was work that could only be done by women, by *white* women – it could not fall into the hands of anyone else. Black women's influence in private Cuban homes threatened the racialized hierarchy that defined Cuban democracy. Thus, writers and public servants interested in domestic science and domestic tasks encouraged white women to manage their own homes, taking the reins of authority firmly in their own hands as opposed to allowing their (black) domestics to take over.

The "abandonment" of middle-class homes and families could result in a takeover by the likes of Delfín's María Antonia. A 1917 cartoon and short story from the illustrated weekly magazine *La Política Cómica* (*Comic Politics*) echoed Delfín's warnings. The cartoon featured Señora Sacramento Berruga de Coronilla, called Sacra, who was on a mission to rescue her priest from a trumped-up scandal. She visited a judge to convince him to dismiss the charges against Padre Rogelio. When she finally returned home that night, she found "a dirty house, abandoned by fault of leadership." Her young son was dragging the family cat around by its tail. Worse, her husband was locked in a passionate embrace with "the *mulatica* [mixed-race woman], Natalia." When Sacra saw them and screamed, Natalia ran back into the kitchen, but her husband calmly said: "As always, you have abandoned your home because you're out in the street attending to things that you shouldn't concern yourself with, and I manage to distract myself the best I can."[35]

Because Sacra took on a cause unrelated to her home life, her home fell apart. The spilled bottle of liquor in the bottom right of the cartoon, the cobwebs in the top left, the broom left abandoned in the center of the room all suggest an abandonment of propriety and domesticity. An abandonment of hygiene was obvious too: Sacra's house was *dirty*. When had she last supervised the washing of the walls, as a domestic science book had advised back in 1906? When had she last put away the laundry that Natalia might have cleaned? Her home had been contaminated likely by

[35] "La Flor de Siguaraya," *La Política Cómica*, May 27, 1917.

FIGURE 3.1. "La Flor de Siguaraya," 1917 (*La Política Cómica*, May 27, 1917).

germs but also by the influence of the *mulatica*. Sacra's husband's pursuit of Natalia was his wife's fault for abandoning him.

Natalia wears house slippers and a simple dress, but she has pearls around her neck, earrings in her ears, and a tiara in her hair. She also has grotesquely exaggerated "African" features: huge lips, kinky hair, and an outsized backside. Is she wearing her mistress's jewelry, having replaced her as the woman of the house? Or is she wearing her own jewelry, an indication of her sexual attractiveness and prowess even as she cleans and cares for the child? The short story never names Natalia as the domestic – she is just called "the *mulatica*." When Sacra catches Natalia and her husband, Natalia flees into the kitchen – the only indication of her job. But the implicitness of her work makes clear that blackness and domestic service are conflated. Natalia is the *mulatica*, which means that inevitably, she is also the domestic.

But Natalia herself was incidental to the moral of this story, which was that white women needed to be careful about how much time they spent pursuing causes – or careers, or education – outside their homes. That they would have domestics was a given, but this cartoon suggested that they could not leave the domestic to control the household without chaos ensuing. The threat already lurked within: Apparently, domestic servants had the ability to destroy white nuclear families.

What could white women do to protect their homes? They could stay there. A 1918 tome entitled *Treatise of Domestic and Agricultural Education* assured its readers that "the soul of the home is the woman." The book's introduction celebrated the first school of domestic economy in Cuba while simultaneously critiquing contemporary feminism, which it argued did not sufficiently consider the natural differences between men and women.[36] Women were the natural caretakers of domestic space, and bedlam could ensue if they did not take their position seriously:

The mistress of the house who is too inclined to go out, more attentive to soirées, and theater, and fashion, and cuisine, and social happenings than to her children and her husband and her home, is not a woman who is fulfilling her domestic tasks; she will likely not be a safe guide for the children, not because she does not love them, but because *she seems forced to turn them over to the care of strangers.* The abuse of that life of forgetting the tasks of the home arrives, in certain cases, to break the happiness of the family.[37] [emphasis mine]

---

[36] Comallonga and Ortiz, *Tratado de Enseñanza Domestica y Agricola*, 5–6.

[37] "La ama de casa demasiada paseadora, más atenta a los saraos, y teatros, y modas, y comidas, y crónicas sociales que al cuidado de los hijos y del marido y del hogar, no es una dama buena cumplidora de sus deberes domésticos; no será probablemente una guía segura para los hijos, no porque no los quiera, sino porque se ve forzada a entregar éstos al cuidado de extraños. El abuso de esa vida de olvido de los deberes del hogar llega en ciertos casos a romper la felicidad de la familia." Comallonga y María de los A. Ortiz, *Tratado de Enseñanza Domestica y Agricola*, 11–12.

It might be expected that a woman of a certain class would leave the care of her children to nannies or nurses, but that woman needed to remain the moral center of her children's lives. This admonishment listed the leisurely activities of bourgeois women as potential distractions from home life, instead of professional or political interests. It was a subtle but effective way of reducing the "distractions" from home life to frivolities that no one could argue were more important than children. This book went on to describe the proper method of furnishing maids' quarters (simply, and with a working washroom so that they would be encouraged to clean themselves), which indicates that the authors did understand that domestic servants were a part of their readers' lives. They simply warned against them becoming too significant a part.

A magazine published in 1920s Camagüey had similar concerns. The *Magazine of the Feminine Association of Camagüey* combined reports on the latest feminist news with advice about home life and standards for domestic success. A 1921 article admonished women for leaving the nutrition of their families up to maids – a carelessness that contributed to untold illnesses.[38] In an introduction to several recipes (including tongue croquettes, rice with clams, and chocolate soufflé), the journalist warned readers not to complain to her about their soft hands and manicured nails being ruined, or about being reduced to the same labor as their cooks.[39] Another column from 1923 discussed time management, scolding housewives who constantly complained that they had no time for leisure activities.

The reporter noted that she had recently met a "pharmacist who had three children, she was an excellent mother, a wonderful housewife, since everything in her house ran with the order of a stopwatch, she didn't have maids, nor did she have a cushy job. She herself mended clothing and hats."[40] The reporter went on to say that it was time for housewives to "wake up from their lethargy." The pharmacist was to be congratulated for being everything to everyone without employing domestic service. Even as it was understood that middle-class Cuban women would employ domestics, it was heavily suggested that this rendered them less-than as mothers and wives. The danger was that they would transfer their own responsibilities over to

---

[38] "Páginas del Hogar," *Revista de la Asociación Femenina de Camagüey*, enero 1921, 16.
[39] "Recetas de Cocina," *Revista de la Asociación Femenina de Camagüey*, junio 1921, 14.
[40] "Páginas del Hogar," *Revista de la Asociación Femenina de Camagüey*, diciembre 1923, 5–6.

a servant class, which because of its racial and class background would corrupt husband, children, and home alike.

Feminists disagreed – not with their assumed reliance on servants but with the supposed danger that entailed. Historian K. Lynn Stoner argued that the feminist movement created "a new facet of the ruling class" in Cuba, one that oversaw issues assumed to be women's domain. Members of this new feminist class believed that they were perfectly suited to take care their own homes *and* to manage Cuban governance of women's issues.[41] The "intellectuals, journalists, teachers and painters" who comprised feminist groups in Cuba could do all of those things and manage their homes.[42] This dual focus was possible because of servants: "Feminist advocates … sensed no conflict between professionalism and motherhood, nor between motherhood and feminism, because, in their own lives and owing to their wealth and existence of a servant class, they never had to exclude one option for the other."[43] Anti-feminists and mainstream Cuban feminists disagreed on women's place, and they disagreed on whether domestics were a sinister or integral facet of the Cuban household. But they agreed that domestics *were* a part of the household, and that their position functioned outside questions of labor. Beginning around the late 1930s, a more radical strain of feminism would emerge in mainstream discourse; feminists would combine anti-racist and pro-labor rhetoric to advocate on behalf of servants. But many early feminists in Cuba relied on the poorly remunerated labor of domestic service.

### 3.3 NATIONALIST PEDAGOGY VERSUS MIGRANT ACTIVISM IN 1920S CUBA

Feminists were no enemies of Cuban home life; in fact, they advocated for the creation of a school dedicated to that hallowed space. In the same year as the railroad strikes, the island's government authorized the creation of schools in Cuba related to "domestic economy." One year later in 1919, the government approved the regulations of "the Superior School of Economy, Art, and Domestic Economy … which will be known as *Escuela del Hogar.*" The *Escuelas del Hogar* (Schools of the Home) were a project of the *Club Femenino de Cuba* (Feminine Club of Cuba), one of the island's first feminist organizations. Founded in 1917, the *Club Femenino* rallied around ending prostitution, creating women's prisons

---

[41] Stoner, *From the House to the Streets.*   [42] Pagés, *En busca de un espacio*, 60.
[43] Stoner, *From the House to the Streets*, 194.

and juvenile criminal courts, and winning women's rights.[44] The goal of
the *Escuelas del Hogar* was

the advancement of women, whose scientific, artistic and practical knowledge
[would] give them general cultural information to prepare them for life in the
home as caretakers and mothers and outside the home as responsible people in
industry appropriate to their gender.

The *Escuelas* would train women in "practical home skills, domestic arts
and sciences, commercial preparation, artistic-industrial lessons, and
occupations and responsibilities appropriate for women."[45]

    The creation of the *Escuelas* passed with bipartisan support and virtu-
ally no protest because the schools did not challenge the patriarchal
system.[46] Rather, the *Escuelas* offered women professionalization in fields
that conservatives deemed completely appropriate for women. Unlike the
history of domestic workers participating in protest, a history of the
*Escuelas del Hogar* is traceable because it was what lawmakers in Cuba
wanted to see: women behaving as they believed women should behave.
No matter that domestic workers and students at the *Escuelas* performed
the same work: Students took classes in cooking, cutting and sewing, and
laundering, among other topics. The work itself mattered less than the
manner in which those who performed it behaved.

    And just five years after the creation of the *Escuelas del Hogar*, at least
one labor union was inviting domestic workers to militancy. The Union of
Antillean Workers, formed in the summer of 1924 in the eastern capital of
Santiago de Cuba, released a bulletin which read in part:

The woman worker: cook, nanny, hand servant and dedicated to other labors,
there is still not any association in
    Cuba – that defends your rights; for this reason the Union of Antillean Workers
welcomes the woman – forsaken until recently! – but who now with the constitution of this workers' entity has someone to defend her.[47]

    The Santiago newspaper *Diario de Cuba* published an editorial about
the Union of Antillean Workers' overture to domestic workers. The writer
was scornful of the idea that maids needed union representation:

Undoubtedly, it is necessary to fill the hole that this society feels because of the
lack of a union of cooks, nannies, maids, etc.
    It must end, this misunderstood liberty that exists now and that permits maids
to work where they feel like it, earn in accordance with the services they offer and

---

[44] Ibid., 57.    [45] Ibid., 135–136.    [46] Ibid.
[47] "Notas del Momento," *Diario de Cuba*, 18 mayo 1925, 2.

mold themselves to the customs of each house, in which she idiotically ends up feeling like a member of the family.

We have to stop with all that . . .

For everything there will be a set of rules and regulations dictated by the Union . . .

In sum, the hour of the clock of civilization has arrived in which the maids govern the houses in which they serve and in which, in addition to taking for their own houses enough food for their children, they have at their service the hateful "bourgeoisie" that pay them . . .

Glory to Creole Bolshevism!

And may God have pity on the maids so that they don't commit the nonsense of falling into the tyranny of a union![48]

The editorial's sarcasm made clear what the newspaper thought of union-izing domestic workers: It went against everything that domestic service should have been. Without unions, maids had freedom to choose their employers, their hours, their salaries, their circumstances. Within unions, these choices would have been stripped from them. These arguments were not original in the context of anti-union sentiment, but they played on the perceived informality, freedom, and familiarity of the unregulated domes-tic servant arrangement.

The idea that a domestic worker might experience a work-related accident, for example, was apparently absurd. The editorial specifically mocked that possibility, sarcastically listing what the utopic union of domestic workers could offer its members:

Additionally, the obligation to insure all maids against work-related accidents will be specified, for example tooth pain produced by the heat in the kitchen, the bite of a child during a punishment, a straw in the eye when she's drying the walls, etc. etc.[49]

The *Diario de Cuba* was openly scornful of the idea that maids might have such grievances.

The anti-union editorial also suggested that the Union of Antillean Workers' call was especially irresponsible given that Cuba was experi-encing a shortage of domestic workers:

Because . . . for what other reason can a union for maids establish itself except so that the maids – whom today are fewer than the number needed because the Cuban women who before were maids today dedicate themselves to typing and teaching – dream of such stupid utopias?

[48] Ibid., 2.   [49] Ibid.

Although a "lack of maids" was a common trope used by employers of domestics in periods of anxiety about labor rights and demands for higher wages and better treatment, in 1920s Cuba it was actually true that fewer women were electing to go into domestic work. Increasing educational opportunities for women, including the *Escuelas del Hogar*, presented more options than had ever before existed for women.[50]

The decline in domestic service among native-born Cuban women corresponded to a stark increase in immigration to the island; it's telling that the Union of Antillean Workers invited domestic workers to join their ranks. Anglophone and Francophone Caribbean workers migrated to Cuba in record numbers during the 1920s – about 300,000 between 1917 and 1931 – mainly to work on sugar plantations.[51] Many of these workers found themselves without gainful employment during the *tiempo muerto* (dead time), when there was no sugarcane to harvest. Anglophone Caribbeans had luck finding work as domestics during these times because many North American families lived there, people who owned cattle ranches or sugar plantations, or worked as professionals at those sites. These English-speaking families preferred that their domestic help also speak English. British West Indians were also more likely to travel to Cuba as couples, meaning that there were more female British West Indians who searched for work.[52]

Henry (Enrique) Shackleton, a British West Indian man, helped found the Union of Antillean Workers. He attended several labor conferences in Havana in the mid-1920s and garnered the attention of British officials in Cuba with his regular denouncements of the British consul, who did little to protect foreign workers from abuse. From the beginning the union crossed national and gendered lines – the founding president was Haitian, and at the inaugural meeting the national anthems of Cuba, England, the United States, Haiti, France, and the Dominican Republic were all played. The Union of Antillean Workers was short-lived, only existing until the 1930s and apparently never expanding outside Santiago de Cuba. But in that brief time, it passionately defended Caribbean immigrant workers, regularly lobbying British, French, *and* Cuban officials to improve the situation of migrant workers by tightening regulations on migration and improving working conditions.[53]

The pan-Caribbean bent of the Union for Antillean Workers, which published one of the earliest recorded overtures for domestic servants to

---

[50] See page 80.    [51] de la Fuente, "Two Dangers, One Solution," 34.
[52] Fondo Escuelas del Hogar, AHPC.    [53] McLeod, "Undesirable Aliens," chap. 3.

unionize, contrasted sharply with the nationalist aims of the *Escuelas del Hogar*. In 1926, author Maria Paniagua de López argued that girls educated in Cuban domesticity were bulwarks against foreign influence. The massive and growing influence of the United States had seeped into Cuban family life: "The glorious tradition of the Cuban home is lost, imperceptibly, to the modern tendency to live outside of the house." By teaching Cuban girls how to arrange, clean, cook in, and manage their homes, the *Escuelas del Hogar* had the potential to rescue "the future of Cuban society, that runs the risk of dissolution if the worship of familial community is not restored."[54] Paniagua was one voice among many; by the 1920s critiques of encroaching US culture were common.[55] But cultural traditions began at home, so the *Escuelas del Hogar* had an important role to play in resisting North American – and possibly Caribbean – mores. Retaining Cuba's cultural identity and educating girls in the domestic arts were laudable goals.

Several women I interviewed in Santiago de Cuba and Camagüey had Anglophone or Francophone Caribbean roots. Edilinda Chacón Campbell's grandmother, Edith Coleman, left Savanna-la-Mar, Jamaica, for Cuba in the 1920s. Chacón's grandmother, grandfather, and great-aunt were pushed out of the labor market in Jamaica by the growing South and East Asian workforce there. Her grandfather's labor history was typical of the time – he had helped to build the Panama Canal and then moved back and forth between Cuba and Jamaica until settling in Cuba with his wife. Edith Coleman worked as a washerwoman for workers at a sugar mill in San Germán, a town some seventy miles northwest of Santiago de Cuba. In the early 1950s Edith moved with her daughter, Mónica, to Santiago, where Mónica worked as a cook in two different homes. Mónica was Edilinda's mother. In 2015, Edilinda was a history professor at the University of the East in Santiago.[56]

Margarita Pérez García, a practitioner of natural medicine when I spoke to her in 2015, was born in 1926 in Camagüey to two Haitian parents who'd come to the island in the early 1920s. She was raised by the wealthy couple who employed her mother as a washerwoman – Margarita described the couple as a *guajira* (farm girl) who married the son of a slaveowner. Graciela López Offis's father was Haitian, and her mother was born in Guantánamo to Haitian parents. She remembers her

[54] "La Escuela del Hogar de la Habana y la Dra. Angela Landa," abril 1926, 13–19.
[55] Pérez, Jr., *On Becoming Cuban*.
[56] Interview with Edilinda Chacón Campbell, April 17, 2015, Santiago de Cuba.

mother washing clothes in a river in Camagüey in the early 1950s; she remembers that later, when her mother worked for a family who owned a local cookie factory, they sometimes fed her with stale cookies.[57]

These mothers and grandmothers of the women I spoke to might have benefited from the protection that the Union of Antillean Workers offered back in 1924. In 1925 the Santiago workers' magazine *La Voz Obrera* (*The Working Voice*), a stalwart supporter of the Union of Antillean Workers, pointed out the racism inherent in all discussions of migrant workers: "Daily they accuse those industrious workers, for the mere fact of not being white nor Spanish, of carrying epidemics and corrupting our customs, when in reality, those poor things … are victims of everyone they come across."[58] Domestic workers across Cuba did experience problems that labor unions were envisioned to resolve. This, despite *Diario de Cuba*'s insistence that domestic service was marked by ease and flexibility, and despite the fact that *Escuelas del Hogar* taught domestic labor to middle-class and aspiring middle-class girls.

The *Escuelas del Hogar* were *not* meant to train women for domestic service, unlike schools with similar pedagogical content across Latin America.[59] Rather, they trained women to be middle-class homemakers or to teach domestic sciences and domestic economy to girls like themselves. In her rebuttal to Gerardo del Valle's critique of black Cuban women discussed in Chapter 2, Catalina Pozo y Gato asserted that many of her black female friends were highly educated, with degrees from *Escuelas del Hogar*, but that they were reduced to working in domestic service.[60] Life as a maid was not the intended goal for such a degree. And in the records for the *Escuela del Hogar* in Camagüey, which began with the 1939–1940 academic year and ended in 1959, the overwhelming majority of girls who enrolled were white, from households with two married parents.[61] By 1943 the majority of Cuban domestic workers were African-descended, so it is unlikely that these white, middle-class *camagüeyanas* were enrolling in their local *Escuela del Hogar* to work in other people's homes. Rather, the *Escuelas del Hogar* were an expression of the same project discussed in Chapter 2: Domesticity and proper hygiene could and should be taught to aspiring housewives and mothers.

---

[57] Interview with Graciela López Offis, March 27, 2015, Camagüey; interview with Margarita Pérez García, March 27, 2015, Camagüey.

[58] *La Voz Obrera*, May 25, 1925, 1, in McCleod, *Undesirable Aliens*, 115.

[59] A Brazilian example can be found in Gomes da Cunha, "Learning to Serve."

[60] Pozo y Gato, "La mujer negra y la cultura," *Diario de la Marina*.

[61] Fondo Escuela del Hogar, AHPC.

The *Escuelas del Hogar* linked domestic science education to nation-building and the enforcement of gender roles, while radicals and labor activists increasingly linked the work of paid domestic service to other labor and acted accordingly. Despite the fact that men and women had been doing the things that *the Escuelas del Hogar* taught for centuries, the Cuban government used the *Escuelas* to elevate the study of the domestic sciences and locate them in the realm of middle-class white womanhood. The *Escuelas del Hogar* and the Catholic Church initiatives formalized women's preferred role in the private sphere even as women's prospects in Cuba were expanding beyond their homes and domestics were beginning to organize.

The celebration of the *Escuelas del Hogar* and conservative fears about the feminist movement betrayed the swirling anxiety around middle-class status itself. Other historians of Latin America have confirmed that self-identification as middle-class had little to do with a family's net worth.[62] The category invoked professional, nonmanual work, as well as a certain morality and, as the twentieth century continued, an orientation toward consumption. Domesticity was an important part of class status. The *Escuelas del Hogar* sought to ensure that domesticity would remain distinctly Cuban in the face of aggressive American influence. Discourse about femininity and domesticity simultaneously made clear that part of being middle class in Cuba was employing at least one servant; in this way, too, the island distinguished itself from the United States, where servants were far less common. Given the persistent erasure of male domestic servants from discussions of domestic service and the routine portrayal of all servants as women, we can assume that the ideal middle-class family had a *female* servant. The middle-class ideal encompassed conservative notions of racial and gendered dominance, embodied in at least one *criada* – but not one with too much power.

Bryan Owensby argued that in mid-century Brazil, novelists cast the middle-class home as a respite from the chaotic politics of that time – neither conservative nor liberal parties offered the middle-class Brazilian a better way forward than his or her own ambition. This might have been the case in Cuba as well; a well-appointed and secure home could offer refuge from politics outside. But as the Great Depression loomed, there would be no sufficient refuge from politics. And by the end of the 1920s, radical action would overshadow liberal solutions.

---

[62] See, for example, David S. Parker, *Latin America's Middle Class*; Ricardo-López, *The Making of the Middle Class*.

### 3.4 NOT LEGALLY LABOR: DOMESTIC SERVICE AND PROGRESSIVE LEGISLATION

But the radicalism would not immediately come from the state. Cuba's third National Labor Congress convened in Havana in 1925. There, the first national labor federation – the *Confederación Nacional Obrera de Cuba* (National Workers' Confederation of Cuba) – formed. In October, a commission under the auspices of the Secretary of Agriculture, Commerce, and Work proposed a General Administration of Labor in Cuba. This administration would

gather, classify, and submit to the Executive Power as much information as necessary for the reform of labor legislation; monitor the execution and observance of this code and of industrial regulations; organize and direct the corresponding services of inspection; and promote and channel social action and initiatives in favor of the well-being of workers and of the harmony between them and their employers.[63]

In pursuit of this harmony, the administration would form provincial tribunals – one in the capital of each province – and one national tribunal in Havana to hear complaints from workers and employers about misunderstood expectations or pay cuts. Each tribunal would include three laborers in different fields, three employers in different fields, a lawyer, and a professor.[64] This movement toward labor reform was part of President Gerardo Machado's 1924 campaign promise of meaningful change within a corrupt and graft-ridden government.[65]

However, not all Cuban workers would enjoy the benefits of this new administration. To pursue a case in the tribunal, one would have to be a member of a labor union. Among those excluded from the right to unionize would be "those who work in a family and inside a domestic home, with independence of any boss ... [they] will not be admitted into any union which could correspond to the home-based industries that they work in."[66] Other excluded groups were lawyers in the public interest, public employees, and homeowners who did not run a business from their homes.

---

[63] "Recoger, clasificar y suministrar al Poder Ejecutivo cuantos datos sean necesarios o convenientes para la elaboración y reforma de la legislación del trabajo." Comisión Nacional Codificadora, *Proyecto del código del trabajo*, 15.

[64] Ibid.   [65] Pérez, Jr., *Cuba: Between Reform and Revolution*, 187.

[66] Comisión Nacional Codificadora, *Proyecto del código del trabajo*, 20.

Interestingly, the law did not directly prohibit such people from pursuing a case in the tribunals. Rather, it indirectly prevented that situation from arising by disallowing such persons from joining a union that would have represented their labor interests. So much rhetoric about why domestic servants have historically been less likely to organize than other groups has to do with their supposed isolation within private homes and their inability to meet each other and commiserate.[67] This proposed law presents a different possibility: Domestic workers did not organize because laws prevented them from doing so.

Outside of Cuba, too, national governments disassociated domestic service from formal labor. In 1927 an American official in Haiti wrote to the Secretary of State about the yearly exodus of Haitians to Cuba, which Haitians colloquially referred to as "the slave traffic." As a result of such traffic, certain parts of Haiti were regularly "completely denuded of men." The United Fruit Company was a key culprit in robbing Haiti of its healthiest and strongest male laborers, often in ways that were not within the bounds of agreements between company and nation.[68]

Haiti passed a law that year seeking to limit the number of men traveling as migrant workers to foreign countries. It prohibited laborers from leaving the country outside of the regulations of established customs houses, and it established strict rules regarding when they could leave, for how long, from where, and with whom. Article 2, establishing the definition of a laborer, read:

The word laborer as used in the present law means a person whose livelihood is wholly or substantially derived from manual labor, exemption being made of a personal servant when departing from Haitian territory with or in order to join an employer for whom he has worked as a personal servant for not less than 90 days.[69]

Cuban sugar planters feared losing the migrant labor that kept their mills running, and Cuban workers feared losing their jobs to such cheap foreign labor, but as long as a Haitian was a domestic servant, he could come and go from the island as he pleased. The Haitian government and its small towns feared that emigration – which one newspaper editorial called a "vampire" – would irrevocably transform its landscape and

---

[67] See Elena Gil Izquierdo's quotation on page 134.
[68] Russell, Translation of Haitian Law, Despatch No. 1113, October 28, 1927, RG 59 837/504/312, NARA.
[69] Ibid.

ability to produce.[70] Still, neither side was concerned with the movements of domestic workers.

Much changed between 1927 and 1933: Machado bullied and bribed his way into another term as president, which led to the violence and chaos described in this chapter's introduction. His administration fled in 1933, and Grau's 100-day government took over; the latter administration ended when the military officer Fulgencio Batista worked with the US government to oust Grau and install Carlos Mendieta as president in January of 1934. The United States, which had never formally acknowledged Grau as president, recognized Mendieta almost immediately. The Cuban revolutionaries who had supported Grau did not surrender, however. Strikes and protests against the Batista-Mendieta coalition continued through 1934 and into 1935.[71] In May, the Cuban army assassinated Antonio Guiteras, the most important anti-government leader of the youthful cohort that carried on Grau's radical politics.[72] That same month, President Carlos Mendieta resigned, ceding power to Batista. Labor reforms continued amid prolonged political turmoil. A law establishing paid vacation days for workers passed in February of 1935.[73] Again, it explicitly excluded domestics.

Despite these legal exclusions, outside analysis of domestic service from the mid-1930s suggests that even in the fifteen years between 1918 and 1933, understandings of the work had shifted. *Problems of the New Cuba*, a report written by the (American) Foreign Policy Association and commissioned by President Mendieta in 1934, found that wages in the 1930s were much lower than they had been in 1909–1910. Domestic servants were making eight dollars per month in Havana and four dollars per month in the interior. The fact that the authors of *Problems of the New Cuba* chose to explicitly list the salaries of domestic workers in a discussion of falling wages is significant – demonstrating their understanding that domestics were workers, in some capacity.[74] A description of the strikes that rocked Cuba after Machado's fall is even more telling: "In some *centrales* the cooks, laundresses, nurses and other house servants declared a strike and called for higher wages ... For a time the whole population seemed to have assumed an economic

[70] "It Urges the Stopping of Emigration," *Le Temps*, October 21, 1927, 2, RG 59 837/504/312, NARA.

[71] Pérez, Jr., *Cuba: Between Reform and Revolution*, 209.      [72] Ibid., 210.

[73] Calella Sanz, 47. The law also excluded agricultural workers.

[74] Commission on Cuban Affairs, *Problems of the New Cuba*, 183.

offensive."[75] In 1918, Mr. Morson of the Cuban Railway Company noted that servants "refused to work"; in 1935, American experts on Cuba described such action as a strike and grouped domestics in with all Cubans in their "economic offensive." Perhaps due to the actions of domestics in 1918, overtures toward domestics by worker syndicates in 1925, and a general political sea change in the early 1930s, outside observers of the Cuban political economy increasingly acknowledged that domestics were workers, even if the government and media would not.

### 3.5 CONCLUSION

By the end of 1934, Batista had solidified his hold on Cuban politics, and the next twenty-five years would become known as the *pax Batistiana*. Between the 1933 and 1959 Revolutions, Batista was Cuba's kingmaker. No political force emerged or thrived without his permission. While many Cubans embraced the political reality that emerged out of 1933, a feeling of listlessness persisted as well. What good had the political revolution been? Had politics in Cuba changed at all, for all the violence?

The answer was yes. The strikes of the early 1910s, the labor activism of the 1920s, and the political upheaval of 1933 had all irrevocably shifted Cuban politics. It had made even conservative elites aware of the demands of workers in factories, on sugarcane fields – and in wealthy homes. In the early twentieth century, only the Catholic Church reached out to domestic workers, and the participation of domestics in strikes was studiously ignored. But by 1935 foreign analysts of the Cuban economy acknowledged the economic precarity of domestic workers. Contemporary coverage of the 1933 mill occupations acknowledged that cooks and maids were full participants. And secular organizations formed to protect the interests of domestic workers.

Laws, however, continued to ignore domestic workers. It might seem as though lawmakers saw domestic service as too unimportant to warrant legislation: It was the realm of women and of foreigners, according to most discourse. But in reality, domestic service was *too important* to risk legislation. It was too necessary to the functioning of Cuban society and the self-identification of the middle class to regulate. With all of its racialized and gendered baggage, to upend domestic service would have been to upend Cuban society (which is exactly what would happen after

---

[75] Ibid., 184.

1959). The emotional logic of domestic service had become even more important in the aftermath of a violent revolution; it was important to maintain the myth of racial harmony after 1934. Domestics themselves likely knew that.

The shifts that did occur between 1910 and 1933 had everything to do with domestics' own actions. As their numbers diminished from the first decade after independence, they became more vocal about their rights as workers, perhaps intuiting that their employers had fewer options than they had once enjoyed. Once used as an excuse to control the movements of freedwomen after abolition, now a "lack of maids" lent advantage to the demands of the remaining maids. They could and did negotiate formally for higher wages, clear job descriptions, and legal protections, but they also likely negotiated interpersonally with their employers, knowing that finding a replacement would be more difficult than it had been previously.[76] Domestics would only become more vocal and more radical as the 1930s continued, joining the ranks of domestic servants across the Americas who regularly implored their employers and their governments to understand their work as work. They had always been workers; now, they hoped, their employers would see and be grateful for their labor.

---

[76] For an in-depth discussion of the value of intrapersonal negotiations between domestics and employers, see Ally, *From Servants to Workers*.

# 4

## Patio Fascists and Domestic Worker Syndicates

### *Communism, Constitutions, and the Push for Labor Organization*

"*La negra Pilar*" was born a slave to the Count and Countess of Peñalver. She left them when she was twelve and worked for another family for five generations, as a nanny and a cook. When she died at the age of 90, she was buried at the famous Colón Cemetery in Havana, at the family mausoleum. Pilar was a model of deference and propriety. So was Roxa, a Galician woman who worked as a nanny to the fifth generation of the same family. She was "loyal, good and simple, without long hair or short skirts." Ricardo Cortés, a *pardo* (brown-skinned) cook employed by this family, was so proud of his employers that he bragged about their literary and cultural accomplishments as if they were his own.[1]

*Diario de la Marina* columnist Federico Villoch wrote about his family's servants in 1945. "The old servants of yesterday were like members of the family," he reminisced. Without laws and policies that put them at odds with their employers, domestics were circumspect and respectful, grateful for what they were given and always working harder to receive more. In what Villoch called "the golden age of domestic service," servants worked for the same families for years and years, quitting only because of old age, the desire to marry and begin a family, or to start their own small business. In 1945, "servants enter and leave in an interminable single-file line, like travelers at a train station." Once, people ate food at home that was prepared by their cooks; in 1945, they ate food prepared by strangers at bars or cafeterias.[2]

---

[1] Villoch, "Aquella Antiguo Servidumbre," *Diario de la Marina*, 27 junio 1945.
[2] Ciro Bianchi Ross, "Federico Villoch, postalista," *Juventud Rebelde*, 24 marzo 2018. Accessed 19 December 2018, http://www.juventudrebelde.cu/suplementos/el-tintero/lectura/2018-03-24/federico-villoch-postalista.

Villoch longed for an era before Cuba's hyper-industrialized and increasingly anonymous present. He illuminated the difference between *then* and *now* through his discussion of domestic servants. His nostalgia for "good girl" *gallegas*, for *negras* who knew their place and stayed there, and *pardo* cooks who bragged about their employers' accomplishments exemplifies the emotional and racially charged reactions of many economically comfortable Cubans to political transformations that began in the late 1930s. As domestic workers demanded formal labor protections, middle- and upper-class Cubans vocally longed for the days when servants (supposedly) would ask for no such things.

By 1943, domestic service had been thoroughly feminized in Cuba: Seventy-six percent of domestic workers were women, when just 36 percent had been in 1919. Cuban-born black women did dominate in the field by 1943, comprising 40 percent of the domestic service workforce.[3] Strangely, Villoch's nostalgic image of what domestic service had been like at the turn of the twentieth century more closely resembled the demographic makeup of servants in 1945, when he wrote. But one difference was probably the basis of his lamentation: Whereas 23 percent of working Cubans had been domestic servants in 1899, just 3 percent were domestics in 1943. There were far fewer servants than there ever had been in Cuba previously. And the ones who were left fully understood themselves to be workers deserving of the rights and protections afforded to other workers.

This chapter traces "the golden age" of domestic worker activism. In 1938, a decree granted paid vacation to domestic servants but was rescinded one week later in the face of mass outrage. Coinciding with the mass deportation of Caribbean migrant workers in Cuba, the response to the 1938 law revealed just how deeply attached Cuba's bourgeoisie was to unregulated domestic service. In the 1940s and 1950s, however, domestic workers and feminist and Communist allies came together to address the inequities of the work in unprecedented ways, even advocating for the inclusion of domestic worker protections in the 1940 Constitution. These radical activists' demands coincided with the organization of new domestic worker civic groups in Havana, whose impulses ranged from charitable to solidary. By the time of the 1959 Revolution, domestic worker unions were publicly pledging their loyalty to the 26th of July movement, confident that the revolutionary

---

[3] República de Cuba, *Censo de 1943*.

government would bear their interests in mind. A 1960 census that encouraged domestic worker participation suggested that, finally, domestic workers' time had come.

This chapter focuses on Cuban law's relationship to domestic labor and in so doing explores how the tension between radical demands and a resistant employer class shaped the Cuban republic's legal culture. Decree 1754 sought to reverse policy set in place after the 1933 Revolution and was rescinded; delegates at the 1940 Constitutional Convention deftly avoided discussing domestic service, with the result that the new constitution did not award labor protections to domestics. One analysis of the constitution's exclusion of domestics frames it as an oversight or failure. Another analysis – the one I think is true – suggests that the erasure was intentional. Domestic workers' continued exclusion from labor laws was not anomalous in the face of the radicalization of Cuban labor politics. It happened *because of* the radicalization of Cuban politics. Workers in factories, mines, or offices could call for improved labor conditions and get them in post-1933 Cuba; their access to minimum wage or maximum hours would not unsettle middle- and upper-class Cubans' sense of self-worth. Having to cede such protections to their nannies, cooks, maids, and gardeners *would*. For people who could employ domestics, the work was as much about performing social hierarchies as the actual labor being performed.

Cuba's failure to protect domestic workers as laborers parallels the same failure in countries like the United States and Mexico in the middle of the twentieth century. As in those countries, the unregulated nature of domestic service upheld a racialized and gendered hierarchy. This chapter advances the conversation about domestic labor globally by framing the unrealized efforts of domestics and activists not as a mistake on the part of the government but as a calculated strategy to maintain servants' subordinance. From the US New Deal to Cárdenas's rise in Mexico to Cuba's 1940 Constitution, this was supposedly an era of progressive reform in all three nations, in which citizens would be guided by laws rooted in justice and the social good. And yet, in all three countries, domestic workers were excluded from the protections accorded other workers from the 1930s to the 1950s. Societal conceptions of hierarchies and the social order proved to be just as important as theoretical conceptions of justice in shaping Cuban law in the mid-twentieth century. And in Cuba, traditional conceptions of hierarchy and social order remained ingrained in the century prior.

## 4.1 COLONIAL FOUNDATIONS FOR DOMESTIC
## SERVICE LEGISLATION

Since both nostalgic conservatives and radical activists in the 1940s connected domestic service to Cuba's slave society past, it's useful to briefly revisit the work in Cuba's colonial era. Far from the utopian situation that conservatives envisioned, the dire state of domestic service was grounds for conservative complaints even in the late nineteenth century. In May of 1878, the conservative Havana periodical *Revista Económica* (*Economic Magazine*) published a series of articles on domestic service in postwar Cuba. The sins of Havana's domestic servants were many, but the first and most egregious was their misrepresentation of themselves in classified advertisements:

Often some black woman who has never known anything other than hoarding sugarcane in the mill advertises herself as an *excellent handmaid* or *general cook and washerwoman*, and [an advertisement for a] *pardita* or *mulatica* [light-skinned, mixed-race woman] *of some age to take care of children or serve, with the condition that she does not have to go out on the street*, is really a *pardita* who knows Havana's corners as well as any coachman, and ... has already been a mother two or three times.[4]

By now, the stereotypes that emerge in this nineteenth-century article are familiar to the reader. Most domestics were actually men around the end of the nineteenth century, but the writer's deployment of a female archetype allowed him to express his anxieties about the sexuality of African-descended women.[5] He implied that this archetypal woman was deceitful, pretending to be experienced with working as a maid, a cook, or a laundress when she was not. Additionally, she claimed innocence when she had none: Why, he asked implicitly, would a street-smart woman who had already given birth several times feign the desire to stay off the streets? Domestics also asked for too much money, insisted on sleeping in their own homes with their partners and children when it would have made more sense for them to sleep at their employers' homes, and quit at a moment's notice.

Another article published weeks later linked access to "good" domestic service to the survival of the peaceful colony and called for a passbook system, already utilized in Spain and Puerto Rico, to monitor and regulate

---

[4] "El servicio doméstico en Cuba," *Revista Económica*, 25 May 1878.
[5] United States War Department, *Report on the Census of Cuba*, 404.

the movements of former slaves. The writer suggested that respect for the law by all Cubans – enslaved and free, black and white – was necessary to maintain the tenuous peace that had just been established in February of 1878 (and would be broken by the next year). By "peace," the *Revista Económica* meant the social order as it supposedly had been before the chaos of the Ten Years' War, in which blacks were subservient to whites. Domestic servants who asked for more money than they deserved and quit for no reason threatened that "peace" by flaunting their newfound freedom. The magazine insisted that they would harbor no judgment if "Juan or Pedro" understood the value of work and their responsibility to others, but the "class dedicated to domestic service" did not understand these things. Thus, just as children required education, so too did the "*big children*" who comprised the domestic service workforce.[6] Ignoring the fact that free African-descended people worked as domestics, the *Revista Económica* conflated domestic servants with former slaves and subtly called for a path toward freedom that would keep enslaved and free people under the thumb of the state.

A third article printed on September 28, 1878, published the "Regulation of Domestic Service" in Santiago de Cuba, which was to serve as the model across the rest of the island. The most important component of this law was a domestic service registry, which all free or enslaved people who wanted to work in domestic service had to sign. Upon registering, they would be given an identification card known as a *cartilla* identifying their birthplace, parents, occupation, and physical appearance. Employers would not be allowed to hire domestics without identification cards. Once hired, domestics would hand over their *cartillas* to their employers for safekeeping, to be returned when domestics quit, or when they were fired.

A domestic servant who wished to quit had to give his or her employer three days' notice. For failing to do so, he or she would incur a fine of two pesos. The domestic's former employer would give back the *cartilla* upon the date of the domestic's exit, and the domestic had twenty-four hours to submit the *cartilla* to the appropriate government branch of his or her city. Failure to take *this* step would result in a fine of two pesos as well. Essentially, these *cartillas* gave employers of domestic servants complete control of their movements, whether the servants were enslaved or free.[7]

---

[6] "El servicio doméstico en Cuba II," *Revista Económica*, 14 September 1878. Italics in original document.

[7] Ibid., III.

For all its detail, the proposed plan forcing domestic workers to carry *cartillas* failed; the Spanish colonial government tried to reintroduce passbooks for domestic workers in 1889 but failed again.[8]

Prior to Cuban independence, the Spanish government attempted to regulate domestic service not for the benefit of domestics but for the benefit of the stable colony, which required a compliant workforce of domestic servants, whether they were enslaved, free, or not quite either (as many found themselves during the *Patronato*). Such attempts failed, as evidenced by the bitter tone of the *Revista Económica*'s coverage and the failure of the passbook system. But these attempts reveal that regulating domestic service was about regulating Cuba's racial hierarchy and controlling the labor and movements of African-descended Cubans. Colonial-era domestic service regulations were about protecting the status quo, not the workers themselves. In the late 1930s, a law that attempted to regulate service once more had the reverse intention. Backlash to the law, however, would reveal that the same racialized fixation on the status quo that had plagued colonial administrators consumed Cuba still.

### 4.2 *PATRONAS* VERSUS *FÁMULAS*: DECREE 1754 AND ITS BACKLASH

In early 1937, Fulgencio Batista quickly pivoted his image as a violent repressor of anti-government protests to a generous enforcer of pro-worker policies. Historian Robert Whitney describes the years between 1937 and 1944 as Batista's populist phase, during which he attempted to create a state that fulfilled the promises of the 1933 Revolution. Policies such as social security and workers' compensation that had been suspended after Grau's ouster were reinstated. In early 1937 Batista announced his *Plan Trienal* (Three-Year Plan) for Cuba, which would include "the recovery and survey of land owned by the state, survey of communal lands (realengos), abolition of large estates, a new national banking system, crop diversification, and co-ordination of the sugar industry through a profit-sharing mechanism among millowners, colonos and labour."[9] And new pro-worker laws emerged: Decree 798 of April 13, 1938, on the "regulations of labor contracts" identified contracts between workers and their employers as the heart of social justice legislation. Unfortunately, the new regulations clarified that

---

[8] Casanovas, *Bread, or Bullets!*, 60–61.
[9] Whitney, "The Architect of the Cuban State," 442, 444.

employers of domestic workers were not obligated to create labor contracts of any kind. The decree also explicitly denied paid vacation days to domestic workers.[10]

But just three months later, Decree 1754 of August 25, 1938, stated that "there exists no reason that authorizes the exception of domestic service from the benefits of social legislation." It continued unequivocally:

The government should exercise its tutelary action when dealing with workers who, because of the characteristics of their work, remain disunited and at the mercy of the employer, economically powerful and with excessive labor power at his disposal.[11]

It was the government's responsibility to regulate the obligations and responsibilities of both employees and employers in order to prevent controversies from arising. To resolve all these problems, Decree 1754 allotted four 24-hour periods of paid rest to domestic servants per month and two hours of paid rest per day, identifying the households that had to comply with the law as those "employing one or more servants, cooks, chauffeurs, nurses or permanent domestic personnel." Of the four days of rest, two had to be Sundays; the other two could be decided upon mutually by the employee and employer. The law also required that employers provide "healthy and sufficient food" to domestics, even on the days they had off, with no decrease in their salaries. It stipulated that employers must provide an "appropriate resting place" to domestic servants for the two hours of rest they earned daily. Finally, violators of the law would be fined at amounts ranging from fifty to five hundred pesos per infraction.[12]

The new law irritated US State Department personnel in Cuba. One official wrote that the law was "a clear illustration of the confused indefinite way in which the Cuban government is forever advancing upon positions that it shortly discovers are untenable." Another dispatch from the State Department called the law "remarkable" and noted that the first WHEREAS clause of the law – quoted above – was a "blast at the economic supremacy of the employers over domestic servants." From

---

[10] Comisión Nacional Codificadora, *Proyecto del código del trabajo.*

[11] Borges, *Compilación ordenada y complete de la legislación cubana (1899–1934)*, 995.

[12] "Logra el descanso con retribución el servicio doméstico," *Diario de la Marina*, August 26, 1938, 3. "Dicta Trabajo Reglas para Descanso de Obreros Domésticos," *Diario de Cuba*, August 26, 1938, 1. Regarding the two hours of paid rest per day, the law did not specify how it defined a day.

the US perspective, the domestic service rest law was "another gesture by the Administration to Leftist elements."[13]

The Cuban media was incensed. Less than a week after protections for domestics became law, major newspapers condemned the enactment of Decree 1754. The Havana daily *Información* (*Information*) published an editorial on August 31 entitled "Only the Powerful Will Be Able to Have Maids." Because of the exorbitant fines for violation of the law, the editorial argued, Cubans of middling means would simply opt not to have maids rather than make themselves vulnerable to accusations of poor treatment. This would result in a fundamental change in the middle-class Cuban family. These families would move into apartments or guesthouses instead of houses. They would send their children to boarding houses and be forced to eat cold cuts or to eat at work canteens because domestic service was no longer available to them. Ultimately, the middle class in Cuba – the society's foundation – would be destroyed.[14] According to US State Department sources, the decree caused such "a furor" that "numerous complaints about the original law brought about its revision."[15]

On September 2, 1938, the government rescinded Decree 1754, citing "nearly unanimous opposition" to it. Two days later, longtime *Diario de la Marina* columnist M. Álvarez Marrón applauded the law's deroga- tion.[16] He drew the same conclusion that *Información* had: Faced with the threat of expensive fines and the imagined complication of finding domestic servants who would not extort them, most employers of domes- tic servants would choose to forego the service, moving into serviced apartments and leaving the women whom the law sought to protect unemployed. Álvarez Marrón assured his reading public that he had always been an advocate for the "domestic class," but this law would harm domestic workers rather than help them.

Álvarez noted that while the law mentioned *patrones* (bosses), it would be more accurate to include *patronas* (female bosses), "whose interests in this business are infinite."[17] Subsequently Álvarez only referred to the relationship between domestics and employers as one between women. According to him, a certain leniency and benevolence among *amas* and a

---

[13] Memorandum, September 9, 1938, RG 59 837.504, NARA.
[14] "Sólo los potentados van a poder tener criados," *Información*, August 31, 1938, página Editorial.
[15] Note, September 8, 1938, RG 59 837.504, NARA.
[16] Alvarez Marrón, "Burla burlando," *Diario de la Marina*, September 4, 1938.    [17] Ibid.

certain humility and comportment among *fámulas* (a very old-fashioned word for maid) had always flourished. This law would eliminate the warm relationship that had previously characterized domestic service and replace it with hostility and distrust.

Both *Información* and *Diario de la Marina* stripped the question of domestic servants' paid rest of its relation to labor, as *Diario de Cuba* had done thirteen years earlier. Álvarez's use of feminine pronouns and his assertion that domestics and employers enjoyed a familial relationship underscore his attempt to depoliticize the work. Even in 1938, *work* was not seen as women's true realm, and domestic work was not understood as work in the same way that working at a tobacco factory was. Readers of Marrón's column might have understood the relationship between a male *patrón* and a female domestic as a labor relationship. They might have understood it as a labor relationship if he had mentioned *patrones* and male domestics, who, in 1943, still comprised more than 20 percent of the domestic service workforce – and had been a shocking 92 percent of that workforce 7 years prior to Decree 1754.[18] By making the issue one about relationships between women when men would have comprised a significant portion of the people affected by the law, Marrón, drawing on cultural stereotypes, trivialized the issue.

*Información* asserted that maids were "almost like one of the family," given food, room and board, and additional financial and material support on a fluctuating basis. The editorial argued that formalizing such things as shelter, food, and paid rest would have confused and sullied the naturally intimate relationship between domestics and the families for whom they worked.[19] Tropes of intimacy and female closeness were hardly original in discussions of domestic service: Domestic workers worldwide have often been cast as slightly subordinate family members rather than workers. In post-1933 Cuba, however, conservatives actively deployed that characterization to protest the granting of rights to domestic servants and ultimately to rescind those rights once granted.

At least one newspaper did support Decree 1754 and lamented its reversal: Communist daily *Noticias de Hoy* (*Today's News*). Tomás A. Rodríguez wrote his column, he said, at the behest of his friends who were domestic servants. He insisted that the law, which lasted so briefly, would have helped

---

[18] República de Cuba, *Censo de 1943*, 781; *Censo de población, Estadísticas industrial y Agrícola de Cuba, 1931*, Tabla No. 21.
[19] "Sólo los potentados," *Información*, August 31, 1938.

girls between the ages of eleven and fourteen, employed in houses to clean, run errands, wash some things, dust, and when they go to their respective houses, just in case, they are allowed to take some cold soggy food to feed their poor siblings (they miserably earn $1.50 or $2 a month).[20]

Rodríguez lambasted the *Información* editorial published a week before his own for drumming up sentiment against the law, which he noted "absolutely no one" attacked or defended before *Información* proclaimed itself the "valiant defender" of the middle class. The vulnerable young women he described deserved the protection the law would have granted them, not because they were vulnerable young women but because of "the quality of their work."[21] *Noticias de Hoy* supported the law because it would have protected people they understood to be *workers*. Ultimately, the refusal of most Cubans to see domestics as workers caused the decree's derogation.

President Laredo Bru called for the Secretaries of Labor and Justice to convene to come to an appropriate resolution. The result was Decree 2174, passed on October 15, 1938. The new law still mandated four days of rest during the month, but instead of requiring food and room and board, it mandated that domestic servants be given what they were usually given by their employers – which could mean a healthy substantial meal or nothing at all. And while this new law did state that the "head of the family" would be held responsible for any infractions, it did not specifically mention any fines.[22] The compromise left far more of the relationship between a domestic worker and his or her employer up to the employers and employees, ultimately handing power over to the *patrones* and *patronas*.

An American report released in December did mention specific penalties: "For infractions of the decree the head of the family is punishable, under the Social Defense Code, by 1 to 60 days' imprisonment or a fine of 1 to 60 quotas, or both."[23] And the report drew a chronological line from October of 1933, when the first law that guaranteed workers paid rest passed (and excluded domestic workers); to August 1938, when Decree 1754 passed and was derogated pending investigation; to October 1938, when the new law passed. Like other coverage, it glossed over whatever conflict occurred over the law's passage.

---

[20] Rodríguez, "Ley de Servicios Domésticos," *Noticias de Hoy*, September 6, 1938, 11.
[21] Ibid.
[22] Borges, *Compilación ordenada y complete de la legislación cubana (1899–1934)*, 1085.
[23] *Monthly Labor Review*, December 1938, 1286–1287.

The US State Department's final analysis of the paid rest law for domestics shared the Cuban media's skepticism of domestic workers. American Vice Consul George F. Scherer wrote that "Since domestic servants are now in a position to bring charges against their employers, there is a likelihood that numerous bothersome suits will be instituted by incompetent servants who are dissatisfied with their condition."[24] Like the Cuban press, Scherer assumed incompetence on the part of domestics and skepticism that any complaints they might have could be based in reality. He also took the opportunity to favorably compare Americans in Cuba with the natives:

In Cuban families it is understood that servants are required to work for long hours without rest, and if the law is enforced there should be some amelioration in their condition. On the other hand, most of the American families living in Cuba follow the customs observed in the United States concerning granting days off to servants, and it is believed that such rest periods are more liberal than those required by the present decree.[25]

Scherer's rather nationalist assertion that Americans were superior employers was dubious. In eastern Cuba, American sugar corporations turned cities like Banes into company towns. American families often hired British Caribbean servants because of the shared native language and created an English-language bubble consisting of American families and their servants.[26] Anecdotal evidence does not indicate that those servants were treated any better or worse than Cuban servants working for Cuban families; but Americans in Cuba were hyper-aware of the fact that employing servants was a benefit of being in Cuba, a privilege they would likely not enjoy in the United States.[27] In any case, Cubans and Americans who opposed the law insisted that employers of domestic servants could be counted on to treat their servants well without the restrictions of the federal government. Hadn't they been doing so since the abolition of slavery, and even before that institution's end?

Apparently, Batista himself was one of the law's few supporters. Just after the derogation the Office of the President released a statement:

---

[24] "Cuban Decree Regarding Rest Periods for Domestic Servants," October 17, 1939, RG 59, Box 5946, 837.504, NARA.
[25] Ibid.      [26] Skelly, *I Remember Cuba*, 123.
[27] Ibid; Jo Werne, "I'm Happy Here, But I Miss...," *Miami Herald*, June 26, 1966, 3. In her letters to her family in the United States, the modern dancer Lorna Burdsall – married to Manuel Pineiro – regularly mentioned her nannies and maids, and acknowledged that women in Cuba had maids to help with domestic labor. Burdsall Family Papers, Collection 5311, CHC.

Effectively, the Government established that domestic workers had the right to enjoy four days of rest per month. This is humane and it is not new, because it exists in all civilized countries.

Nevertheless, public opinion was clamorously against this measure. In the government there was only one voice of applause. It was the lone voice of Colonel Batista that was present in the meeting about servants' paid rest.[28]

It was certainly in the political interest of the Office of the President to claim that only Batista had pushed forward this controversial law. Doing so served the dual purpose of distancing President Laredo Bru from its unpopularity *and* burnishing Batista's populist reputation. But even considering the probability of some exaggeration, it is true that, more so than many of his contemporaries, Batista understood that to maintain power in a post-1934 Cuba it was necessary to placate and control labor. Legacies of his reign over Cuban presidencies included the reinstitution of pensions, social security, and maternity leave.[29] Batista's failure to protect domestic service matters as much as his successes because it demonstrates that while Cubans were ready for protective labor legislation, they *were not* ready for legislation that protected paid domestic labor. That labor was sacrosanct, outside the appropriate areas on which governments could legislate.

In other countries, it was not so sacrosanct: Decree 1754 "regulated domestic service in the same form in which it was done in the majority of democratically organized nations."[30] Batista might have been trying to keep up with the development of nations to which Cuba compared itself, nations that were vocal and powerful members of the Latin American cohort. Also in 1938, domestic workers in the Mexican city of Torreón demanded union inclusion so that they could "enjoy all the benefits of the [Mexican] Revolution," and they received it within less than a year.[31] Alongside the Catholic Church, mixed-sex domestic work unions in Chile

[28] "Efectivamente, el Gobierno estableció que los componentes del servicio doméstico tenían derecho a disfrutar de cuatro días de descanso al mes. Eso es humano y no es nuevo, porque existe en todos los países civilizados.
  "La opinión pública se produjo sin embargo en contra de esa medida de un modo clamoroso. Al oídos del Gobierno solo llegó una voz de aplauso. La sola voz de Colonel Batista que estuvo presente en la reunión donde se trató al descanso de los sirvientes." "El Decreto Sobre Descanso a los Obreros Domésticos fue Suspendido por el Pdte.," *Diario de Cuba*, 3 septiembre 1938.
[29] Whitney, "The Architect of the Cuban State."
[30] Borges, *Compilación ordenada y complete de la legislación cubana (1899–1934)*, 1007.
[31] Olcott, *Revolutionary Women in Postrevolutionary Mexico*, 145.

began organizing conferences and staging strikes in the 1920s.[32] In Argentina, Juan Perón's government demonstrated that advocacy for domestic workers need not represent disdain for luxury or consumerism. The "Hogar la Empleada General San Martín" opened in December of 1949 in the heart of downtown Buenos Aires. Residents, who included domestics and other female workers, had access to medical and dental services, counseling, and recreational activities.[33] Mexican, Chilean, and Argentine societies were no less hierarchical or fixated on class; and yet domestic workers in those countries had made gains in demanding rights for themselves. But the precarity of Cuba's middle class in the aftermath of the Great Depression, combined with the history of African slavery that was still so deeply embedded in Cuban domestic service, made unfettered access to servants vitally important to the self-understanding of the bourgeoisie.

The Cuban aristocracy's wealth had peaked in the mid-nineteenth century, and the economic boom of that era – the last true boom on the island – had been won on the backs of enslaved people. The independence wars essentially destroyed Cuba's aristocracy, and a class of ambitious Spanish immigrants and upstarts from Cuba's inland provinces replaced them. Culturally and economically, upper-class Cubans were insecure in their elite status. The depressions of 1920 and 1930 had demonstrated how easily the fluctuating world sugar market could wipe out fortunes. Only a few families were landed; only a few Cuban families had family wealth that had survived the independence era.[34] To placate anxieties about their status and wealth, these Cubans needed domestic servants. They needed to be the kind of people who employed domestic servants.

Domestic servants with labor protections mandated by the state would not do. How could middle-class, professional Cubans distinguish themselves from their servants if their servants had the same kind of occupational benefits they themselves enjoyed? Adding to the anxiety was the "new-money" air of much of the Cuban bourgeoisie. Many of the wealthiest Cubans by the late 1930s were not from the dozen or so "best families," who had owned sugar estates in the nineteenth century.[35] They were upstarts, "self-made people."[36] Upper- and middle-class Cubans were not secure in the knowledge of their societal superiority. To know who they were, they needed to surround themselves with people who were less established than they were.

[32] Hutchison, "Shifting Solidarities."    [33] Elena, *Dignifying Argentina*, 138.
[34] Padula, "The Fall of the Bourgeoisie," chap. 1.    [35] Ibid., 34.    [36] Ibid., 47.

Part of that superior social status was racial dominance. The columnists
who wrote against Decree 1754 were careful not to refer to domestic
workers as anything other than "girls" or "women"; but domestic service
continued to be highly racialized work. In 1943 domestic service was the
largest employer of foreign white women, native black women, and foreign black women in Cuba.[37] These ethnic markers rendered the archetypal domestic servant an "other" in Cuba, either because she or he had
not been born in the country, or because she or he was of African descent.
Racial distinctions were not supposed to exist in post-independence Cuba,
but the racial hierarchy of domestic service masked inequalities that might
have been more difficult to hide outside of the home.

Back before Cuban independence and during the drawn-out abolition
of slavery, enslavers had also balked at laws that deprived them of
unrestricted access to servants. In 1881, Doña María de Jesús Yesquera
of Trinidad contested the freeing of her *patrocinada* Caridad Hernández.
The Trinidad *Patronato* had freed Hernández after she proved that her
late mother had given de Jesús 300 pesos for her liberty. De Jesús disputed
this, saying that the money had been given to Hernández's former *patrona*
and had nothing to do with her. She also argued that Hernández's work
was her only source of income and that she survived on Hernández's
earnings as a day worker.[38] Her claim of impending poverty was irrelevant to the question of whether Hernández's freedom had been paid for,
but de Jesús's deployment of it demonstrated her deep sense of posses-
siveness over Hernández's body and labor. Prior to the *Patronato*, heirs of
slaveowners had regularly taken possession of their deceased relatives'
human capital with little regard for whether those men and women had
been manumitted.[39]

A sense of possession also emerged in an 1882 complaint from Don
Francisco Baguer of Havana. The *Patronato* of Havana had freed his
*patrocinada* Donata because of his failure to pay and clothe her. Baguer
disputed this, arguing that three of his neighbors could testify that he had
indeed provided all the required amenities for Donata. He had paid her
"religiously" on the first of every month, and she had a trunk full of shoes
and clothes. Additionally, Donata had been with his family since she was

[37] *Censo de 1943*, 1043. The largest employer of native white women was "Industrias y
comercios no clasificados."
[38] "Demanda de Doña María de Jesus Yesquera, contra un acuerdo de la junta de Patronato
de Trinidad, que delcaró libre a la patrocinada Caridad Hernandez," Febrero 20 de 1883,
Fondo Consejo de Administración, Legajo 65 Num. 6583, ANC.
[39] Chira, "Affective Debts," 21.

thirteen (her current age was not listed) and had been "part of the family" since that time. The trope of familial membership suggests that Donata, like Caridad in Trinidad, was a domestic for the family from which she extricated herself.[40] The quite literal sense of ownership that *patrones* felt over their *patrocinadas* was a pattern that would replicate itself over and over again in twentieth-century Cuba, including during the controversy over Decree 1754. Employers of domestic servants insisted that their domestics' labor was not something that the state had any right to regulate or restrict.

In the twentieth century, those invested in maintaining the domestic service status quo drew on the nineteenth century to make their arguments. Nostalgia and a fixation on preservation became rhetorical weapons against reform. Don Francisco Baguer called Donata "family" as he tried to stop her from obtaining her legal freedom; the columnist Villoch used precisely the same language as he reminisced about his servants in the 1945 column that began this chapter. *Información* warned that Law 1754 threatened to disintegrate the Cuban family. The elite Cuban "family" had always included African-descended Cubans in a subordinate position. In the late 1930s, conservatives were as desperate to keep domestics subordinate as *patrones* had been in the early 1880s. Their suggestion that the intimacy and informality between domestics and employers rendered oppression impossible suggests that many of them did not believe that slavery had been so terrible. How could it have been, when black and white Cubans had lived in such harmony?

Anti-black discrimination was compounded for foreign domestic workers of African descent, whose presence in Cuba also shaped the debate over domestic service. Two laws had passed in 1933 that endangered Caribbean workers' presence on the island: the Fifty Percent law, which mandated that all Cuban industries employ at least half Cuban-born workers, and Decree 2232, which authorized the forced repatriation of destitute or unemployed foreigners from Cuba.[41] In the 1930s, some 38,000 Haitians were deported from the island.[42] *El Avance Criollo* (*The Creole Advance*), a politically moderate Havana daily, reported on September 6, 1938, that the Secretaries of Labor and Health were jointly preparing what the newspaper described as "concentration camps" in

---

[40] "Demanda de D. Francisco Baguer contra una resolución de la Junta de Patronato de esta Provincia por la que se declara escenta del mismo en la patrocinada Donata," 5 diciembre 1882, Fondo Consejo de Adminstración, Legajo 88 Num. 8101, ANC.
[41] McCleod, "Undesirable Aliens," 255.     [42] Ibid., 5.

Camagüey and Santiago de Cuba to house 50,000 Caribbean workers before they were deported to their home countries.[43] The *Diario de la Marina* reported in the same month that as many as 1,274 Antilleans were living in Havana, the majority of whom were Jamaican domestic workers. The paper believed the true number to be higher, but since 1936 over 300 Antillean workers had failed to renew their foreign residence cards.[44]

British Caribbeans managed to mostly escape the deportations that Haitians suffered, even though they should have been subject to the same treatment under the law: While 5,700 Haitian men were repatriated back to Haiti in the last months of 1938, no British West Indians were.[45] Their exemption from deportation was not coincidental; rather, it was tightly bound to the failure to regulate domestic service at the same time. Both the fallout of Decree 1754 and the Haitian law that exempted servants from emigration restrictions (see Chapter 3) suggest that because domestic work was not considered *labor*, it did not need to be regulated. It logically followed that foreign domestic workers in Cuba did not need to be deported, since they were not *working*. We saw anecdotal if not statistical evidence of Haitians working as domestics in Chapter 3; they, too, managed to stay in Cuba. The status of domestic service as essential but formally unrecognized labor ironically allowed migrants to stay in Cuba when, if they had worked on sugar plantations or in factories, they likely would have been deported.

In my research across Cuba and the United States – in national and regional archives in both countries – the documents I have analyzed here are the only ones I have come across about the short-lived Decree 1754. I have found no documentation of legislative debates against the law. While it is possible that those debates exist in an uncatalogued or secret corner of a library or archive, it is also possible that there *was* no legislative debate – that Batista pushed it through with little regard for standard processes for lawmaking. After all, little of the previous five years had comprised standard lawmaking or governmental succession. These were the in-between years of twentieth-century Cuban history, after the conflagration of 1933 but before the genuinely radical transformations that 1959 would precipitate. Until quite recently, historians

[43] "Ultima la repatriación de antillanos la Sctría. de Trabajo," *El Avance Criollo*, 6 septiembre 1938, 2.
[44] "1,274 Antillanos residentes en la Habana se dedican a los trabajos domésticos," *Diario de la Marina*, September 2, 1938.
[45] McCleod, *Undesirable Aliens*, 267–268.

have mostly paid attention to this period only in the context of how it propelled the lead-up to 1959. An almost humorously short-lived law about maids, of all people, was unlikely to attract much attention.

Both possibilities I've named – that no legislative debate existed or that I have been unable to find it – speak to political acts of silencing. If Batista pushed this law into existence via "unorthodox" means, he was employing authoritarian tendencies that he had displayed during the 1933 Revolution and its aftermath and that he would display in 1952, when he staged a coup to install himself as president once more. Possibly lawmakers approached then-president Laredo Bru personally to tell him that Decree 1754 could not stand, unwilling to make a statement in an official capacity knowing that Batista was pulling the strings. Or possibly a legislative debate did happen and was published and is currently languishing in the back room of a regional or national archive in Cuba. All archives have uncatalogued material; the missing 1938 debates might comprise part of such material in a Cuban archive. But the fact that little mention of domestic service is found in the published 1940 Constitutional Convention makes that possibility less likely.

Progress and forward movement are principles deeply embedded in national archives, especially so in Cuba's case. If a nationalist project by definition promotes the notion that the nation moved *forward* politically, failures to progress must be quieted or silenced. Archives make choices about what must be catalogued, what should be catalogued, and what could perhaps be catalogued one day. Maybe 1938's legislative sessions have never risen to primary levels of importance. For our purposes, the supposed "unimportance" of this year and this law compounds the chronic "unimportance" of documenting domestics' lives. We can access so little that would have affected the lives of people about whom we know so little. Scholars of slavery know this dilemma well, and yet some of the most brilliant analyses of enslaved lives dive headfirst into the dearth. Scholars of the twentieth century would do well to take note of the possibilities in scarcity.

## 4.3 CONSTITUTIONAL DEMANDS, COMMUNIST SUPPORT: DOMESTIC SERVICE IN THE 1940S

After 1938, domestic workers and their allies publicly linked their work to racism and found a political ally in Communism. In 1939, the Communist-run *Confederación de Trabajadores de Cuba* (Confederation of the Workers of Cuba, or CTC) created the *Sindicato del Servicio Doméstico*

(Union of Domestic Workers).[46] That April, at the Third National Women's Congress, Elvira Rodríguez, a domestic servant herself and a representative of the new *Sindicato*, spoke about the problems facing domestic servants in Cuba.[47] Edith García Buchaca, the General Secretary of the Executive Committee of the National Women's Congress at which Rodríguez spoke, gave a speech at the 1940 Constitutional Convention that called for the "strict fulfillment of the laws which protected the woman worker and the extension of those laws to domestic workers."[48] The National Federation of Cuban Societies of Color, which encompassed historically Afro-Cuban social and intellectual groups, similarly called on the Convention to create a Labor Code that especially protected women, children, and domestic servants.[49] For leftist groups in Cuba, the protection of domestic servants and the regulation of domestic service had become a standard tenet of their politics.

The 1940 Constitution was one of the most progressive constitutions ever passed in the Americas, codifying many of the rights that protesters had demanded during the 1933 Revolution. It wrote women's suffrage into Cuban law and declared access to work the privilege of all Cuban citizens. It signaled the end of a decade mired in violence and corruption. With the political sphere more open than it had ever been before – Batista had legalized the Communist party in September of 1938 – the 1940 Constitution represented a turn toward a Cuba governed by laws and fairly elected officials, not by military despots and backroom deals.[50] Eighty delegates representing nine different political parties attended the Constitutional Assembly. Of the five African-descended delegates – one of whom was an Afro-Cuban woman – three were members of the Communist Party, which made its commitment to working-class Cubans clear early and often during the assembly's meetings. The party's popularity was also obvious: Two of the six delegates attending the assembly who had received more than 30,000 votes across the island were Communists.[51]

[46]  de la Fuente, *A Nation for All.*
[47]  Brunson, "Constructing Afro-Cuban Womanhood," 259.
[48]  Speech given by Edith García Buchaca at the 1940 Constitutional Convention, 8 March 1940, *Fondo Convención constituyente de 1940*, Legajo 15 Num. 4, ANC.
[49]  Under the heading "Derechos Sociales: Trabajo," the document listed as its fifth priority "Código del Trabajo con especial protección para la mujer, el niño y el sirviente doméstico." P 5, *Federación Nacional de sociedades cubanas de la raza de color.*
[50]  Pérez, Jr., *Cuba: Between Reform and Revolution,* 214.
[51]  Henderson, "Black Activism in the Red Party," 82.

But the 1940 Constitution did not address domestic service. Communists and other party members debated the language of Article 78 of the constitution, which allowed workers paid rest (the topic of Decree 1754) and paid vacation days. The debate centered on whether *all* workers would receive such vacation days. Article 77, which established a forty-four-hour workweek, was also controversial: Delegates argued about whether such a work week was appropriate to all kinds of labor, citing agricultural labor and public service as possible exceptions. The final version of the law allowed for the adjustment of hours depending on the kind of work performed, without mentioning domestic labor. It seems that no convention delegates ever specifically brought up domestic service.[52]

James Holston, in his work on property laws and squatting in twentieth-century Brazil, argues that ambiguity has a specific function in law. Gaps or silences in law are not necessarily evidence of a legal system's ineffectuality. Those gaps and silences can be understood as intentional and effective.[53] Just as when Decree 1754 was replaced with the toothless Decree 2174, the 1940 Constitution's silence on domestic service left the situation as it was: beneficial to the employers of domestics. Sara Hidalgo has found that the post-revolutionary legal apparatus in Mexico degraded the work status of domestics through laws that revised the explicitly inclusive labor laws of the 1917 Constitution and then through Supreme Court decisions that distinguished between domestic labor and protected labor.[54] In Cuba, the constitution never addressed domestic service. There was no need for subsequent laws or rulings on its relationship to other forms of labor. The silence benefited the powerful.

Cuban activists were not blind to this. In February 1944 the workers' magazine *Carga* argued that the constitution's prohibition of discrimination merely allowed discrimination to flourish under the façade of equality and that the press perpetuated a classist morality that kept subjugated groups oppressed. *Carga* highlighted domestic service as one of the most harmful sources of discrimination in Cuban society and called on domestics to organize, asserting that "in their hands there is as much power as in those of the most apt employee."[55] *Carga*, unlike *Diario de la Marina* and *Información*, recognized that the connection between labor and race profoundly affected the experiences of domestic workers.

---

[52] República de Cuba, *Diario de Sesiones de la Convención Constituyente.*
[53] Holston, "The Misrule of Law."    [54] Hidalgo, "The Making of a 'Simple Domestic.'"
[55] "La Ley y los Hábitos Mentales," *Carga.*

The Catholic Church and the *Escuelas del Hogar* persisted in these years, and new organizations emerged to help domestic servants. But the public controversy about Decree 1754 and the national conversation about the 1940 Constitution ensured that conciliatory overtures to domestic workers would now be matched by radical demands from domestics themselves. Cuba's awareness of workers' suffering and their tolerance of radical worker politics had expanded since 1918 – and nannies, cooks, and maids were prepared to take advantage. Radical activists – mostly associated with the Popular Socialist Party (as the Communist Party was formally known) – were prepared to help them.

In 1946, Elvira Rodríguez contributed an op-ed to the *Organizational Bulletin of the Federation of Havana Workers*. Rodríguez disputed the propaganda with which "fascists of the patio, the reactionaries and the descendants of black slavers, in their uncouth determination, try to continue enslaving domestic workers and vigorously distort all that represents liberty, hygiene, organization and culture." One Havana paper had recently published an article arguing that domestics were treated well and justly. Rodríguez insisted that this was the exception rather than the rule, which was

the salaries of hunger and misery ... the exhausting days that [domestics] have to endure daily in an environment saturated with discrimination, poor upbringing of the children of the men and women and the arguable good or bad manners of the men of the house ... we'll stop there because to list it all would be endless.[56]

She ridiculed the relentless trope that domestics were considered "part of the family," describing the often-horrible rooms they were forced to occupy in the homes of their employers.

After dispelling the notion that domestics had it good or better than other workers, Rodríguez pivoted to the true point at hand: that domestics had organized under the CTC-backed union in which she served as General Secretary and deserved legal protection. Domestic workers now "understood the extremely important role that they are playing in the life of the country as well as the obligations that they have to their brothers in struggle and to the paths of progress which the national and in particular the provincial proletariat signal." She called on current president Ramón Grau San Martín – who had presided over the 100 Days' Government,

---

[56] Rodríguez, "Domésticos, no Esclavos," *Boletín de organización: órgano official de la Federacion de Trabjadores de la Habana*, Agosto 1946.

which passed labor legislation excluding domestic workers – to recognize
the demands of the Syndicate of Domestic Service and to meet with her.[57]

Rodríguez drew a clear connection between domestic service and racial
discrimination. Her column was entitled "Domestics, Not Slaves," and
she referred to those who would deny domestics legal protection as the
descendants of slave traders. She wrote that domestics endured "slave-like
conditions" because they were under the authority of "despotic and
reactionary employers." Scholars of contemporary domestic service
around the globe regularly compare the work to slavery. But in 1946
Cuba, slavery was barely a generation past. Rodríguez's evocation of
slavery was no rhetorical flourish. It was an indictment of Cuba's failure
to protect domestic workers from the indignity of an unfree labor system
that had been abolished so recently. Domestic workers, enslaved or free,
had always demanded better for themselves. Rodríguez was naming that
injustice and that connection. In the same month that her article was
published, Rodríguez met with the Cuban Secretary of Labor to advocate
for the extension of workers' rights to domestic servants.[58]

One year after Rodríguez's column, her union was causing controversy
in Havana:

> The Syndicate of Domestic Service has converted into a ghost which rises before
> the eyes of the comfortable and carefree "society ladies," to "end their tranquil-
> ity," or rather to end their system of considering their servants something sub-
> human, without a right to rest, retirement, or healthcare: the ancient slave concept
> which has persisted among the "grand" families throughout almost a century of
> the end of slavery in Cuba.[59]

The union's progress and aims had caught the attention of "the inveterate
defender of slavery, the *Diario de la Marina*." The *Diario* had recently
accused the Syndicate of Domestic Workers of expelling several members
for attending meetings of *Acción Católica* (Catholic Action), a Catholic
social justice group.

It was typical of the conservative press to color attempts at labor
organization with suggestions of discrimination or militancy. Journalist
Sarah Pascual went to the local offices of the Syndicate of Domestic
Service to verify the claim. Maria Sardiñas, a washerwoman, set her
straight: "It's a big lie. We have never expelled anyone for the religious

[57] Ibid.
[58] "Visitan domésticos al Carlos Azcárate," *Noticias de Hoy*, August 9, 1946, 3.
[59] Pascual, "Las Trabjadoras Domésticas Hablan," *Boletín de Organización de la Federación de Trabajadores de la Habana*, febrero 1947.

beliefs they profess. The faith which interests us is that of the unity of the syndicate."[60] At the offices, located in the neighborhood of Vedado (where many domestics might have worked), Pascual met washerwomen, cooks, handservants, and a home seamstress. One young woman told her that with the support of the Confederation of Cuban Workers, domestics were beginning to change their own destinies. Although María Sardiñas denied to Pascual that anyone had been expelled from the *Sindicato* because of their religious beliefs, this young woman *did* scorn the *Acción Católica*. She said that their señoras wanted to domesticate them with conferences like the one at the *Acción Católica*. She did not oppose Catholicism so much as its conciliatory nature toward poor working conditions for domestics. The girl welcomed the CTC's explicit support of their labor.[61]

Communism's role in domestic worker organizing was an important feature of its trajectory in the 1940s. The Popular Socialist Party (PSP) was the political party that took racial justice and inequity most seriously before 1959.[62] *Boletín de organización*, the organ for the Federation of Workers of Havana and the publication in which both Pascual's and Rodríguez's columns were published, was a PSP publication. The PSP acknowledged the connections between discrimination and job access, which made the group a logical advocate for domestic workers, many of whom, as black women, were shunted into that field.

Sarah Pascual herself was a known Communist.[63] On the day she visited the *Sindicato*, members were gathered to hear a speech from Edith García Buchaca, also on the US State Department's watch list because of her own ties to Communism.[64] In 1948, García pressed other feminists to acknowledge the centrality of domestic service to their worker-centric politics. In a speech in which she warned that female workers were facing hard times, with cigar and textile factories closing, she noted that many women who now worked in these industries had in

[60] Ibid., 21.     [61] Ibid., 23.

[62] de la Fuente, *A Nation for All*; Henderson, "Black Activism in the Red Party," 119.

[63] Pascual was identified as a writer for the magazine *Revista de la Mujer*, which was the editorial arm of the "women's Communist front organization," Asociacíon Pro-Enseñanza Popular de la Mujer. J. Edgar Hoover, "Survey of Communist Activities in Cuba," March 17, 1944, RG 59 Box 5573, 837.00B/3-1745, NARA.

[64] García Buchaca was identified as the president of the *Federación Democrática de Mujeres Cubanas*, which the Embassy Counsel described as "Communist-inspired, Communist-controlled and Communist-directed." Lester D. Mallory, "The Cuban Women's Democratic Federation (FDMC)," January 31, 1949, RG 59 Box 5578, 837.00B 1-3149, NARA.

the early to mid-1930s worked as domestic workers. The reserves of domestic workers, she said, "grew extraordinarily," and their wages remained low. García warned her fellow Communists against allowing the Cuban political milieu to return to a time when women's labor was so cheaply bought.[65] Mainstream discourse around domestic servants connected them to sex workers, but Edith García Buchaca acknowledged their ranks among cigar and textile workers. Communist labor advocacy allowed domestic workers and their allies to frame their grievances as those of workers, not those of "fallen" or vulnerable women. The national conversations of the previous fifteen years, led by domestic workers and their leftist feminist allies, had made domestic workers part of "the working class."

### 4.4 THE RADICAL BECOMES MAINSTREAM: EVOLVING DEMANDS FOR SERVANTS IN THE 1950S

At the same time as demands were made at the constitutional convention, the *Sindicato* was formed, and Elvira Rodríguez's editorial came out, a quieter organization of domestic servants was happening in the Havana region. Such organizations were not exclusive to Havana and had formed before 1933. After 1933, however, organizations that collectivized domestic servants' interests proliferated like never before. Domestic worker organizations formed between 1940 and 1958 and recorded in the national Registry of Associations toggled between staunch labor activism and charitable uplift. Some promised to morally uplift the poor – an impulse with roots in the colonial era; others promised to make demands on the state to improve labor protections for domestics – an impulse that gained traction after 1938. Some organizations promised both. These were years of stagnation and chaos in Cuba's larger political economy, and it's possible to read the impulse toward cultural uplift as skepticism about the state's capabilities, and the impulse toward demanding state action as optimism. The charters of these organizations do not mention specific political allegiances or beliefs. But the proliferation of these groups in the twenty years before 1959, simultaneous with the radical activity outlined in the last section, certainly demonstrates heightened awareness across the political spectrum of servants' needs and demands.

---

[65] *Informe de la compañera Edith Buchaca en la reunión nacional de mujeres, celebrada el 17 de junio de 1948*, Instituto de Historia.

The Union of Domestic Servants represented the kind of beneficent aid to domestic workers typical of earlier decades. Founded in 1943 in Havana, the *Unión de Servidumbres Domésticas y sus Similares* aimed to

achieve unity, protection and aid to all people who dedicate themselves to Domestic Service, laboring through all mediums that tend to the progress and improvement of the class of domestic servants ... inside the diverse beneficent ends of this noble profession, as much in the social, moral, and intellectual order and especially in the economic order inside the most fervent brotherhood.[66]

Members of the union, who could be foreign as well as Cuban, were offered financial and material help in times of need as well as medical care. The *Unión* also promised help in placing domestics and representing servants in cases of eviction. It worked with families who wished to hire domestics: Through a paper slip sent with each servant to a prospective home, the organization "answered for the honor and morality of all the servants that we send to a house."

Additionally, the *Unión de Servidumbres* also created a cultural institution for the children of domestics. The institution would offer classes and room and board for the children of union members. Classes offered would include vocational ones –bookkeeping, stenography, and typing – but also more traditional classes –calligraphy, grammar, English, arithmetic, and preparation for entering university. Beyond subject matter, however, the school's mission betrayed the union's *ultimate* goal: No other society [for domestic servants] addressed the

future of children, which would avoid the relaxation of public customs, which cause grave damage to national institutions which are representative of the sovereignty and the independence of the country. The Union of Service ... works for the reaffirmation of Cuban nationalism and refinement [?] and culture of the poor.[67]

The union's concern with the children of servants and with the "cultural refinement of the poor" betrays an insidious and age-old assumption about domestic servants: Servants were morally deficient and needed to be "lifted out" of their cultural morass. This organization would create a

---

[66] "Lograr la unidad, protección y ayuda a todas las personas que se dediquen al Servicio Doméstico, laborando por todos los medios que propendan al progreso y el mejoramiento de las clases de las servidumbres Domesticas y sus similares, dentro de los diversos fines beneficios de esta noble profesión, tanto en el orden Social, moral, intelectual y muy especialmente en el orden económico dentro de la mayor fraternidad."

[67] Reglamento de Unión de Servidumbre Doméstica y sus similares, fondo Registro Civil, legajo 277, exp 7577, Fondo Registro de Asociaciones, ANC.

kind of bubble around the work, connecting servants to homes, providing for them when their own resources were insufficient, and educating their children. The charter of the *Unión de Servidumbres* never mentioned petitioning the state to protect domestics in the same way that, by 1943, it was protecting other workers.

Despite relatively progressive worker protection laws, in the 1950s the instability of Cuba's economy and its failure to provide trained citizens with well-paying jobs became undeniable. The country's elite, supported by the United States, could afford to ignore the contradiction between their way of life and Cuba's almost nonexistent economy. But the middle classes could not. Young people flocked to new political parties like the Orthodox Party, founded in 1947 and led by the hugely popular radio host Eduardo Chibás. Chibás, a former member of Grau's Auténtico Party, railed weekly against corruption within that party and across Cuban politics on his radio broadcast. Lillian Guerra argues that the *Ortodoxo* Party, whose platform was mainly anti-corruption, did not so much create political fervor among Cuba's youth as funnel it into a specific cause and person. Young Cubans were fed up with corruption and decadence in government before Chibás emerged; he was an avatar for the promise of a new Cuba.[68]

*El Comité de la Lucha del Servicio Doméstico en la Provincia de la Habana* (Committee for the Struggle of Domestic Service in Havana Province) formed in 1950. The *Comité*, which would fight for "equity and justice," assigned two representatives from each neighborhood in Havana province to agitate for the demands of domestic servants, which the *Comité* defined as any man or woman who worked as a maid, nanny, washer, or cook.[69] The Committee also retained lawyers for its members. In the same year María Oltmans, Micaela Morales, Uldarica Alonso, and Rosa López founded the *Asociación Cívica de Amas de Casa* (Civic Association of Housewives). Among other goals, the *Asociación* planned to

oblige the government to create Vocational Schools for the education and preparation of servants, so that their services are suitable and effective, both in the material and moral senses; and to constitute also protection for these same servants, obtaining for them the adoption of measures that will produce a human

[68] Lillian Guerra, *Heroes, Martyrs, and Political Messiahs in Revolutionary Cuba*, 28–29.
[69] Reglamentos del Comité de la Lucha del Servicio Doméstico en la Provincia de la Habana, formed November 7, 1945, Fondo Registro de Asociaciones, ANC.

relationship, with the necessary remuneration for domestic work, with social laws for insurance, nullity and old age.[70]

Both groups demanded legal protections for domestic workers on a state level and in so doing distinguished themselves from the moral uplift-centric aims of the *Unión de Servidumbres*. It's not difficult to imagine these group's founders being inspired by Chibás's new political party, which promised to "clean up" Cuba's corrupt politics, and his weekly radio show in which he called out politicians by name. Perhaps in Chibás and his followers, labor activists envisioned a future in which the Cuban government *would* pass legislation regarding domestic service.

But in 1951, Chibás shot himself in the stomach while recording his live radio show and died in the hospital eleven days later. His suicide left a gaping hole in the Cuban political fabric. And on March 10 of 1952, former president and kingmaker Fulgencio Batista took over the Colombia military base in Havana and declared himself president of Cuba, unseating then-president Carlos Prío Socarrás. Batista promptly cancelled the national elections that had been scheduled for November of that year. In late July 1953, a group of young professionals staged a disastrous attack on the Moncada army barracks in Santiago de Cuba with the intention of wresting national power away from Batista. Dozens were killed in the aftermath; some were tortured by Batista's military. At his trial, the ringleader of the group – a lawyer named Fidel Castro – dared the jury to condemn him, assuring his audience that he would be absolved by the jury of the future.[71]

Two organizations that formed after Chibás's suicide, Batista's coup, and the disastrous Moncada attacks sought to protect domestics but made no claims on the government to do their part. In 1954, the Association of Domestic Service organized in the Havana neighborhood of La Víbora. Benefits of membership included medical care, legal consultation, education and culture, and dental surgery. The organization would also "extend and diversify, through the Section of Education and Culture, patriotic ideals, defending in each moment the compliance of the

---

[70] "Recabar del Gobierno la creación de las Escuelas Vocacionales para la educación y preparación de la servidumbre, de modo que sus servicios sean idóneos y efectivos, tanto en el orden material como en el moral, y constituya también protección a la misma servidumbre, recabando para ella la adopción de medidas que produzcan un trato humano, con la debida remuneración para el trabajo doméstico, con leyes sociales de seguro, invalidez y vejez." Reglamentos de la Asociación Cívica de Amas de Casa, formed December 11, 1950, Fondo Registro de Asociaciones, ANC.

[71] Pérez, Jr., *Cuba: Between Reform and Revolution*, 237.

Laws and Fundamental Letter of the Republic, contributing to the growth and tidying-up of the social conglomerate."[72] The National Association of Domestic Employees of Cuba, founded in 1955, also offered medical and legal assistance to its members. Members could also seek help in finding domestic service jobs, an ID card identifying them as part of the National Association.[73] It's unclear whether the Association of Domestic Service's reference to "tidying up" the social body through an organization aimed at maids was intentional wordplay or whether it intentionally harkened back to the *Ortodoxo* Party's use of an illustration of a broom on its propaganda. But when compared to the plans of the Committee and the Civic Association of Housewives, these association promises sound like a retreat from the optimism of 1950.

But not all activists responded in the same way. *La Convención Nacional de la Mujer por la Seguridad y Felicidad del Hogar* (National Convention of Women for the Security and Felicity of the Home) convened in Havana in the last days of January in 1954. The *Convención* proclaimed as one of its goals "the strict application of the laws that protect women workers and the extension of their rights to farmer women as domestic workers"; another goal demanded maternity leave for domestics.[74] Elena Gil, Vice-Secretary General of the founding committee of the Convention, would play a major role in the trajectory of domestic service after 1959.

Dejection and resolution, cynicism and hope collided in the last years of the 1950s. As he had predicted, Fidel Castro's profile only grew after he was convicted in 1953. Batista granted Fidel and his brother Raúl early release from prison provided that they leave the country, and they did, traveling to Mexico in 1955. But they never intended to stay away from Cuba. In December of 1956 they and some eighty other revolutionaries sailed back to Cuba's eastern coast on a luxury yacht called the *Granma*. The trip, like the attack on the Moncada barracks, was a disaster: Batista's military anticipated the group's landing and decimated their numbers. But the 26th of July movement, as they called themselves, survived and began to grow their ranks through 1957 and 1958.

[72] *Asociación de Servicios Domésticos*, 20 diciembre 1954–2 septiembre 1960, legajo 162 expediente 7234; *Asociación Nacional de Empleados Domésticos de Cuba*, octubre 1955–septiembre 1960, legajo 159 expediente 2871, Fondo Registro de Asociaciones, ANC.

[73] *Asociación Nacional del Servicio Doméstico*, 21 junio 1958–21 agosto 1960, legajo 137 expediente 2024, Fondo Registro de Asociaciones, ANC.

[74] *Mujeres Cubanas*, Año 3, Num. 23, Nov–Dic. 1953, 3.

The National Association of Domestic Service, formed in 1958, promised to promote

the material, social, cultural and athletic improvement of all its members. To achieve its goals it will use all the fighting methods of the working class and develop its course of action over the terrain of that class struggle, laboring for the interests close to workers in domestic service and to the goals of all workers in general.[75]

The National Association of Domestic Service celebrated the working class for its activism instead of disparaging its supposed cultural atavism. Unlike other organizations, it appears to have had actual domestic servants as members of its governing body: The organization's assembly was divided into cooks, chauffeurs, handservants, and gardeners. Perhaps the association was influenced by the heady politics of the late 1950s. All over Cuba, anti-Batista guerrilla groups and organizations were seeking ways both nonviolent and violent to overthrow the despotic government, and the working class was essential to any one group's victory. However, beyond soaring rhetoric, the association offered no indication that it would attempt to change the legal status or protection of domestic workers.[76]

Possibly domestic workers would always have to rely on charity, some organizations seemed to suggest; maybe a government would emerge that could protect them as it protected other workers, other organizations implied. All agreed that domestic servants needed more aid – mutual, legislative, or charity-based – than what they were currently receiving. These organizations would not go so far as Communists did in tying domestic service to slavery and promoting a workers' state, but such groups clearly saw the 1940s and 1950s as a time when legal protection for domestic service was a political possibility. Ironically, the political and legal structures that radical activists lobbied for and liberal leaders seemed resigned to were about to be utterly transformed.

### 4.5 SALARY PLEDGES AND CENSUS DATA: DOMESTIC SERVICE, 1959–1960

On New Years' Eve 1958, his forces having suffered a decisive blow from Ernesto "Che" Guevara's troops in the central city of Santa Clara, Batista fled Cuba for the Dominican Republic. He would spend the rest of his life

---

[75] *Asociación Nacional de Servicio Doméstico*, legajo 137 expediente 2024, Fondo Registro de Asociaciones, ANC. Translation mine.
[76] Ibid.

in exile.[77] Meanwhile, the 26th of July movement and especially Fidel Castro emerged as the new leaders of Cuba to raucous celebration. As the 1950s wore on, many Cubans had become weary of Batista's increasingly brutal efforts to repress resistance to his regime. They welcomed the emergence of these seemingly mythical men and women who had come down from the Sierra Maestra mountains and made promises about restoring democracy, protecting workers, and lifting Cubans out of abject poverty.[78]

On February 17, 1959, the *Asociación de Sirvientas* (*Hogar La Sirvienta*) – Association of Servants (Servants' Home) – formed, with the aim of securing "housing for associates during the time that they find themselves without a job, and their civic, social, and cultural development."[79] If they paid their monthly membership fee, which was sixty centavos each month, members of *Hogar la Sirvienta* could stay in the home for free for three days each month, paying only for their meals. If their need for housing extended past those three days, they could stay for longer and pay twenty centavos per night. *Hogar la Sirvienta* was one of the first initiatives regarding domestic workers after the 26th of July movement took power, and the men and women who formed the executive committee of the organization were thinking of ways to improve conditions for domestic workers.

The aims of *Hogar la Sirvienta* were not quite as radical as those of other Cuban groups that formed in the 1940s and 1950s and promised to advocate for changed legislation regarding domestic service. Its aims were more in line with the groups active in the 1920s, which also explicitly expressed their desire for domestics' "moral and cultural development." Perhaps the founders of *Hogar la Sirvienta* did not feel the need to call for changed legislation or improved protections for domestics. In the same month that *Hogar la Sirvienta* formed, members of the *Sindicato del Servicio Doméstico* all pledged to donate part of their monthly salaries to the "industrialization of the nation."[80] Very early on, domestic service and revolutionary fervor could happily coexist. This was not the 1930s or 1940s. It was 1959, and the new government had promised to change everything.

---

[77] van Gelder, "Batista, Ex-Cuban Dictator, Dies in Spain," *New York Times*, August 7, 1973.

[78] Pérez, Jr., *Cuba: Between Reform and Revolution*, 243.

[79] "Reglamento del Hogar la Sirvienta," Legajo: 137 Expediente: 2035, Fondo Registro de Asociaciones, ANC.

[80] "Frente Sindical," *Revolución*, February 22, 1960.

At first, it seemed as though the government would change everything. By January of 1960, one of the higher-ups in the new government was calling for servants to be given an eight-hour workday, paid vacations, sick leave, social security, and a minimum wage. But a familiar backlash ensued: This proposal alone so disturbed the Cuban bourgeoisie that the Minister of Labor at the time felt the need publicly to dispel the rumor that servants would be given a minimum salary of sixty pesos per month.[81] The same month, as part of a new labor law, the new government embarked on the creation of a labor census, the first one of the Revolution and one that would truly include *all* Cubans. Maids were enthusiastically encouraged to participate.

Still in January, advertisements in the *Diario de la Marina* continued to solicit and offer domestic servants. "A young single woman, moral and reliable, is solicited," one proclaimed from the Havana suburb of Luyanó. "White, between 25 and 35 years old. For all household chores. Must know well her obligations; if not, don't bother."[82] Under the "*Se Ofrece*" ("Offering") heading, one young woman proclaimed that she was "a Cuban cook, young woman of color, with passport and references, available for general work with a Cuban family or an American family in the United States."[83] In 1960, through the newspaper, Cubans solicited maids, cooks, and washerwomen, and Cubans advertised their services as maids, cooks, washerwomen, chauffeurs, and gardeners. Not quite everything had changed.

The 26th of July movement mouthpiece *Revolución* promised that the labor census would be the first step toward ending unemployment, distributing jobs effectively, identifying the need for certain production centers, and eliminating racial discrimination.[84] This census was part of Organic Law of the Ministry of Labor, approved in January of 1960. With the information the census provided, the labor ministry would "create a national registry of job seekers in which the unemployed would be randomly assigned a number. Only the ministry could fill vacancies."[85] Thus, all hiring (for protected labor) became the purview of the state; unions and employers no longer had the right to fill jobs as they saw fit. With one law, job access in Cuba became race blind.

---

[81] Padula, "The Fall of the Bourgeoisie," 537.
[82] *Diario de la Marina*, 3 enero 1960, 15-B.    [83] Ibid.
[84] "Ayuda el censo laboral en la campaña contra el desempleo," *Revolución*, April 9, 1960, 4.
[85] de la Fuente, *A Nation for All*, chap. 7.

FIGURE 4.1. Advertisement Encouraging Domestics to Participate in the Labor Census, 1960 (*Revolución*, April 16, 1960, 13).

The census that would form the basis of the Organic Law was to be carried out between the 18th and the 24th of April, and articles ran almost daily in *Revolución* with detailed instructions about who needed to participate as respondents and where they could do so. These articles often dedicated explicit instructions to domestic servants about how they could (and should) participate in the census. Domestics could pick up the survey at the school nearest the place of their work, fill it out, and give it to their employers to sign and return to the school. If their employers refused to sign, domestics could denounce their employers at the nearest police station, sign the survey with witnesses to that effect, and turn it in.[86] Dispersed throughout *Revolución* that month were also advertisements reinforcing the idea that domestic servants needed to participate in the upcoming census.

*Revolución* fell silent about the results of the census after April 24. In January of 1961, Fidel Castro told a crowd that he noticed that at the various night schools he visited, most of the students were domestic workers. These women were making a huge sacrifice to attend the schools because they already worked twelve- or fourteen-hour days. The women in these schools worked in the most aristocratic homes in the city while they existed in bitter poverty.[87]

## 4.6 CONCLUSION

Despite the machinations of a populist-leaning political kingmaker in Fulgencio Batista, legislation regarding domestic service failed in the late 1930s. The reasons for its failure had roots in Cuba's slave past: Domestic service, as a supposed marker of racial harmony and an actual marker of racial dominance, was too vital to the island's social hierarchy to legally protect. State sources were mostly silent about the racial implications of legislation on domestic service, but activists loudly insisted that racial domination was definitional to the problems that domestics in Cuba faced. And by the late 1930s, it was not just native African-descended or foreign white Cubans who dominated in domestic service. Black Caribbean migrants had become a significant portion of Cuba's overall workforce, particularly in the east. The failure of Decree 1754 coincided with one of the largest deportations of Caribbean labor from Cuba in the twentieth century, but the employment of mostly Anglophone Caribbeans as domestics protected many of them from repatriation. Even as their countrymen faced deportation for taking jobs from native Cubans, Caribbean domestic workers escaped scrutiny because of the

---

[86] "Ayuda el censo laboral en la campaña contra el desempleo," *Revolución*, April 9, 1960, 4.
[87] Castaño, "¿Que eramos? Las domésticas. ¿Que somos?" *Mujeres*, August 1973, 8–13.

disassociation of domestic service from formal labor. The construction of a racial hierarchy and the construction of domestic service as informal (and therefore unprotectable) labor reinforced each other amid the law's repeal and mass deportations.

Far from stymieing activism, the failure of Decree 1754 inspired even more action on behalf of domestics in the 1930s and 1940s. Communists allied with domestic workers to publicly link domestic service to slavery and to demand state action to extend protective labor legislation to domestic workers. In the 1950s, civic organizations aiming to protect and uplift domestic workers proliferated; the charters of these groups revealed both liberal and radical strains of thought among those who sought to help domestics. Little changed about domestic service in the year after 1959, but rumors abounded about the work's future as radical change reverberated throughout the island. The new government's passionate appeal to domestic workers to participate in the 1960 labor census portended change, but what shape that change would take was unclear. But the decades of activism that had preceded the 1959 Revolution, during which women like Elvira Rodríguez and Elena Gil organized and agitated, made clear what domestics wanted: acknowledgement as workers and legislative protection.

This chapter traces a previously ignored legal foundation for domestic service reform in Cuba. In doing so, it transforms understanding of the Cuban Revolution's actions regarding domestic service after 1959, disabusing historians of the notion that revolutionary change had no foundation in the republican past. Assumptions about affective female relationships and racialized and ethnic conceptions of labor deprived men and women who worked as domestics of wages and legal protection, even in a period of frenzied and rapid reform in Cuban society. Chapter 5 will explore just how Fidel Castro, the Federation of Cuban Women, and others attempted to change the circumstances of domestic workers without necessarily altering societal assumptions that shaped those circumstances.

# 5

## Pushing the Present into the Past

### *The Revolution's Solution to Domestic Service in the 1960s*

Capitalist to socialist, Catholic to atheist, neocolonial to sovereign: Cuban revolutionaries and anti-revolutionaries alike deploy these binaries to describe changes in Cuban society after 1959. They are not so much inaccurate as simplistic because the transformations for which the revolution is known happened quickly but not instantly. Those transformations in revolutionary Cuba were contingent.[1] The revolutionary government's relationship to paid domestic service is the same story in microcosm. The official post-1959 story is that domestic service in Cuba was racist, bourgeois work that the revolutionary government abolished, saving countless women from lifetimes of drudgery. Actually, domestic workers had advocated for themselves since before slavery's abolition. From the 1920s onward, they behaved far more like other workers than contemporary observers would have had us believe. People who worked in domestic service had lives more complex than the revolutionary narrative let on. They did not need rescuing. But rescue them the revolution did.

This chapter investigates what action the revolutionary government took regarding domestic service from 1961 on. After the 1960 labor census, the newly formed *Federación de Mujeres Cubanas* (Federation of Cuban Women, or FMC) opened training schools for domestic workers that operated for most of the 1960s. Despite rhetoric about how anti-revolutionary domestic service was, the government also used it as punishment and rehabilitation for counterrevolutionary women in

---

[1] See, for example, Guerra, *Visions of Power in Cuba*; Spence-Benson, *Antiracism in Cuba*; Chase, *Revolution within the Revolution*.

the aftermath of the warfare that raged in central Cuba in the 1960s. Such contradictions revealed the government's ambivalent attitude toward the labor itself. Ultimately, the revolutionary government's embrace of full socialism – whereby all domestic labor would be performed collectively – eliminated the need for paid domestic service. From the abolition of slavery to the 1959 Revolution, the majority of Cuban working women had been domestic workers; now, the labor no longer existed.

The authors of the training schools for domestics celebrated the work's disappearance from the landscape of Cuban life. It was a simultaneous victory for women's equality and Afro-Cuban social ascendance. Stories abounded about the achievements of women (it was always women) who attended and graduated from the training schools. But in these stories, the women themselves were not the authors of their own liberation. Elvira Rodríguez and other organizers had been forgotten. There was no more mention of the *Sindicato del Servicio Doméstico*. The story of domestic service in Cuba was seamlessly absorbed into the narrative of the revolution, which allegedly emancipated people unable to save themselves. Women who had worked as domestics surely saw their lives improve. But an important strand of Cuban labor history disappeared in the frenzy of revolutionary advancement.

And a pernicious strand of pre-revolutionary thought continued, even as Cuba transformed seemingly before people's eyes. The stories about domestic service's end that the Cuban media promoted in the 1960s and continues to promote even today follow a classic literary trope: the revenge plot. The former domestic encounters her former employer, who is frozen with shock that the woman of whom he (or she) thought so little has risen so high. The former domestic responds with grace and aplomb. This trope is classic because it distills high emotion into a simple story about two people running into each other. But it is also reductive. These stories of triumph emphasize the chagrin of the wealthy as much as the accomplishments of the formerly downtrodden. The trope does not transform the notion prevalent before 1959 – that domestic service labor issues were actually personal and intimate struggles between women – so much as reverse the winner of that supposedly inevitable struggle. The narratives that the new revolutionary government used to describe massive structural changes often drew on old stereotypes: Domestic workers were all women, the work was undignified, workers were isolated and apolitical. These stereotypes had always been false, but they were as useful to this new government, seeking to erase domestic service, as they had been to republican-era conservatives seeking to maintain it.

## 5.1 WORKING-CLASS UPLIFT AND A NEW LABOR FORCE: THE *ESCUELAS DE SUPERACIÓN*

The conditions that made training schools for domestics possible emerged from several initiatives. One was the April 1960 labor census. Another was the literacy campaign: Beginning in January of 1961, more than 300,000 Cubans enrolled in the *Ejército de Alfabetizadores* (Army of Literacy Teachers) to erase illiteracy from the island. They were briefly trained in the cities where they lived and then traveled to homes throughout Cuba, where they lived and worked with the families they tutored.[2] Many of the newly trained teachers began volunteering at night schools around Havana right away.

Cuban feminists would later point to Castro's January speech about domestic servants in night schools as the seed of the idea for schools specifically for domestics, but Castro's comment is revealing for another reason.[3] Of their own accord, domestic workers were taking advantage of new opportunities that the revolution offered and fitting classes into their severely cramped schedules. Just like the *Hogar la Sirvienta* and the *Sindicato del Servicio Doméstico*, domestics' attendance in night schools before April of 1961 showed that early on their work was not incompatible with the aims of the revolution. Just like the thousands of young people who left their comfortable Havana homes to teach peasants to read as part of the *Ejército de Alfabetizadores*, domestics added revolutionary fervor to their own identities.

In April of 1961 the Federation of Cuban Women opened the first night schools specifically for domestic workers, which corresponded to education they would have received in primary school. In December, the government opened Schools of Specialization for Domestics, which former domestics could enter after completing the sixth grade in night school. At these specialized schools, first located in the private Catholic University of Villanueva and then transferred to the tony Hotel Nacional, former domestics learned jobs like bus and taxi driving, traffic control, typing, and teaching.[4] The FMC reveled in placing domestic servants in luxurious locations, which would previously have been patronized by employers of servants, not servants themselves. By December, there were 60 schools for domestics in Havana with 20,000

---

[2] Guerra, *Visions of Power in Cuba*, chap. 2.     [3] See the end of Chapter 4.

[4] Lockwood, *Castro's Cuba, Cuba's Fidel*; Izquierdo, "Sharpening the Class Struggle," in Chaney and Castro, eds., *Muchachas No More*.

former domestics enrolled.[5] Between 1962 and 1965, some 90 specialization schools for domestic workers operated across the island – 60 in Havana and 30 in the interior.[6]

A woman named María Manuela knew that the training schools were the chance she had been hoping for. The daughter of a widowed cane worker in eastern Cuba, she'd had to start working as a domestic when she was barely an adolescent. She loved school but had to quit to work. When she heard about the schools for domestics, she said to herself, "María Manuela, finally your opportunity to study has arrived." Asela, a teacher at one of the schools in Vedado, remembered the schools as having an "incredible" revolutionary atmosphere. "[The schools] were during the early years, the hard years," she said. She recalled that in the first few years of the schools many women still worked as domestics and lived with their employers, who resisted their education at every turn. The domestics' determination in the face of such condescension united them. A woman named Glafira recalled that classes continued even during the Missile Crisis. She used the word *atrincherados* (entrenched) to describe the women determinedly continuing their classes, linking them with the militarized environment of the entire island during those thirteen days in October of 1962.[7]

A *santiagüera* named Cristina was sixteen in 1959 when she moved to Havana with a family for whom she worked as a domestic. In Santiago, she had run errands for Frank País, one of the most important urban insurrectionary leaders in the 26th of July movement. When she announced to her employers in Havana that she would take advantage of the new adult education schools to learn to read and write, they fired her. Years later, she ran into her former employer and triumphantly informed him that she was both educated and a "worker" – two things she never would have been had she continued to work for him. She said, "I think he liked me better as a servant."[8] Elena Gil Izquierdo, who headed the schools for domestics, recalled a similar incident in which a woman found herself face-to-face with her former maid when she went to the bank to cash a check – her maid was now a teller. She wrote, "That encounter made an impact: a humiliation that wounded her in the deepest part of her being, her sense of class."[9] That story, which Gil recounted in

---

[5] Randall, *Mujeres en la revolución*, 188.

[6] Izquierdo, "Sharpening the Class Struggle," 357.

[7] Castaño, "¿Que eramos? Las domésticas. ¿Que somos?" *Mujeres*, August 1973, 8–13.

[8] Kozol, *Children of the Revolution*, chap. 5.

[9] Izquierdo, "Sharpening the Class Struggle."

a 1989 anthology about domestic service activism in Latin America, also appeared in a 1986 *Granma* article.[10] Stories like Cristina's and the bank teller's vindicated the revolution and bolstered former maids' confidence in themselves as deserving workers. Once subordinate to upper-and middle-class Cubans, they were now their equals.

But the stories' formats also personalized former domestics' triumph in a way that echoed pre-revolutionary tropes about servants and employers. The physical encounter between the domestic and her employer is extremely satisfying on a narrative level because it reduces structural change to a conflict between two individuals, and the underdog emerges triumphant. But the *format* is the same as the format of stories about domestic service before the revolution, when the employers always ended up on top. After the abrogation of Law 1754 in 1938, M. Álvarez Marrón's column also pivoted from political to personal, insisting that personal conflicts between *amas* and *fámulas* did not require legal intervention. Years before that, the *Diario de Cuba* reduced domestics' labor concerns to petty squabbles between women.[11] The revolutionary government, in promoting stories like these in this way, changed the winner but not the game. Domestics' triumph was still the outcome of an intimate conflict, not a hard-fought political struggle; and domestics only won because of the support of more enlightened officials, not because of their own activism and efforts.

The schools benefited the women who attended, but they benefited the government as well. Night schools were integral to the political consolidation of the revolution, as teachers hoped to counteract the counter-revolutionary propaganda that domestics were surely hearing in the homes of their employers. Castro himself had informed the FMC that domestics needed to receive not just a practical but also a revolutionary education.[12] New leaders believed that domestics were uniquely vulnerable to ideas antithetical to the revolution, as Elena Gil Izquierdo wrote:

They were subject to the daily influence of the environment and mentality of the bourgeoisie; they were isolated in the homes of their masters, lacking any contact with the struggle of the working class, without the possibility that this class could defend them ... women in domestic service and peasant women represented the most backward sectors, the ones most subordinated to the ideological influence of the bourgeoisie.[13]

---

[10] Camero, "Las burguesas se quedaron sin criadas," *Granma*, April 10, 1986.
[11] "Notas del Momento," *Diario de Cuba*, 18 mayo 1925.     [12] Castaño, 8–13.
[13] Izquierdo, "Sharpening the Class Struggle."

These training schools not only allowed women to learn skills other than domestic service; they allowed the revolutionary apparatus a chance at securing the loyalty of these women to its radical political project.

Gil, despite having worked on issues of domestic service herself before the revolution, believed that domestics suffered an apolitical pre-revolutionary existence. She wrote in a report to the FMC that Fidel conceived of the schools for domestics to "liberate them from that bourgeois influence through the study of the social realities that had determined their servitude." She also explained that each of the specialized schools was named for a Cuban woman who had fought in the struggle for national independence not only to honor those women but also to "start to show the domestics a world unknown to them: that of struggle: the endless fight of humanity for a better world."[14] Oria Calcines, the director of education for the *Escuelas de Superación* (Schools of Achievement), said that she experienced the same emotions teaching domestic workers as she had when she taught first graders.[15] Thus, Gil and Calcines denigrated domestic workers even as they celebrated their own activism on domestics' behalf.

The training schools for domestics supposedly awakened women's political consciousness, but, as we saw in Chapter 4, many of them were already awake. Cristina's story was framed as an ascent from nothing to something, but, when Cristina was "nothing," she worked for Frank País as a messenger.[16] She risked her life for the revolution when she was still a maid. And even though domestics themselves had been lobbying the Cuban state for the extension of legal rights to domestics for *thirty years*, remarks like Gil's and Calcines's suggested that the state could only see these women as participants in political life once they hung up their uniforms and left the homes of their employers. Activism surrounding domestic work before the revolution sought to convince the Cuban state to recognize the dignity of workers. But the revolutionary state only recognized the dignity of these women once they stopped working as domestics.

Aside from political integration, there was another more prosaic reason for the schools: the staggering loss of skilled labor across the

---

[14] Izquierdo, "La Educación de las Domésticas: Una Agudización de la Lucha de Clases."
[15] Weisman and Vega, "From Maids to Compañeras."
[16] Michelle Chase and Lillian Guerra have both pointed out that the revolutionary struggle in urban areas like Santiago de Cuba and Havana was statistically far more dangerous than being in the Sierra Maestras. Frank País himself was murdered by police in 1957.

island. About 80 percent of the Cubans who reached Florida through 1962 were professionals or skilled workers.[17] Transportation, for example, was a serious problem for the revolution: A former taxi driver who left Cuba in 1964 estimated that only about 5 percent of the 40,000 taxi drivers that were in Cuba supported Castro, and that they demonstrated their dissatisfaction with slowdowns and sabotage.[18] Of about 3,000 Cubans who participated in the 1961 Bay of Pigs invasion, about 550 of them – or 20 percent – were involved in transportation. In February of 1963, the Minister of Transport denounced transportation workers as "the most counterrevolutionary element in our country."[19]

It makes sense, then, that the revolutionary government attempted to replace these "counterrevolutionary elements" with women who ostensibly would be more loyal than anyone else to the revolution. A photo diary from the New Year's Eve 1961 issue of the weekly periodical *Bohemia* – a fierce supporter of the revolution since its triumph – featured women, the "large majority" of whom had been domestics, learning about transportation.[20] An article from the same month entitled "A New Life: The Workers of Domestic Service" profiled former domestics enrolled at technical schools. The photos surrounding the short story featured women learning to file in a "modern office," type, repair cars, and work as chauffeurs.[21] The replacement of male white- and blue-collar workers with former domestics was a revolutionary solution to an acute problem in 1960s Cuba.

While proponents rarely talked about it as such, the training schools for domestics were also part of policy intended to improve the fates of African-descended Cubans. The three primary subjects of "From Maids to Compañeras" – a 1998 documentary about the training schools for domestic workers – were all women of African descent. Mariela Manuela Blanco said of her life then, "I didn't have dreams … what could a black poor woman do besides be a domestic?" Blanco went to work as a maid at the age of eleven. She went to law school after attending the *Escuelas de*

---

[17] Pérez, Jr., *Cuba: Between Reform and Revolution*, 261.
[18] Cuban Labor Bulletin, August 1, 1964 (No. 4) in CCFC Collection, Box 28, Folder "Transportation," Hoover Institution Archives.
[19] Citizens Committee for a Free Cuba Press Release, January 10, 1964, in CCFC Collection, Box 28, Folder "Transportation," Hoover Institution Archives.
[20] Guerra, *Visions of Power in Cuba*.
[21] Guerra, photos by Jose Amador, "La Mujer en el Transporte, *Bohemia*, December 31, 1961; Jorge Luis Bernard, "Una Nueva Vida: Las Trabajadoras del Servicio Doméstico," *Bohemia*, December 24, 1961, 120–121.

En abril de 1961 se crearon las primeras escuelas nocturnas para la superación de las domésticas. A lo largo del país se abrieron 17 escuelas en las cuales matricularon unas 30 000 domésticas. En la foto, una visita a una de aquellas escuelas.

FIGURE 5.1. Image of Schools for Domestics, 1986 (the original caption reads, "In April of 1961 the first night schools for the advancement of domestics were created. Across the country 17 schools were opened in which some 30,000 domestics matriculated. In the photo, a visit to one of those schools." *Granma*, April 10, 1986).

*Superación.* By 1998, she was a judge. Another interviewee, Georgina Herrera, remembered thinking as a teenager that she could only be either a domestic or a prostitute; now, she is a celebrated poet. Elda Ibáñez, who slept on a cot with a sack over her body for warmth even as she lived in and cleaned a mansion, became a cook after she trained in the FMC's schools.[22] For these women, the revolution's training schools were the first step toward a future that was previously unimaginable.

While Blanca, Herrera, and Ibáñez all talked about the racism endemic to Cuban culture, the documentary that featured them did not address the structural racism that pervaded the domestic service industry, nor did it characterize the training schools for domestics as a moment of *superación* specifically for women of African descent. It certainly was that, however. African-descended women comprised a significant percentage of the beneficiaries of the night schools and specialization schools the FMC

[22] Weisman and Vega, "From Maids to Compañeras," 1998.

La Escuela Nocturna de, Superación para Domésticas.

FIGURE 5.2. Image of Schools for Domestics, 1973 (the original caption reads, "The Night School of Advancement for Domestics." *Mujeres*, August 1973.)

organized. Photographs used in articles that memorialized the schools for domestics decades later featured predominantly black women, or at least equal numbers of black and white women. It was in 1961 that Fidel Castro declared racism "solved" in Cuba, so it is possible that the government was reluctant to continue focusing on the anti-racist implications of its policies, preferring to discuss women's rights and workers' power. However, even if discussion of race was taboo in post-1961 revolutionary Cuba, that African-descended women benefited hugely from the *Escuelas de Superación* was undeniable. Additionally, the visual reality of the women's blackness combined with their and others' narration of Fidel's action on behalf of domestics collapsed any space between Afro-Cubans after the revolution and Fidel himself. *He* helped *them*; *Fidel* helped *black Cubans*. Once more, intrapersonal intimacy overtook a narrative that prioritized self-determined activism.

## 5.2 THE SCHOOLS' SKEPTICS

Perhaps because of the anti-racist, anti-sexist, and anti-classist bent of the training schools for *domésticas*, suspicion and skepticism about the political and social ascendance of former domestic workers flourished along with the schools. The Tita Calvar brigade, a counterrevolutionary group based in Oriente province, reported in June of 1963 that the training schools for domestics were nothing more than Communist indoctrination centers, where the "poor girls" were manipulated and lied to. Allegedly, teachers read the women letters stolen from the post office and sent from the United States, which always reported terrible news about the United States.[23] The brigade reported that teachers pressured former domestics into revealing information about the families for whom they worked, like what kind of food they ate and whether their employers bought food at the People's market or on the black market. Girls who resisted tattling were mocked.[24] A Havana resident named "Panchita" wrote to her friend Patricia in October of 1965, "You can't imagine the number of people in domestic service ... who have decided to leave to try their luck in other places. Here they had few prospects because the Schools of Improvement didn't accept them or, if they did accept them, treated them badly."[25]

The Tita Calvar brigade and Panchita suggested that the Cuban government did not treat these women as sovereign citizens fully in control of their destinies. Instead, teachers treated them as sources of information about an enemy class and abused the young women when they resisted. According to anti-Communist sources, the schools merely replaced one source of unwavering authority with another.

Cubans suspicious of the revolution mocked the capacity of former maids to successfully drive buses or taxis. An "anti-Communist Cuban," writing in December of 1962, wanted the Cuban Freedom Committee (CFC) to know that "In Cuba they call the [female] chauffeurs of the People's Transportation las *choferonas,* or the [car] destroyers, because they have destroyed all the cars in six months."[26] Given that this *cubano* wrote just one year after the training of domestics in transportation, it is likely that the "destroyers" he referred to had been maids before the revolution. Another letter, sent from Guantánamo in 1964, lamented the difficulty of finding a maid in those years, noting that "those who before served as maids now are militants or they go breaking cars that

---

[23] The Tita Calvar brigade was apparently a counterrevolutionary group writing from Oriente in the mid-1960s.

[24] Letter dated June 27, 1963, in Cuban Freedom Committee Collection, Box 60, Folder "Cuba-January 1963," Hoover Institution Archives.

[25] Letter dated October 24, 1965, in Cuban Freedom Committee Collection, Box 64, Folder: "Cuba-January 1965," Hoover Institution Archives.

[26] The CFC was a United States-based organization quietly funded by the Central Intelligence Agency to transmit anti-Castro radio broadcasts. For more information on the CFC, see "Cuban Freedom Committee Collection Overview," Hoover Institution Archives, http://www.oac.cdlib.org/findaid/ark:/13030/kt000003off/?query=cuban+freedom+committee. Letter dated December 20, 1962, in Cuban Freedom Committee Collection, Box 60, Folder "Cuba – January 1963," Hoover Institution Archives.

were formerly private taxis and which the revolution stole from their rightful owners."[27] In the same year, the CFC reported on the shortage of transit workers on the island, concluding that "the regime desperately tried to overcome the critical situation by impressing domestic servants into learning to drive confiscated private automobiles and assigning them to routes as 'popular transport.' This merely increased the traffic hazards."[28] Women doing men's work was a boon for the revolution, but disaffected Cubans scoffed at the possibility. These letter writers opposed the revolutionary government generally, but their specific critique of women replacing men as taxi drivers reveals that at least part of their opposition was to gender-switching work assignments.

Taxi driving was not the only thing maids could not do. A woman named Mariepa reported in 1965 that her friend's maid had been through two government scholarships: seamstress and ballet dancer. Mariepa noted that "Because she never received the sewing machine Fidel had promised her, she could not work as a seamstress, and as for the ballet dancing, I think she came out of the Academy better prepared to dance the *rumba* [an African-inflected social dance popular among Cubans of African descent]." Mariepa concluded that this woman was worse off than she had been before, having "overcome" but then being forced to go back to work as a maid.[29] Mariepa's scorn was both racialized and gendered: She added parenthetically that now she was supposed to call the rumba "the mozambique" to honor Africa.[30] For her, a former maid having learned a dance long associated with the Havana slums was a waste of time.

In the novel *The Maids of Havana*, housewives gossiped anxiously and derisively about their maids abandoning them after 1959. One insisted that the whole enterprise would be nothing more than "Queen for a Day" – a popular TV show in which a working-class woman was treated like a "queen" for twenty-four hours. This housewife accused Castro of tricking girls: "They're believing what *that* crazy degenerate still reeking of the bush is saying: that he's going to turn all the maids into secretaries,

---

[27] Letter received March 11, 1964, CFC Collection, Box 61, Folder "Cuba – Copies – 1964," Hoover Institution Archives.

[28] Ibid.

[29] Letter received October 29, 1965, CFC Collection, Box 63, Folder "Cuba – October 1965," Hoover Institution Archives.

[30] For an exploration of dance and politics in revolutionary Cuba, see Schwall, *Dancing with the Revolution*, 2021.

teachers, and doctors. And they believe him!"[31] *The Maids of Havana*
suggests that women who had employed servants were skeptical and
scared of their maids' social ascendance.

Devyn Spence-Benson noted that the fear of speedy and total racial
integration was an oft-unspoken reason that many white Cubans fled the
island after 1959. White Cubans feared that the revolutionary government would allow black Cubans to infiltrate their homes, their social
spaces, their previously segregated worlds.[32] Letters like Mariepa's highlight the racial overtones of resentment around the ascendance of domestic workers. Her counternarrative turned the narrative of *superación* on
its head: Instead of achieving new heights, the revolutionary training
schools supposedly brought maids lower than they had been before.
This was typical of anti-Communist analysis of this period: What the
revolutionary government touted as progressive and good was actually
damaging and sinister.

Libia Rodríguez Roberto, writing in March of 1964, had been a
teacher before leaving Cuba. She reported that many of the *new* teachers
on the island were former domestics who had only gone through six-
month Communist indoctrination programs. She noted scornfully that
"Communism takes advantage of those persons who have the least preparation to use them in its indoctrination plans."[33] Ironically, her estima-
tion of maids' capacity to resist brainwashing was similar to Elena Gil
Izquierdo's, who called maids "subordinated to the ideological influence
of the bourgeoisie." These women, both educators, had conflicting politics yet parallel understandings about maids' ideological vulnerability.

The night schools for maids closed by 1967, once all the students
enrolled across the city had graduated and more general skill-based
schools had opened across the island.[34] Thus, these reeducation schools
were located squarely in the early period of revolutionary politics, part of
the first wave of attempts to absorb all Cubans into the revolution.
Supporters saw this project and others like it as a move toward women's
liberation from the drudgery of "women's work." Opponents, meanwhile, saw it as a cynical ploy to indoctrinate vulnerable women with
Communist ideals. Both sides, however, saw the women involved as
susceptible to the machinations of the other. As much as maids were

---

[31] Pérez-Sarduy, *The Maids of Havana*.       [32] Spence-Benson, *Antiracism in Cuba*.
[33] Letter sent March 23, 1964, CCFC Collection, Box 30, Folder "Indoctrination," Hoover
    Institution Archives.
[34] Randall, *Mujeres en la revolución*, 193.

citizens to be liberated, they were also citizens who needed to be controlled. Revolutionary and anti-revolutionary attitudes about the readiness of former maids to perform other tasks reflected stereotypes about domestic servants that had thrived for centuries.

## 5.3 THE "*LIMPIA DE MATANZAS*," PLAN NUMBER TWO, AND REVOLUTIONARY DOMESTICITY

The Cuban Revolution is in part the story of the Cuban government extending its reach to every single person in the country, a goal that either was not possible or not of interest to previous governments. Getting former domestic servants into school and then into the workforce gave those domestic servants access to new skills and, simultaneously, put them on the government's radar. But domestics were not the only population who had been elusive, and the *Escuelas de Superación* were not the only method the government used to gather information. Rachel Hynson has written about "Operation Marriage," which, through mass weddings, got thousands of Cubans' information to the national government in a matter of months.[35] Other methods resembled the *Escuelas de Superación* but delved even further into what had been the private sphere.

The revolutionary government was obviously very proud of the training schools for domestics and the successful transfer of their labor from service to suffering industries. Viewed as a pragmatic tool to absorb Cubans into the governmental apparatus, however, the training schools were similar to other, less publicized operations, at least one of which outraged Cubans opposed to the nationalization projects of the early 1960s. The Cuban revolution also rehabilitated prostitutes and counterrevolutionary women. These programs shared the goals of training schools for domestics but were not so attractive to the general public.

One can understand prostitution in the twentieth century – and the revolutionary government's attempts to eradicate it – as the unsavory cousin of domestic service. Since Cuba's independence, domestic workers and prostitutes were often assumed to be the same people. The governmental and journalistic studies of prostitution discussed in the first two chapters of this book insisted that the low wages domestic service offered had pushed women into prostitution. The criminal cases in those chapters

---

[35] Hynson, "Sex and State Making in Revolutionary Cuba, 1959–1969."

and their outcomes suggested that republican courts were suspicious of the sexual propriety of women and girls who worked as domestics.[36]

Pilar López Gonzáles, a former prostitute who was "rehabilitated" by the revolution, made the connection between domestic work and prostitution explicit. Pilar started working as a live-in maid when she was thirteen in the late 1940s; her employers forced her to wear a uniform and to address them as señora and *caballero* (ma'am and sir). Pilar got her first work as a prostitute through her second job as a domestic: The brother-in-law of her employers offered her far more money to sleep with him than she got as a maid.[37] Pilar's story was not unique to Cuba; a study of sex work in early twentieth-century Mexico City found that the vast majority of prostitutes had been domestics and turned to prostitution after sexual assault *while* working as maids.[38] Repeating over and over that she couldn't resolve her financial needs with the salary she made as a domestic worker, Pilar highlighted the desperation that went into her decision. She was targeted by a powerful man and drawn into sexual activity. When asked by an interviewer why she turned to prostitution when she seemed so intelligent and independent, Pilar responded that she had no other options: "There was no other work aside from being a domestic."[39]

Although the government preferred to present its reform of prostitution on the island as a top-down, well-organized process, that was far from the case. Community activists and members of the FMC attempted to eradicate prostitution on their own between 1959 and 1961; after that year, a federal ministry took charge of reform efforts. At first sporadic and somewhat spontaneous, the movement to end prostitution in Cuba culminated in 1962 with the creation of several residential training schools for former sex workers. By 1963, the revolutionary government had closed all brothels in all provinces and eliminated the designated areas that had allowed sex work.[40] By 1966, Castro declared that prostitution was "nearly eliminated" in Cuba. Rachel Hynson argued that the

---

[36] See Chapters 1 and 2.

[37] "Part III: Pilar López Gonzales," in Lewis, Lewis, and Rigdon, *Four Women Living the Revolution*.

[38] Bliss, *Compromised Positions*, chap. 1. For a study of prostitution in nineteenth-century Havana, see Tiffany Sippial, *Prostitution, Modernity, and the Making of the Cuban Republic, 1840–1920*.

[39] "Pilar: Interview 8/26/69, pp. 1–84, Spanish, MD," Oscar and Ruth Lewis Papers, University of Illinois Archives.

[40] Lewis, Lewis, and Rigdon, 279.

efforts to end prostitution were far more than just that: Rather, they represented efforts to police *all* women and transform women thought of as outside the bounds of proper revolutionary behavior (prostitutes, but also poor women and African-descended women in general) into good middle-class revolutionaries.[41]

But revolutionary attitudes toward domestic and reproductive labor had created a vacuum that needed to be filled. To encourage women to leave lives of sex work and/or servitude and enter the productive labor force, revolutionary discourse had denigrated the appeal of domestic and reproductive labor. Anthropologist Elise Andaya noted that, if before women had been the moral centers of their homes, "socialist orthodoxy inverted this moral valuation, viewing domestic chores and the nurturance of children as numbing, wasteful, and degrading when performed by unpaid women in the home."[42] Fidel Castro himself compared domestic work to such notorious occupations as bartending and prostitution. Despite this new attitude, however, there was still need in Cuba for the preparation of food, the care of children, and the cleaning of houses.

The government also perceived the need to correct the behavior of wayward women. According to several reports, the revolutionary government used domestic work as punishment for female counterrevolutionaries. The Tita Calvar brigade reported that as early as 1963, "Communists" were razing farmland in Matanzas and sending farm girls to Havana to work as servants.[43] *Free Cuba News* (FCN), a newsletter based in Washington, DC, reported that there had been a protest in the small town of San Carlos in Las Villas province in July of 1964. The people of San Carlos allegedly swung empty pots and pans in protest of food shortages "and other miseries." While the Castro administration admitted that it had sent all protestors to "rehabilitation camps," *FCN* asserted that, "Actually, the women demonstrators were sent to Havana to become servants in government buildings, the men were whisked off to work in concentration camps, and the children were sent to schools of

---

[41] Hynson, "Count, Capture, and Reeducate."

[42] Andaya, "Reproducing the Revolution," 67.

[43] The letter reads, in part, "The communists have razed all the tillable farms in that zone, carrying away all young farm hands, distributing them among several farms in the Pinar del Río province. Farm girls having also been carried away, forcing them to work as servants of the students living in Havana suburbs." Letter dated June 27, 1963, in Cuban Freedom Committee Collection, Box 60, Folder "Cuba-January 1963," Hoover Institution Archives.

Communist indoctrination."[44] In August of 1965, the F.O.R.D.C. – an anti-revolution labor group – reported that 5,000 peasant women were being interned in Havana homes.[45] What the exile press and dissident Cubans likened to forced labor, however, the authors of the peasant women program called "reeducation."

Little has been published in English on the civil war that wracked the central Escambray region of Cuba after 1959.[46] The counterrevolutionary insurgency there was in response to the Agrarian Reform Act, passed in 1959, which famously reduced massive landholdings in Cuba and redistributed land to the poor. Less famously, groups of large landowners, smallholders, former rebels, and landless peasants with aspirations to land ownership in the Escambray mounted a passionate and violent war against the encroachment of revolutionary policy in the region. The insurgents received arms and supplies from the US Central Intelligence Agency (CIA), but also found support among peasants in the region.[47] The Cuban government called the campaign to wipe out those counterrevolutionary forces "Plan Number One." To flush them out, the revolutionary government simply removed the inhabitants of that area. A woman interviewed by the anthropologist Oscar Lewis in 1969 referred to the violent conflict as a *limpia* (cleansing), a term that underscores the extreme violence of the government's subordination of resistant men.[48]

"Plan Number Two" was what the government did with the families rendered homeless in the process of subordinating central Cuba to the revolutionary project. The revolutionary government did not deny their policy of separating families that had participated in counterrevolutionary activity but framed it as necessary to successful reeducation. Plan Number Two was based in Miramar, an exclusive Havana neighborhood, and was entirely female – boys were sent to another part of Miramar to be scholarship students. Peasant women were reeducated:

---

[44] "Cuba: Subversion Capital of the Hemisphere," *Free Cuba News* (vol. 3, n. 10): August 9, 1965, p. 7, in CCFC Collection, Box 34 Folder "FCN Vol. 3 No. 10," Hoover Institution Archives.

[45] "5,000 Peasant Women Held by Castro-Communism," *Cuban Labor* (F.O.R.D.C.), August 1965, CCFC Collection, Box 28, Folder "Women," Hoover Institution Archives.

[46] Exceptions include Guerra, *Visions of Power in Cuba*; Swanger, *Rebel Lands of Cuba*; and Sara Kozameh, "Harvest of Revolution."

[47] Kozameh, "Harvest of Revolution."

[48] "Bueno, Caridad: Interview of 1/2/70, Spanish, pp 1–16, RL," Box 141, Oscar Lewis papers, University of Illinois Archives.

From the moment they enter Plan Number Two, the mountain women spend most of their time being educated in one way or another. They are given careful instruction in how to dress themselves, in cooking, washing, housecleaning, hygiene for themselves and their children. They are taught how to put on makeup.[49]

Peasant women were not the only ones who were educated by the government in domestic arts. Less formally, "wayward girls and former slum dwellers" were sent to agricultural boarding schools to clean residences and bathrooms.[50] The government's version of what happened to peasant women in Miramar clearly differed from what anti-Communist publications and dissident letters claimed. Anti-Communists insisted that peasant women were working as servants for families not their own. The government suggested that peasant women were learning domestic tasks that would help them better manage their own families' lives. Neither claim can be satisfactorily verified through documents. The claims of the F.O.R.D.C. were intended for use as propaganda, as were the Cuban government's claims. But the overlap between the narratives – that of domesticity – offers up a kernel of truth.

Whether they were servants for revolutionary personnel, as anti-Communists insisted, or students of revolutionary femininity, as the government said, women who had been relocated from the Cuban countryside to Havana were learning new forms of domesticity. The revolution's use of domestic work to rehabilitate or punish women located it within a robust tradition in the Americas of using domestic work as a corrective to female behavior.[51] Despite wanting to change everything, the authors of the Cuban revolution drew on long-tested traditions to solve social (and military) problems.

Both narratives of Plan Number Two, conflicting though they were, actually had roots in pre-1959 Cuban history. Anti-Communists interpreted the plan as slavery, whose legacy the revolutionary government was determined to erase in Cuba. The government insisted that it was more like an educational program – rhetoric linking it to the *Escuelas del*

---

[49] Lockwood, *Castro's Cuba, Cuba's Fidel*, 260–262.
[50] Guerra, *Visions of Power in Cuba*, chap. 7.
[51] Throughout the twentieth century, women incarcerated in Mazorra – Havana's most notorious insane asylum – were regularly rehabilitated with domestic tasks. In the nineteenth century, poor girls in Argentina and Brazil were trained in the domestic arts and then shipped out to wealthy families. *Mitanaje*, or unpaid domestic service to wealthy landowners, was a hallmark of Indigenous Bolivian life until 1953, when Indigenous activists made its abolition essential to their support of the Bolivian Revolution. See Gomes da Cunha, trans. Micol Siegel, "Learning to Serve"; Gotkowitz, *A Revolution for Our Rights*; Guy, "Girls in Prison"; Lambe, *Madhouse*.

*Hogar* of decades past. The *Escuelas* had closed in 1961, but the legacy of domestic education lived on.[52] Long before 1959, domesticity could be (and was) a site of power and regulation by the state. Both Plan Number Two and the program for former sex workers reflected Cuba's rapidly evolving understanding of what domesticity was and how it could function in an anti-capitalist society. No longer did domestic labor exist in the context of work and compensation; now its performance was about how to be a "proper" revolutionary woman.

## 5.4 SAN ANDRÉS, FULL SOCIALISM, AND THE ERASURE OF DOMESTIC SERVICE IN CUBA

Just what a "revolutionary woman" was represented a site of bitter conflict between Communist Cubans and their anti-Communist counterparts both in Cuba and in exile. The ideological gap between the groups continued to widen through the 1960s. Anti-Communists in Cuba and in Miami supported traditional femininity, which prioritized women's place in the home above all else, and used metaphors of slavery to define the new labor norms in Cuba. The revolution, meanwhile, unapologetically strove to distance women from the responsibilities of the home so that they could contribute to Cuba's economic growth. Revolutionary actors framed the revolution as the harbinger of women's liberation *from* the home and strove to create utopian Communist towns where all adults engaged in productive labor, the care of their children left to the state. It was a nightmare for Cubans who already feared that the revolution sought to destroy their families and raise their children as communist drones, but, for the government, it was a dream. The institution of paid domestic service became irrelevant as reproductive and domestic labor became part of the collective effort to push the Cuban economy forward.

A 1965 *Miami Herald* article, entitled "Exiles Say Women Forced to Labor," reported that,

Fidel Castro's Communist regime is forcing women in Cuba to work as much and as hard as the men ... The Cuban Student Directorate (ORE) said that thousands of women are being forced to abandon their homes, children and families to help in harvesting tobacco, cane, coffee and other crops.[53]

[52] Vega, "The Last, and Still Proud, Generation of Cuba's 'Hogaristas'," *Miami Herald*, May 15, 2015.
[53] "Exiles Say Women Forced to Labor," *Miami Herald*, March 9, 1965, in CCFC Collection, Box 28, Folder "Women," Hoover Institution Archives.

The abandonment of hearth and home to do Communism's bidding was a constant in critiques of revolutionary labor policies. It was unnatural for women to perform the same jobs as men, anti-Communists insisted, and especially unnatural for anyone to prioritize female "productive" labor over the reproductive labor of childcare. For women who left Cuba in the 1960s and for Miami journalists reporting on Communism, the reconfiguration of women's place in society was one of Communism's most egregious crimes.

Instead of denying that women had to work in Communist Cuba, the revolutionary press embraced that fact. A radio broadcast from International Women's Day of 1968 explicitly tied women's productive labor to the triumph of socialism, and the underemployment of women before 1959 to the decadence of capitalism:

> Before the triumph of the revolution, under the capitalist way of life, no one could have imagined in Cuba that Cuban women would move en masse to the country-side to do agricultural work and play an essential role in the construction of the socialist economic foundations ... When the capitalist base of exploitation was destroyed, the revolution also destroyed discrimination and the prejudices engendered by the former regime by liberating the women. This has made it possible for hundreds of thousands of women to get into production, especially agricultural production, which is our main source of work and in which the great battle of our socialist construction is being waged.[54]

For the Cuban government, women's productive labor *was* liberation. What they did before the revolution – working as housewives or domestics – was forced labor, foisted upon them by the constraints of capitalism. Exiles and dissident Cubans critiqued Cuban labor practices, but the revolutionary government was proud of these accomplishments.

San Andrés de Caiguanabo, in Cuba's westernmost province, was the manifestation of the revolution's desire to socialize reproductive labor. The town became the flagship of a pilot program announced by Castro in January of 1967 to develop new towns as completely Communist.[55] The basic idea of San Andrés and the other towns was the total devotion of its residents to productive labor. In San Andrés, children would be under the care of the state from a very young age; their housing, food, and schooling would be provided by the state so that their parents could work without

---

[54] Excerpts from "The Triumph of the Revolution Was the Triumph of Women," Transcript of Havana Domestic Service in Spanish, 8 March 1968, 1700 GMT, in CCFC Collection, Box 28, Folder "Women," Hoover Institution Archives.
[55] Navarro Vega, *Cuba, el socialismo y sus éxodos*, "Comunismo 'in vitro.'"

the obligations of childcare. At the town's inauguration, five nurseries opened, each with the capacity to care for sixty to eighty children. The town also boasted a central laundromat and kitchen.[56]

The socialization of childcare, once left to nannies and parents, was a hallmark of the Cuban Revolution's transformation of the family. The FMC had organized the first *círculos infantiles* (daycare centers) across Cuba. They initially operated 5 days a week, from 6 am to 7 pm; for a nominal fee, they provided free uniforms and meals to children. In 1962, on a televised roundtable discussion of the new daycare centers, Fidel Castro asserted that the concept of a state-run daycare came from the revolution itself: "Before, for what reason were daycares going to exist? Who was going to concern themselves with the children of the workers?"[57] A full-page spread in a 1967 issue of *Granma* about completely free daycare centers noted proudly that, "Now not only will mothers go to work without worrying about the care of their children, but they will also enjoy an increase in their home economy."[58] San Andrés, with its municipal capacity to care for 400 children, was a clear reflection of the state's desire to absolve women of household responsibilities so that they could perform productive labor. In a speech outlining the goals of San Andrés, Castro gloated that women in the town would be liberated, no longer "prostituted" by capitalism.[59]

Of course, enemies of Cuban Communism saw things differently. A *Miami Herald* article, which called the San Andrés plan "pure Communism," asserted that while Castro claimed that San Andrés and its sister cities across the island were to be the first of their kind in the world, there was a distinctly Cuban historical parallel: slavery. The reporter noted that, as in San Andrés, Cuban slaves were fed, clothed, and treated for sickness by their masters. The only difference this reporter saw was that while enslaved Cubans were able to live with their children, the residents of these experimental towns would be unable to.[60]

[56] Rojas, "San Andrés," *Granma*, January 29, 1967, in CCFC Box 29, Folder "Pinar del Río," Hoover Institution Archives.
[57] Leiner, *Children Are the Revolution*, 54.
[58] Manresa y Naon, "Las Simientes: Gratiutos los Círculos Infantiles en todo el país, desde enero," *Granma*, 17 enero 1967.
[59] Leighton, "Castro's 'True Communism' Plan Puts All Children under Care of State," *Miami News*, 1967, in CFFC, Box 30, Folder: "Indoctrination," Hoover Institution Archives.
[60] Martínez, "Pure Communism Project to Start in Cuba," *Miami Herald*, March 5, 1967, in CCFC, Box 30, Folder: "Indoctrination," Hoover Institution Archives.

Given the strides that the Cuban government had made in erasing structural inequities between black and white Cubans even as early as 1968 and given the horror many white Cuban exiles had expressed at the prospect of full racial integration on the island, the reporter's reference to slavery was ironic. His audience comprised precisely those Cubans who, though they might decline to admit it, were partially driven to exile by their racial prejudices.[61] It was also unoriginal, since the anti-revolution press constantly referred to the forced labor of Cuban women on the island. His comparison of San Andrés to slavery was rooted not in reality but in a cynical (and widely shared) desire to denigrate the new Cuban government's efforts to transform society. It also subtly indicated that not *all* of slavery was bad. At least slavery, the logic went, allowed for some closeness among families and between enslaved people and their masters. Proponents of this logic extolled the supposed intimacy of plantation slavery while blithely ignoring the violence lurking underneath.[62]

In 1968, the government launched the Revolutionary Offensive, whereby *all* businesses were nationalized.[63] San Andrés, apparently, had just been a preview: The Cuban government wanted to make all of Cuba more like the ideal version of San Andrés, where reproductive and domestic labor were the concerns of the state. There were exceptions. Some Cubans had servants well into the 1970s and 1980s, referring to them obliquely as "a woman who helps me." But by the end of the training schools and the Revolutionary Offensive, domestic service was no longer a prominent part of life in Cuba. In 1959, servants had donated their union dues to the cause of the revolution; in 1973, the women's magazine *Mujeres* published a retrospective on domestic service in Cuba entitled "What Were We? The Domestics. What Are We?" that located domestic service squarely in Cuba's pre-revolutionary past. After fourteen years, domestic service had become part of the national memory. "Full socialism" contributed to the movement of domestic service from reality to memory.

### 5.5 CONCLUSION

Inocencia, one of the women profiled in Oscar Lewis's acclaimed *Four Women Living the Revolution: An Oral History of Contemporary Cuba*,

---

[61] Spence-Benson, *Antiracism in Cuba*.
[62] Villoch, "Aquella Antiguo Servidumbre," 27 junio 1945; for an analysis of Cabrera's writings, see Chapter 6.
[63] Guerra, *Visions of Power in Cuba*.

had worked as a domestic for much of her life. She was a staunch supporter of the revolutionary government. In a 1969 interview he conducted himself, Lewis attempted to connect Inocencia's work as a domestic with her revolutionary zeal, first asking her what she thought of the fact that she had worked as a domestic until 1959. She corrected him: She had stopped working as a domestic in 1950. Lewis tried again, asking if her work as a domestic "planted seeds" within her of identification with the poor. After she hesitated, he acknowledged that the question was complicated and clarified again: Did Inocencia see some connection between working as a domestic and her revolutionary attitude today? "No," Inocencia answered flatly, insisting that if she had been rich her attitude would have been the same.[64]

Exchanges like these, where women refused to make a neat line from their pre-revolutionary ignorance or backwardness to their post-revolutionary model behavior, were common in the interviews that Lewis and his team performed. Inocencia refused to let Lewis impose a logic to her life that she disagreed with, but she could not stop the revolution's overall narrative. Government officials and authors of the training schools for domestics relished the idea that before the revolution domestics had been downtrodden and invisible. The training schools, and by extension the FMC and Castro himself, had saved them. This narrative, alive in Cuba today, completely elides the activism and self-advocacy of domestic workers before 1959. The erasure of domestic service from Cuba's economy is touted as an unmitigated good, but the history of demands for the extension of labor rights to domestics in the 1940s and 1950s has been ignored, cutting off a potentially fruitful debate about whether the racism and sexism in domestic service could have been resolved *without* the work's elimination.

Women who were maids before 1959 received access to education and technical training because of the *Escuelas de Superación*. Once ensconced in the new economy, they had healthcare and access to affordable housing, just like all other Cuban workers. Their children had opportunities beyond their wildest dreams; they would never clean floors on their hands and knees or be paid in leftover food.[65] These schools opened doors that

---

[64] Oscar Lewis, "Interview." Folder: "[Inocencia]: Interview of 12/13/69, Spanish, pp 1–25," Oscar Lewis papers, University of Illinois Archives.

[65] See the opening anecdote to de la Fuente's *A Nation for All*, in which a former maid reunites with her employer in 1993. The former maid's children had become an engineer and a doctor.

had been closed. But the meaning that the revolution imposed on the schools erased the story of pre-revolutionary activism. It deprived generations of Cubans of the names of women and men who organized in the 1920s, 1930s, and 1940s. The banishment of paid domestic service made the work itself – childcare, cleaning, laundering – more tightly associated with female identity, so much so that by the mid-1970s, even women extremely loyal to the revolution were complaining about the pressures to excel in productive, reproductive, and revolutionary labor.[66] And the banishment of the *memory* of domestic workers' pre-1959 activism allowed a certain kind of nostalgia about domestic service – and, by extension, race relations in Cuba – to flourish on and off the island. The next chapter will explore the repercussions of that post-revolutionary nostalgia.

[66] Andaya, *Conceiving Cuba*, 38.

# 6

## Conjuring Ghosts

### *Domestic Service's Remains after 1959*

This book has argued that throughout the twentieth century, elites wielded nostalgia to form arguments against legally protecting domestic service. Nostalgia rests on memory – the topic of this final chapter. I use memory as a vector through which to understand the transformations and stagnations of domestic service in Cuba after the 1959 revolution. Memory appears in several forms, including oral history interviews I conducted myself, the transcripts of oral histories taken down in 1970s Miami, and memories encapsulated in personal letters and personal papers. Lydia Cabrera makes another appearance, as several of her unpublished speeches and interviews address the topic of domestic service in pre-revolutionary Cuba.

This chapter expands both the chronological scope of this book – by moving into the second decade of the twenty-first century (more extensively discussed in the conclusion) – and the geographical scope – by integrating Miami into this study of Cuba's long relationship to domestic service. Memory functions as methodology and argument. Cubans' and Cuban-Americans' memories of domestic service regularly erased the political content of the work, favoring instead lessons about emotional intimacy, family ties, and – implicitly – racialized hierarchy. This elision of the politics of domestic work paved the way for the work's return to Cuban society, with many of the same attendant inequalities and dangers, in the twenty-first century.

Social histories can fit awkwardly with histories of emotion and of intimacy: Census data and hard numbers collide with conflicting memories and unwavering loyalty to a very specific interpretation of reality. Unlike the majority of this book, this chapter consists mostly of oral

histories. Other oral historians have found that emotion – not political
or economic transformations – typically fuel the narratives of people's
memories.[1] A need for one's life to make sense can supersede any
dedication to fleshing out the political context of one's past, as social
historians are contracted to do. But emotions are an essential component of the social history of domestic service; thus, oral histories are
essential to the story.

The women I interviewed in Cuba in 2014 and 2015, who had worked
as or employed domestics, mainly remembered the closeness they felt to
their employers or employees. Memories from late twentieth-century
Miami yielded the same kinds of emphasis on emotional ties. Almost to
a person, no one's memories included activism. It seemed like everyone
had forgotten, or never knew, the political work that has always swirled
around the labor of domestic service. Instead, people remembered their
ties to other people. The use of oral histories and memories is invaluable,
as much for what it erases as for what it reveals; the erasure of political
activism *on both sides* of memories of domestic service in Cuba suggests
that domestic service plays a pivotal role in what Steve Stern called
"emblematic memory." Emblematic memory "refers not to a single
remembrance of a specific content ... but to a framework that organizes
meaning, selectivity, and countermemory."[2] Domestic service as a pro-
vider of emotional intimacy is part of the emblematic memory of
twentieth-century Cuban history. The emotional logic of domestic service
scaffolds the way that Cubans have understood race relations on the
island since the colonial era.

The emotional logic of domestic service dictated that racial interactions
between Cubans of African and European descent could be harmonious,
affectionate, and even loving as long as each party remained in his or her
designated role. Within a hierarchy based on who paid whom and often
who was dependent on whom for food and shelter, there was plenty of
space for a close emotional relationship to flourish – and often it did. But
a mutually understood racialized and gendered hierarchy made such
affection possible. Domestic service, which upheld racial stratification in
the home, perpetuated that stratification in Cuba's public sphere even as
Cuba proudly presented itself as a racial democracy. This chapter uses the
memories of domestic servants and their employers to explore how the
emotional logic of service continued well past the 1960s. As Alejandro de

[1] Stern, *Remembering Pinochet's Chile*; James, *Doña María's Story*.
[2] Stern, *Remembering Pinochet's Chile*, 105.

la Fuente argued about anti-racist revolutionary policy, I argue that the programs to eradicate domestic service struck at the branches but not the roots of the underlying lessons about authority and subservience that service taught.[3] What we might call "ghosts" of domestic service persisted and even thrived in post-1959 Cuba.

## 6.1 THE POLITICAL USES OF LOVE

Before 1959, domestic service was a capitalistic relationship fueled by the exchange of goods and labor. By the early 1960s, the revolution had (mostly) successfully severed that relationship, through the training schools and through elite exile. Emotional bonds persisted, though, and sometimes became politically advantageous. In the decades after the near eradication of domestic service, former domestics and their employers propagandized emotional loss in service to their political perspectives.

In 1966, a New Orleans-based Cuban exile named Isabel wrote to an anti-Castro political group called the Citizens Committee for a Free Cuba (CCFC). She enclosed a letter from her former servant, who had worked for her for twenty-five years and was "completely uneducated" but honorable and worthy. The servant, Agustina, was married to a card-carrying Communist – and Isabel had loved him despite that – but even *he* could not abide what Castro had done to his beloved island.[4] The New Orleans exile wanted to show that Castro's social revolution had failed to totally alienate the bourgeoisie from the working class: Her cook still loved and missed her. She ended her letter by writing: "I should indicate that we're talking about *blacks* here. The way that this *señora* expresses my treatment of and affection for her does not reflect the hatred that Castro proclaims that we felt towards blacks."[5]

A set of nesting dolls comes to mind when one considers all of the motivations that got Agustina's letter (from Cuba) to Isabel (in New Orleans) to the CCFC (in California). The innermost doll, the smallest one, must be Agustina's reason for writing to Isabel. Throughout the note she begs Isabel to write back to her, noting that she has written twice with no response. She laments: "Since you went away I have aged enormously; my hair has turned completely white due to the sorrows and sufferings.

---

[3] de la Fuente, *A Nation for All.*
[4] Letter sent to Dr. Isaac Casariego dated 17 September 1966, Box 64, CFC, Hoover Institution Archives.
[5] Ibid.

I never go out anymore, not even downtown. I don't feel like seeing or talking to anyone, as no one loves me anymore."[6] Having only this three-page letter from Agustina, in which she reports news from Havana – things are terrible – and begs Isabel to write back to her, our only option is to take her at her word. She misses Señora Isabelita, as she calls her in the letter.

There's no reason to imagine that Agustina would know of Isabel's intention to send her letter to such an organization as the CCFC. Isabel's motivations enclose Agustina's, like the second, slightly larger nesting doll. The CCFC was founded in 1962 to lobby the US government to act against the Castro regime in Cuba. The CCFC followed Cuban politics closely throughout the 1960s, analyzing radio broadcasts and public speeches for policy changes or potential weaknesses within the Communist government. The organization also received thousands of letters from self-identified *"gusanos"* (worms) inside and outside Cuba about the turmoil and chaos of Communist Cuba.[7] From New Orleans, Isabel decided to send her former cook's letter to the CCFC so that they could use it as part of their propaganda. She was savvy enough to make clear that her former servant was black, thus refuting Castro's characterization of Cuban exiles in the United States as racist.

Then, the CCFC excerpted and translated the most moving parts of the letter from Agustina for their internal dispatches, forming the outermost doll and completing the set. Agustina's letter was translated twice, from a plea for communication to an example of how Castro had ruined everything to that same message in English, ostensibly for American policymakers. Apparently, those policymakers would not be concerned with full accuracy, because the internal document erroneously called Isabel's former servant "Justina." Agustina no longer worked for Isabel, but she continued to serve. And one has to ask – did Isabel ever write back to her? Isabel's and Agustina's relationship easily became rhetorical weaponry for the anti-Castro diaspora in the United States just seven years after the takeover of Cuba by the 26th of July movement. As the years wore on without the political turnover that so many Cuban exiles expected, memories likely became even more potent and loaded with meaning.

---

[6] Letter sent to Señora Isabela, dated 22 August 1966, Box 64, CFC, Hoover Institution Archives.

[7] The CCFC was founded by Paul D. Bethel, a World War II veteran who had been the head of the US Information Agency in Cuba in 1959. He moved to Miami after the revolution triumphed. John Simkin, "Paul Bethel."

## 6.2 MEMORIES ACROSS THE STRAITS

Exiles from Castro's Cuba settled in New Orleans, New York, and California – but most ended up in Miami. Twenty years after the Cuban revolution, researcher Diana González Kirby interviewed sixty Cuban-American women living in Miami for a research project called "Ethnography of Cuban Drug Use." Kirby took down their life stories and their experiences with licit and illicit drugs. Interviews about drug usage might seem a strange repository for the kinds of memories of interest to this study of domestic service, but Kirby's papers – housed at the University of Miami – are a valuable lens into the memories of women negotiating their identities as Cubans, as Americans, and as immigrants. Because Kirby was interested in why and how her interview subjects used drugs, her interviews delved into the women's (often traumatic) pasts and sources of pain. A common source of trauma was the economic backslide experienced when middle-class families left Cuba for the United States. Domestic servants and the loss of access to them was a regular component of that backslide.

Relationships with domestic workers taught young women in this interview group about power and authority, and who had the right to wield it; these early experiences informed how the women understood race, class, and gender at the time of their interviews. Oral histories must contend with the present to usefully probe the past. These women's memories of family and home life were unquestionably shaped by the city they called home in 1979. Thus, in addition to insights about domestic service and memory, these interviews offer us a brief glimpse of a hugely important component of post-1959 Cuban history, frequently siloed away from national histories: the story of Cuban Miami.[8] Cuban exiles transformed the city, and the city transformed them in ways that reverberated in their memories of domestic service on the island.

The first question that Kirby asked interview subject #167 was about her childhood and how she grew up, and, within two sentences, the woman was talking about the nannies who raised her: "It's from then on that I've had great tenderness for the black race, because in general they were black." This woman's family left Cuba very early in 1959, and her family's maid stayed in the house at first because her father believed that Fidel Castro would be gone within six months. Her family actually

---

[8] For a study that brilliantly integrates the story of post-revolutionary Cuba with the post-revolutionary Cuban diaspora, see Bustamante, *Cuban Memory Wars*.

continued to pay their maid from exile, with money from a bank account her father had left open. They moved first to Los Angeles, where her father worked as a dishwasher until he died. His daughter believed that the downgrade in social status caused his premature death.[9]

She also believed that her father's empathy for people less fortunate than themselves benefited them once they left. He had been a lawyer in Cuba, the son of wealthy people with a farm in San Antonio de los Baños. In the 1950s, he had taken more of an interest in the rural people living on his family's property. He sold off some of the farm to interested families and gifted parcels and houses to the people who'd lived there for a long time. Interview subject #167 said her father's kindness was never forgotten: "And we have lovely letters from [one of the campesinos] after we left. Many families, when they left, their servants hated them. That was not our case. Our servant raised me for thousands of years, and I don't know what she's doing now, but she loved us so much."[10] Interview subject #167's memories of her family and her father echo a longstanding interpretation of class difference across Latin America. Her father was a benevolent landholder, and his "inferiors" loved him for it. In exchange for kindness, her family received gratitude, even as other servants turned against their employers after 1959. Like Isabel, writing in 1966, she is eager to show off how her family's kindness insulated them from resentment. If subject #167 cast her father as a classic patriarch, bequeathing gifts and goods to his inferiors from on high, other interviewees described their experiences with servants more intimately. Both tropes of domestic service – the generous benefactor to a large staff *and* the quasi-friendship between an *ama* and her *fámula* – were familiar ones in Cuba, the former harkening back to plantation days and the latter to a mythic mid-twentieth-century ideal.

Even in the late 1970s, these memories about race and gender were never squarely in the past for the women interviewed in Miami. Interview subject #199, born in 1933, had a "*negrita*" (black) domestic growing up for whom she still yearned. She called the woman "delightful," but explained in the same breath that across the world, black people lacked a motivating impulse. Her own domestic worker was literate and educated but "chose" to remain a servant. For subject #199, this demonstrated an inherent laziness rather than lack of access to other work.[11] Race and job access were volatile topics in 1979 Miami, when this 46-

[9] Kirby papers, "Interview subject #167, 12/11/79," CHC.     [10] Ibid.
[11] Kirby papers, Box 5, Folder: "Interview subject #199, 5/14/80," CHC.

year-old woman was interviewed. Since the initial wave of political refugees in 1959, Cuban men and women had regularly displaced black and other non-white Miami residents. Buoyed by financial subsidies from the federal government, Cuban men and women could afford to take extremely low-paying jobs, edging out black Miamians who needed living wages.[12] Inclined to be sympathetic toward her compatriots, this woman might have understood black Miamians' refusal to work for low wages as the same kind of "laziness" she saw in her beloved "*negrita*." Or, perhaps, the tensions between black Miamians and Cubans in 1960s and 1970s Miami had influenced the way she reminisced on her past life.

Younger women, who were girls when they left Cuba, learned racialized lessons about how to wield authority. One interviewee, a woman born in 1956, left Cuba when she was 10 years old. As a little girl, she had blackmailed her nanny for years. Her nanny was actually a distant relative of her family from the island's rural interior, and she had a *mulato* boyfriend, which her parents would have strongly disapproved of. The interview subject said her constant refrain was, "If you don't let me do this, I'm telling my mother about your boyfriend."[13] Another young woman who was born in 1955 and was twenty-four when she was interviewed played out her own struggle with racialized understandings of people during the interview itself. Speaking in English to her interlocutor, she remembered being sickly as a child and growing up with a lot of what she called "sitters." She never got along with them, never liked them. When she was five or six, she went after one of these "sitters" with a broom and acknowledged in the middle of her own sentence that the woman was actually a servant. Her interlocutor asked if the woman she attacked was black, and she responded,

Yes she was. Yes she was. And let me tell you, that's never been something I've ever had any kind of hard feelings to or anything like that . . . As a matter of fact, most of my sitters were black, and it was not a question that I didn't get along with them, not at all . . . on the contrary, I loved them, I was all over them all the time and this and that, and I never saw any kind of distinction, something that I've seen here in the United States . . . My father and my mother have always, you know . . . some of their best friends were black, black people.[14]

This young woman clearly internalized the power dynamics at play in her childhood, even as she denied their existence and tried to shift a critical

[12] Connolly, *A World More Concrete*.
[13] Kirby papers, Box 5, Folder: "Interview subject #139, 3/18/80," CHC.
[14] Kirby Papers, Box 5, Folder: "Interview subject #205, 4/10/80," CHC.

racial lens onto the United States. The lessons employers and beneficiaries of domestic service in Cuba learned about race and power stayed strong, even after twenty years of living in a different country.

But it's important to note the specific context of twenty years in a different country. These women interviewed in 1979 Miami had experienced twenty-some years *in* Miami, a city with its own story. If the story of 1960s Miami was the mass migration of Cubans to the city and the attendant unification of those Cuban exiles' political position against the island's revolutionary government, the story of the 1970s was one of division and disintegration. By the 1970s, a generation of Cuban descendants had been born in the United States. It was clear to many that the socialist Cuban government would not be toppled as had been envisioned a decade earlier. A generational and political divide plagued Cuban-Americans in the city. The exile movement was splintering, and the city was more violent than ever – between 1973 and 1976, more than one hundred bombs detonated in Miami.[15]

Thus, it was not just the racialized lessons of their childhoods or pasts in Cuba that these interview subjects reflected as they spoke. Women in 1970s Miami reflected the racial and class tensions of that city as they remembered their Cuban childhoods or early adulthoods. It's a Sisyphean task to unravel what portion of their memories and what portion of the lessons they learned came from Cuba itself and what came from their experience in the diaspora. But the diaspora is an inextricable part of the story of twentieth-century Cuba. The political context of Miami – and the Hudson in New York and Washington, DC – matters too. Understanding those exile communities' relationships to their new homes is essential in analyzing oral histories of Cuba, even if interview subjects insist that their memories of home are pristine.

### 6.3 POWER AND LONGING IN BLACK AND WHITE

María Antonia Castañeda Álvarez (*not* the fictional María Antonia from Chapter 2) could be considered the mirror image of Agustina, who wrote that plaintive letter to her former mistress in New Orleans. Born in 1942, María Antonia worked as a domestic for two families: For one, she cleaned and washed dishes; for another, she cleaned, washed dishes, and ironed. After 1959, both families left Cuba. María Antonia waited

---

[15] Bustamante, "Anti-Communist Anti-Imperialism?", 84.

until her children were old enough before she attended the night schools offered to domestics, but she completed three months of primary school and then a course in taxi driving. María Antonia won prizes for her driving during the four years that she was a *taxista*. Subsequently, she worked in a cafeteria, and in 2015 she worked for the Casa de la Americas, a publishing house, as a caretaker for the American study abroad students that the Casa hosts each semester. The students, who came to Havana to study from schools like Brown University, were too old for María Antonia to be considered their nanny, but she cooked for them and cleaned the public spaces of their apartments.[16]

María Antonia exemplified the dominant post-1959 narrative of domestic service. She was a maid turned revolutionary, celebrated by the egalitarian government. Her life *improved* once her employers left, and she was absorbed into the revolutionary project. However, the truth of her time as a domestic is more complicated than that revolutionary tale. Far from being abused, neglected, or condescended to, María Antonia loved the families for whom she worked, one in particular. They loved her so much, María Antonia said, that when they left Cuba for the United States in 1963 they offered to take her *and* her baby and send the baby to school when it was ready.

María Antonia mentioned this at the beginning of our conversation and said that she declined their invitation. When I asked her why she did not go, she replied scornfully, "What was I going to do there [in the United States]?", suggesting that she never seriously considered going. We continued our talk, discussing the experiences of other women she knew who worked as domestics. We came back around to the invitation that her employers extended to her, and *this* time she said that she had wanted to go to the United States. Her new explanation for why she did not go was that her mother and grandmother did not want her to. These days, she said, young girls could ignore their mothers' wishes, but that was not the case when she was young.[17]

María Antonia had been reluctant to contradict the official revolutionary narrative about domestic service before 1959. That narrative, featuring a downtrodden woman being treated poorly by her employers and only finding dignity in the embrace of the revolution, left little room for genuine affection between employers and employees. Her first answer – that she did not want to go to the United States – falls in line with that

---

[16] Interview with María Antonia Castañeda Álvarez, February 24, 2015, Havana, Cuba.
[17] Ibid.

official narrative, or at least does not contradict it. Her second answer – that her mother and grandmother would not let her go – *does* contradict a narrative suggesting that all service relationships were only based on power and authority. I interviewed María Antonia in 2015, in the loft apartment where she looked after Brown University undergraduates. It was just three months after then-US President Barack Obama had announced the normalization of relations between the United States and Cuba. Possibly, this was one of the first times that María Antonia felt comfortable admitting that as a teenager she had wanted to leave Cuba for the United States. In the 1970s, or the 1990s, such an admission would not have been politically palatable.

María Antonia's story is complicated further, though, by how it ends. I asked her if she felt like "part of the family" for whom she worked, knowing by this point that it was a common trope in domestic service relationships. Instead of responding personally, she told me about a friend of hers who nannied a child, now grown and living in Philadelphia. Every two years this man came back to visit his former nanny. He also regularly sent her money. I pressed further, and she told me that the children in the family she worked for – two boys and one girl – adored her. "What they didn't tell their mother, they told me," she remembered. But after they left Cuba, she never heard from them again.[18]

María Antonia and Agustina had very similar experiences on the surface: They were two black women who worked as domestics and stopped doing so when their employers left for the United States. Both developed intimate relationships with their employers. But while Agustina's experience was deployed by her former employer to impugn Communist Cuba in the 1960s, María Antonia was able to make sense of her own life to me in the twenty-first century. More directly: Agustina's story was used in service of anti-Castro politics; María Antonia used hers to celebrate the revolution. Agustina seems the more impenetrable – we only have one letter of hers, while I talked to María Antonia for hours. But María Antonia was speaking to me through barriers too – through the barrier of having been a beneficiary of the early revolution and then enduring the extreme poverty of the 1990s in Cuba. The truth she spoke to me in 2015 was likely not her truth in 1963, when she was invited to the United States. Daniel James wrote that people tell stories to maintain a "coherence of the self" –narratives that allow them to make sense of their

---

[18] Ibid.

own lives.[19] In one conversation with María Antonia, she needed to interpret her experience with domestic service in two contradictory ways to maintain the coherence of her own life story. Such fluctuation illuminates the rapid changes that Cuba experienced in the second half of the twentieth century.

Other narratives I heard in Cuba forefronted enduring connection and tradition, not loss. But those stories, too, revealed that race and racial hierarchies inevitably nested inside understandings of domestic service. A woman named Zenaida, born in 1942 in Santiago de Cuba, began to work for the Poll Cabrera family when she was thirteen years old. Zenaida's single mother found the job for her through her own position as a cook in a different home. Zenaida moved out of her mother's house to live in the Santiago neighborhood of Sueño with her new employers, where she stayed until she was seventeen.[20] The Poll Cabreras were like family to Zenaida: She loved them and their children, whom she took care of for most of her teenage years. She remains in touch with them even now that they live in Panama, while she remains in Santiago de Cuba. Whenever they return to Cuba to visit, they come to see her.[21] She repeats emphatically, "They *still* help me," indicating that her former employers send her money to this day.

Whatever remittances they send her now, however, are significantly more than what she made when she actually worked for them, because while she worked for them the Poll Cabreras did not pay her any wages. She dismissed this detail by saying, "It wasn't so formal as that." She explained that they fed, sheltered, and clothed her, and sent her to school. Her work was also highly regulated: She was the nanny and did not have to perform any other kind of domestic service. The Poll Cabreras also had a washerwoman and a cleaning woman, neither of whom lived with them. Despite accruing no salary, Zenaida enjoyed a privileged position in this wealthy family's household. (Another woman I interviewed in Camagüey remembered being told, about the other servants who worked for the family, "They are of the street, but *you* are of this house.")[22]

Zenaida made clear, however, that she enjoyed her position of privilege and her intimacy with the family because she understood the limits of their relationship. When asked how her relationship was with the Poll

[19] James, *Doña María's Story.*
[20] Interview with Zenaida García Salas, April 20, 2015, Santiago de Cuba, Cuba.
[21] Ibid.     [22] Interview with Margarita Pérez García, March 27, 2015, Camagüey.

Cabreras, Zenaida said immediately that it was wonderful, that there was mutual adoration – but that everyone needed to stay *"allí en la línea* [there in the line]." The Poll Cabreras were white; Zenaida is of African descent. She explained that they were never racist and always treated their employees well but that there was an understanding that such camaraderie and intimacy could only exist if people of different races understood the gap between them and respected it. Zenaida said her mother, an illiterate domestic worker, taught her that lesson. Zenaida is the foremost authority on her own life. But what she understood to be a fair exchange of services for goods is what we now call wage theft, perhaps even child labor; the lesson that her mother taught her about lanes is what many have always called racism. Economic and relational violence quietly thrived in loving homes.

Rosaura, who lives in Santiago de Cuba and has employed domestic servants her entire life, expressed unease with the state of domestic service today in a way that echoed Zenaida's reminder that people must stay in their rightful places. Born in 1934, Rosaura was descended from Spaniards. Her family had employed several domestics when she was a girl, always treating them like family; she very fondly remembered a "fat, black" woman named Micaela. Micaela worked for Rosaura and her husband until the 1980s. In 2015, Rosaura still employed a woman who cleaned and laundered for her.

She said that after 1959, an equality of rights emerged, "which brought with it its own problems." For example, Rosaura said, an illiterate person would never be equal to an intellectual, and there was no need to pretend that was the case. She lamented that respect had been lost in the turmoil of the revolution but cited her own domestic, Alicia, as a refreshing exception to that rule: She and Alicia had met decades before, when Rosaura was a teacher in Santiago and Alicia cleaned the school where she worked. Even today, Alicia insisted on calling Rosaura "Señora Vázquez." Rosaura also told me about her grandmother's domestic worker – a Jamaican woman who always wore a white uniform and white cap. She noted – approvingly – that this kind of respect and attention to detail was a legacy of slavery in Cuba.[23] For Rosaura and for Zenaida, the intimacy that domestic service engendered was shot through with an understanding and apparent approval of racialized hierarchy.

---

[23] Interview with Rosaura Vázquez Pérez, April 27, 2015, Santiago de Cuba.

Zenaida and Rosaura both remembered good things about being a domestic worker or about employing domestic workers; neither of them had anything bad to say about anyone for whom they worked or who worked for them. However, their pleasant memories and experiences were rooted in a deeply unequal – and arguably violent – understanding of social hierarchy in Cuba. The stories they told me and the conclusions they drew – that transracial social interaction works if everyone "stays in their lane," that today's Cuban culture lacks respect – reflect not only the reality of the past but also that of Cuba's chaotic present. The economy has expanded and contracted dozens of times in the last thirty years. Foreign investment has skyrocketed. People who, twenty years ago, would have been called criminals for their black-market dealings now run successful and legal businesses. At least, women like Zenaida and Rosaura seemed to be saying, things made sense back then, even if that sense was rooted in a racialized and gendered hierarchy that stretched all the way back to Cuba's slave society past.

## 6.4 THE ANTHROPOLOGY OF POWER: LYDIA CABRERA'S DOMESTICS

The revolution broke social and material bonds when it (mostly) eradicated domestic service. At least one Cuban intellectual attempted to rehabilitate the narrative of domestic service in Cuba, rejecting the revolution's dismissal of it. Lydia Cabrera, the famed anthropologist and author of *El Monte*, a seminal study of Afro-Cuban religion, frequently used domestic service to explain the supposedly benign nature of relations between Cubans of African and European descent. She argued so vigorously for a rosy picture of pre-revolution Cuban race relations because she understood the Cuban revolution to be a referendum on all that had come before, *including* race. As a white anthropologist of Afro-Cuban life and culture, her work's legacy was at stake along with the meaning of her nation's history.

In an undated but likely post-1959 speech entitled "The Domestic Slave in Cuba," Cabrera muses that the speech could also be entitled "Why the Black in Cuba Smiles as in No Other Country." She explains that racism was never as deeply rooted in Cuba as it was in, for example, the United States. Well-born Cubans in the nineteenth century grew up with a black nursemaid, black servants, and black cooks – all of whom were deeply embedded within the elite family. It was typical for one "Tata" or "Nana" to raise three generations of the same family.

Cabrera went so far as to suggest that it was often these black women who truly controlled such households, the patriarch of the family often having grown up at their breasts.[24]

In a different speech entitled "The African Influence in Cuba," Cabrera attempted to rehabilitate the notion of paternalism:

We say "paternalism" derisively today, but that mutual affection that united [slave and master] gave honor to the slave and now would cause envy among the new slaves of a modern slave regime. It is the rare Cuban family that does not have buried in its pantheon with the remains of its grandparents and parents, those of these black men and women who were so loved.[25]

Defining "paternalism" as "mutual affection" stripped the term of its dark connotations, leaving only a fatherly love that would have truly benefited enslaved Cubans. By using the image of enslaved Cubans buried alongside the ancestors of elite Cuban families, Cabrera argued not only for the mutually beneficial relationship between blacks and whites in the past but for the endurance of that mutual affection centuries into the future.

Cabrera also discussed the republican era in Cuba, continuing to argue that domestic service was a phenomenon that softened the blow of racial stratification. In a draft of her rebuttal to a book entitled *Area Handbook for Cuba* in 1963, she rejected out of hand the idea that domestic service might have been marginalized work: "It can be affirmed that in the upper classes the servant was very well-paid; he had, in addition to his salary, food with the traditional excessive abundance of the Cuban table, good lodging and free clothing; and habitually medicine and medical attention if he became sick."[26] The memories and advocacy of domestic workers themselves completely contradict Cabrera's quick analysis of domestic service.

This argument about the benign nature of domestic service was not just political for Cabrera; it was personal. Born to an elite family in 1900, Cabrera grew up surrounded by domestic servants – the most important of whom was her beloved nurse, Gertrudis Juncadella, whom Cabrera called Tula. In several speeches and interviews, she tells the story of when she first learned about the toxic race relations in the

[24] Cabrera, "El esclavo doméstico en Cuba," undated, Box 48, Folder 17, Lydia Cabrera Collection, CHC.
[25] Cabrera, "La Influencia Africana en Cuba," undated, Box 32, Folder 16, Lydia Cabrera Collection, CHC.
[26] Cabrera, untitled manuscript, undated, Box 32, Folder 2: *Area Handbook for Cuba*, 1963, Lydia Cabrera Collection, CHC.

FIGURE 6.1. Gertrudis Juncadella, Known as Tula, Lydia Cabera's Nurse (Lydia Cabrera family photos, private collection).

FIGURE 6.2. Cabrera's Family with Juncadella (Lydia Cabrera family photos, private collection).

United States: She was ten and traveling to New York with Tula when they were forced to ride in separate cars because Tula was black. Cabrera owed her illustrious career to the servants of her family: It was from them that she heard the Afro-Cuban fables and traditions that formed the basis of her scholarship.[27] Because of the deep affection she felt for her domestics and perhaps because of what she owed them professionally, Cabrera needed to affirm that domestic service was a job that brought Cubans together, not one that reinforced a racial hierarchy. She weaponized her memories and used them as a tool to reject what the revolution had to say.

Through letters, memories, remittances, and, in Cabrera's case, essays, Cubans asserted the importance of the relationships they formed through domestic service. Cabrera's essays reveal her urgent need to legitimize her own closeness to her domestic workers and to reject the idea that their relationships were tarnished by hierarchy or racism. Of course, this chapter demonstrates that relationships between domestics and their employers could be both affectionate and intimate, *and* tarnished by hierarchy.

---

[27] Interview with Cabrera, Box 13, Folder 7, Lydia Cabrera Collection, CHC.

## 6.5 CONCLUSION

Alejandrina Hierrezuelo was born in 1917 in Santiago de Cuba. When she was four years old, she moved with her mother and two sisters to the Miranda sugar mill about forty miles away from the city. Her mother and sisters worked as domestics there, and, when she was about ten years old, Alejandrina began to work for a Spanish woman called Doña Lola. She ironed, cleaned, and learned cooking and baking. Alejandrina worked for Doña Lola for about five years, after which she began to work in the home of the machine manager of the sugar mill.

In 1959, when Alejandrina was forty-two years old and had two daughters of her own, she moved back to Santiago de Cuba. She sensed the societal opening that was coming, and she was correct. One of her daughters, María Cristina, completed secondary school and university, which would have been impossible at Miranda, where schooling only went to the sixth grade. María Cristina chose a degree in accounting because it was relatively short; she wanted to get a job as quickly as possible, so that her mother could stop working as a domestic.[28] This is the story that María Cristina, who is now a historian of slavery at the University of the East in Santiago, told me. It is the dominant story told in Cuba about domestic service: The revolution halted the seemingly inevitable procession of women of African descent into the work. María Cristina's memory was precise, backed up with names, numbers, and locations, and I trust it completely. But there is another way to tell this story, too.

If Alejandrina began to work for Doña Lola at the age of ten, she began work as domestic in 1927. But calling it "work" is generous because she was not paid. Doña Lola fed, clothed, and schooled Alejandrina, but she did not give her a salary. If Alejandrina left Doña Lola's house when she was fifteen years old, she switched jobs in 1933, the year of a political revolution that reverberated across Cuba and became about much more than who was president. Readers might remember from Chapter 4 that the Miranda sugar mill was plagued by strikes in that year, and that domestics at the mill swore their loyalty to the mill workers.[29] Might Alejandrina have made the loyalty oath too?

Might it have affected her decision to switch employers? Her second employer, for whom she cleaned and cooked, paid her twenty-five pesos

---

[28] Interview with María Cristina Hierrezuelo Planas, April 11, 2015, Santiago de Cuba.
[29] See Chapter 3, note 3.

per month. Possibly the salary came because of the training she had
received with Doña Lola or because of her no longer being a child. But
it could have come from a new knowledge of the worth of her work,
inspired by the militancy of the men and women all around her. If this is
the version of the story closer to the truth, then the moral changes in a
subtle but important way: It was not in 1959 that it occurred to
Alejandrina to seek a better life for herself and her daughters, and it
was not the revolution that caused her to consider it. She had pursued
something better as a teenager, back in 1933, and we cannot know how
long before that workers' dissatisfaction had brewed. In this narrative,
Alejandrina is the protagonist of her life's story, not a secondary character
in the story of the 1959 revolution.

   Which is not to say that the revolution's tales of triumph are false: The
1959 revolution and its attendant initiatives and programs *did* change the
life trajectories of countless Cubans, including and perhaps especially
those of black women. In unprecedented numbers, they went to school
and then to more school, becoming doctors, teachers, politicians, and
historians. Their children went to school, too. By the 1980s, many
markers of inequity in a society had been erased in Cuba: African-
descended people achieved parity in measures of health, income, and
education.[30] The end of domestic service was tied to all of this.

   But it is imperative to acknowledge the erasure of political activism in
memories. In memory, domestic service lived on; but the strikes, the
organizing, the lobbying, the laws failed to. Cubans on the island and in
the United States put their memories to use. Memories of service bolstered
anti-Communist arguments, insisting that race relations before 1959 in
Cuba had been *fine*. They reinforced the notion of a Cuban family that
transcended racial difference. Memories of domestic service also bolstered
pro-revolutionary arguments, as people pointed out how the new government had bequeathed dignity and meaningful work onto marginalized
and powerless women. Neither side allows for the possibility that domestic servants accurately interpreted the injustices of their labor and, like
many other workers, acted against them.

   That possibility, however, was the reality of domestic service in Cuba
from the abolition of slavery through the 1960s. Histories of labor and
activism often overemphasize the importance of success in defining a
movement. Before 1959, domestic worker activists did not succeed in

---

[30] de la Fuente, *A Nation for All*, 307–313.

securing the protections they wanted, but that does not mean they did not try. And the reasons for their failure – outlined in this book – point to a profound and illuminating truth about their work and their island: Domestic service upheld a racialized gender hierarchy that elite Cubans were loath to relinquish. The men and women – native and foreign-born, white, African- and Asian-descended – who cleaned, cooked, and cared for children in Cuba did not face a fair fight when they proposed unionization, helped occupy mills, or merely asked the Cuban government to compensate them for relatives' deaths. Along with slavery's legacy and the relative wealth of their employers, nostalgic memory impeded any progress toward recognition of their work as dignified labor.

*Hierarchies at Home* has provided a new history of Cuban domestic service, one that challenges the emblematic memory of the work, which the powerful in Cuba have always put to such effective use. All histories can be manipulated in service of a particular narrative, but perhaps this new history will be of more use to workers than to those who would oppress them.

# Conclusion

## Cuban History from Inside Out

A central tension in histories of the Americas has been the persistence of racialized hierarchies in the context of democratic governments. Cuba is an extreme example of this tension, given the explicitly anti-racist rhetoric of the independence movement and the erasure of racial distinctions from the 1901 Constitution. But in North and South America, too, national governments have passed race-blind or anti-racist legislation, only to see their starkly segregated societies persist. *Hierarchies at Home* has revealed that alongside the determinedly "raceless" rhetoric dominant in republican Cuba, a racialized nationalist sentiment continuously reinforced itself in the domestic sphere. Publicly, the Cuban government might have extolled the nation's modernity and commitment to liberty and development. Privately, a Cuban ideal *based on a master–servant relationship* persisted. It was able to persist because of its location in the domestic sphere, understood to be a nonpolitical space occupied by women.

Demographically, Cuban servants were all kinds of people – Spanish, Chinese, and British Caribbean men and women. In the island's national imaginary, however, domestic servants were Afro-Cuban women. *Hierarchies at Home* has historicized that image, showing that the steady association of blackness, femaleness, and domestic servitude had material consequences for women of African descent. The parallel tracks of *cubanidad* described above – a public track of modernity and racelessness and a private one of master/servant hierarchy – reinforced each other. The racialized dominance in private homes, cloaked with the language of familial closeness and intimacy, made a "raceless" political orientation possible because employers of domestic servants reasserted their racial superiority in that most intimate of spheres.

The radical 1959 revolution disrupted the political track of "raceless" *cubanidad*, explicitly condemning anti-black racism early on and implementing anti-racist measures in the economic sphere. Although the creation and implementation of training schools for domestics disrupted the domestic counter-*cubanidad* by literally moving servants out of the domestic sphere and into the "productive economy," those schools did little to challenge or disrupt the essence of domestic service as it was understood by much of Cuban society. Chapter 6 explored memories of domestic service from as recently as 2015 that illustrated the tight hold the essence of domestic service continues to have on and off the island. For many Cubans, even and perhaps especially for those in exile, the relationship between a white *ama* and a black *criada* remains the quintessential symbol of Cuban unity and familial race relations – the nostalgic site of *cubanidad*.

*Hierarchies at Home* has offered a political history of interior spaces, tending to the lives and activities of a racialized servant class while illuminating the anxieties and demands of a precarious upper class. Studies of Cuba that span 1959 have tended toward more masculinist orientations, following the *barbudos* from the Sierra Maestra mountains to the National Assembly and fixating on foreign military policy. This book has reoriented the lens through which we view Cuban history, beginning in the domestic sphere and asking how the hierarchies established at home reverberated into the public sphere and into public policy. A focus on the domestic sphere shows that changes the Cuban revolutionary government implemented paled in comparison to the radical demands of domestic workers, particularly black women, over decades. It is entirely possible to write a history that begins with familial or quasi-familial relationships and ends with radical political transformation.

This intervention is one that scholars of slavery know well. Historians of the colonial Caribbean have leaned into the documental dearth to highlight both the strategic silence of enslaved women involved in resistance movements and the archival violence of documenting only the beatings and killings of black women in slave societies, and other crimes against them. These silences also persist throughout the history of domestic service in Cuba because of the perception of domestic service as apolitical, the erasure of men (supposedly inherently political subjects) from the ranks of domestic servants, and the lack of interest in black women's historical experiences. By questioning these silences in the case of Cuban domestic workers and interrogating archival documents that refuse to understand domestics' actions as political, I have exposed a vein of counter-*cubanidad* that, until now, has quietly coexisted with the public-facing narrative of raceless Cuban nationalism. Alongside masculinist narratives of racial democracy (or after 1959, the end of racism), Cubans absorbed a parallel sense of racial *difference* that contributed just as strongly to the national sentiment. Cuba's racial hierarchies were enshrined in the relationships between domestic servants – always imagined to be Afro-Cuban women – and their employers. The domestic sphere – imagined as apolitical, familial, and outside history – naturalized racial inequality as an essential part of the Cuban identity, as important as, though far less analyzed than, notions of racial democracy.

Important aspects of domestic service remained constant over decades. Throughout the twentieth century, domestic service evoked the violence of intimacy, albeit in changing ways. During the *Patronato*, the violence was sometimes literal: Domestic *patrocinadas* endured beatings from their *patrones*. In the republican era, the violence was more frequently rhetorical: By insisting on intimacy between domestics and employers, conservative elites, journalists, and policymakers enacted economic violence. Cubans insisted that the closeness between domestics and employers mitigated any tensions between the two classes, but that very closeness *was* the danger.

The perception that domestic service and domestic service relationships exist outside the policies and politics of a certain nation – in the realm of the personal and domestic – is one that benefits governmental and societal elites invested in maintaining the status quo. Relegating any kind of labor to the "domestic sphere" allows abuses and injustice to go unchecked. With one notable exception in 1938, the pre-1959 Cuban government responded to the actions of domestic workers by trying to limit their power or the protections to which they had access. The government remained silent on domestic service even as workers in other fields gained labor protections and rights. Cuban media cosigned that silence by regularly insisting that domestic service was work unlike any other, more like an arrangement between family members than employment. These institutions worked in concert to leave domestics vulnerable to abuse.

The work's tight links to slavery held well after abolition. At the peak of domestic service activism in the 1940s, the work's advocates loudly insisted that little had changed in domestic service since Cuba was a slave society. In the 1970s and 1980s, Cubans on the island and in exile related domestic service to slavery, albeit for competing purposes. While revolutionary Cubans linked the work to slavery to highlight the corruption of the republican era and celebrate the *superación* that began in the 1960s, exiled Cubans and their descendants deployed the trope of domestic service to explain the supposedly benign relationships between Cubans of European and African descent, insisting that domestic service relationships of the slave era solidified ties of affection and loyalty over generations. Any time that domestic service's informality was threatened – by unionization or legislation – opposing voices became hysterical, insisting that the very fabric of the Cuban nation would be torn apart if the nature of domestic service changed. The fabric of the Cuban nation, apparently, had been sewn by enslaved Africans.

The feminization of domestic service was also notably continuous throughout the twentieth century. In Cuba, domestic service was linked to womanhood and femininity long before women made up the majority of domestic workers. The 1943 Cuban census was the first to list women as predominant in the field. But, since the nineteenth century, discussions of domestic service had almost always centered on women. *Hierarchies at Home* has pointed to moments where it was likely or possible that the domestics in question were men, as in the 1918 solidarity strikes; however, such instances left no documentary evidence behind. Domestic service as feminized work is not a universal phenomenon. On the African continent, for example, domestic servants were popularly understood to be men for much of the twentieth century.[1] That the work in Cuba was so regularly presented as feminine even when men did most of it is conspicuous.

Domestic service's links to slavery, to violent intimacy, and to women all remained at the forefront of discussions and perceptions during the twentieth century. Even when domestic servants were mostly men and when the population of domestics was not majority African-descended, these links held strong. This book has used newspapers, novels, government decrees, magazines, and more to prove these continuities. But it is important to reiterate that, while such perceptions shaped the work itself and made life more difficult for domestic servants, we cannot naturalize (as so many Cubans did) the racialized and gendered stereotypes about domestic service. That is, we cannot ourselves unproblematically associate black women with servility and paid domesticity.

*Hierarchies at Home* has demonstrated that this association was a dominant phenomenon from the end of slavery through the Cuban Revolution, but pointing out the association is distinct from endorsing

---

[1] See Introduction, note 7.

it. Most working black women indeed were domestic workers before 1959; that had to do with the legacy of slavery and with structural racism that impeded their access to education and other jobs. But those working black women were not domestic servants because of any inherent tendency. They did the jobs they were paid to do, but as other workers radicalized from the 1910s onward, domestics – black women – radicalized along with them. Black women were domestic workers – but that statement is not tautological.

Loosening that naturalized association – a primary goal of this book – has revealed the implications this study has for and beyond Cuban history. Once we separate a racialized and gendered identity from the archetypal "domestic worker," we can see how hard the Cuban government and economic elites worked to maintain that association. We can see how valuable the black/white, master/servant relationship was to Cuban society and how important its memory is, even after 1959. We see domestic workers as *workers* who continuously advocated for themselves as such, albeit in evolving ways over the twentieth century. In other nations, the work tightly associated with a certain racialized group might not be domestic service – it might be working a food cart or busking – but interrogating that association can reveal concerted action on the state, societal, and intrapersonal levels to subjugate that group through identification with that work.

Some important aspects of domestic service in Cuba did transform. Most dramatic was the steep decline in domestic service in Cuba overall. The number of Cubans working as maids, cooks, nannies, gardeners, and private chauffeurs declined precipitously in the twentieth century. After 1961, the work itself no longer officially existed. *Hierarchies at Home* has highlighted the inverse relationship between the number of domestic servants in Cuba and the attention the work received: The late 1940s to the late 1960s saw the most passionate activism on behalf of domestic servants, whose numbers were apparently so few. As numbers of servants declined, those left apparently grew more confident in the increased value of their labor. Employers of domestics clung ever more desperately to the idea of a "traditional" family structure with a maid or servant.

Another change was what domestic workers did: This book has both troubled the notion of "activism" *and* shown how activism transformed between the first and sixth decades of the twentieth century. During the *Patronato*, domestic servants advocated for their freedom from *patrones* on grounds of abuse or some violation of the laws that guided the institution. In the first decade of independence, domestic servants demanded the pensions or inheritances of their male relatives who had died fighting for Cuban sovereignty. Domestic servants appeared in criminal cases as survivors of physical and sexual violence. There was no period in the twentieth century in which domestics did not, in some way, press the Cuban state for the same rights and protections other Cubans enjoyed.

However, beginning in the 1910s, servants' activism became rooted in their identity as workers: first in solidarity with other workers and then on their own terms. After the failure of Decree 1754, radical domestics worked with Cuban Communists to form a syndicate and formally press the government for labor protections that extended to servants. In the 1950s, mutual-aid organizations for domestic workers proliferated, particularly in Havana, and even employers of domestic servants demanded equal labor rights for them. Members of the Syndicate for Domestic Servants were among other workers who pledged their membership dues to the fledgling revolutionary government that emerged in January 1959.

Historically, domestic workers have been vulnerable to assumptions about "false consciousness" and supposedly inevitable impediments to organizing: "Unions, reformers, policy makers, and others have assumed that household workers are difficult or impossible to organize because of the home location, scattered worksites often isolated from other workers, and the proximity of workers to their employers."[2] This book contributes to a growing body of scholarship that rectifies the erasure of domestic workers from the realm of labor history based on such standards of activism. Cuban domestics used a variety of strategies to survive. Sometimes they used what James Scott called "weapons of the weak," but, in moments when it was possible, they behaved like unionized workers.[3] Cuban domestics' modes of activism changed with the politics of the republic, adapting to what was possible. Domestic workers were always aware of the value of their labor. What changed was how they made it known.

I hope that *Hierarchies at Home* will inspire other projects and cover ground that I have not been able to here. Such ground includes a detailed study of domestic service between 1970 and 1990. Officially, the work disappeared, but it seems that everyone in Cuba knew someone with a *"mujer que me ayuda"* ("a woman who helps me") during this time. Paid domestic service was never explicitly outlawed, but such arrangements

---

[2] Boris and Nadasen, "Introduction," 5.     [3] Scott, *Weapons of the Weak*.

would have existed on the "gray" market. In 1974, the island's government passed the Family Code, codifying the equal division of labor
between married couples. This was in response to the growing desperation of Cuban women who complained about the "third shift" – a
variation on the "second shift" of domestic labor that working women
in the West had to manage. Cuban women had the "third shift" of being
good revolutionaries, which meant attending meetings for local
Committees for the Defense of the Revolution (CDR) and harvesting
sugar on weekends.[4] A study of paid service during this time would
investigate femininity, family, and revolutionary potential during the
institutionalization of the revolution, as well as the tension between that
institutionalization and the undisputed necessity of the black market.

Further studies could address changes in the physical labor that domestic servants performed. What it meant to clean a house or wash a family's
laundry changed drastically between 1901 and 1961. As appliances like
refrigerators, vacuum cleaners, washing machines, and microwaves transformed domestic life in Cuba, they changed the work of servants, too.
Additionally, a regional study would yield fascinating information about
the differences between eastern, western, and central Cuba. A study of
domestic service that focused on Santiago de Cuba and its surrounding
cities, for example, would give us a useful perspective on how colonial
differences between East and West affected labor in the twentieth century.
*Hierarchies at Home* is a national study, biased toward Havana as so
many national studies of Cuba are (particularly ones in English). A study
grounded in a specific city or region would enrich our understanding of
this understudied and ubiquitous labor.

Domestic service was and remains essential to Cuba's self-understanding
in distinct and sometimes antagonistic ways. It is the work that a large
portion of the island's population did to survive during the first six decades
of independence; thus, domestic workers themselves made up a large part
of Cuba's population. At the same time, the employment of domestic
workers was essential to maintaining the slave society hierarchy that had
guided elite Cubans for centuries. Domestic service was important to some
Cubans because it was the work they did; it was important to others
because the performance of the work *for them* made them feel secure in
their societal preeminence. These dueling motivations behind actions
regarding domestic service confronted each other in bedrooms, kitchens,

---

[4] Alexis Baldacci, "Consumer Culture and Everyday Life in Revolutionary Cuba,
1971–1986."

gardens, and alleyways; they reverberated to courtrooms, capitol buildings, and revolutionary outposts in eastern mountains.

The history of domestic service in Cuba continues as I write this conclusion. In 1993, Cuba passed Decree 141 to expand private business. The unprecedented move was in response to devastating need after the Soviet Union's collapse: Between 1990 and 1993 Cuba's economy shrank by more than 40 percent. During the "Special Period in the Time of Peace" – as the period of extreme scarcity during the 1990s was known – many of the gains the Revolution had made reversed, and many societal vices the government was so proud to have eradicated returned.[5] The island reluctantly implemented reforms oriented toward a more market-based economy. Decree 141 listed paid domestic service as the thirty-second option on a list of newly legal labor fields in which people could work.[6] The work has proliferated across the island since then. In the twenty-odd years since the advent of the Special Period, Cuba's past has rapidly collided with its present.

The situation of Cuban domestic workers in the twenty-first century is so complex that making any simple comparison to the domestic workers of the twentieth century is difficult. The work is now legal and therefore protected, but many domestic workers prefer to labor under the radar of the Cuban government. While many insist that they are far less dependent on and less tied to their employers than their counterparts were before 1959, others note that they regularly enter into agreements with employers only to end up performing far more tasks than they had initially agreed to. Women and Cubans of African descent are no longer restricted from educational or professional opportunities; domestic service is no longer anyone's only choice. However, in the twenty-first century domestic workers regularly make more money than teachers, lawyers, or doctors, so domestic service might seem like anyone's *best* choice.

Given Cuban domestic workers' unique relationship to the island's state-controlled economy, it might seem odd to assert that domestic workers on the island are an ideal group to study as a harbinger of the future. But it is precisely their precarious relationship to the state that makes them vital to understanding Cuba's current political economy. *Hierarchies at Home* has argued that domestics spent the twentieth century in Cuba demanding that the state recognize their work as labor and protect it as such. Now, in the twenty-first century, domestic workers who have the option to register as

---

[5] Pérez, Jr., *Cuba: Between Reform and Revolution*, chap. 13.
[6] Romero Almodóvar, "El Trabajo Doméstico Renumerado a Domicilio en Cuba," 76.

independent contractors but still receive social benefits and some protection from the state regularly decline to do so, taking cash under the table for their services instead. Rather than making demands on the state, they walk away from it. Cuban domestic workers might prove to be early adopters of a new reality in Cuba. The island passed its first Constitution since 1976 in 2019. The 1976 Constitution promised to "build a communist society," but the new Constitution drops that language "and ratifies the adoption of a new model of a mixed economy in which not only private property is legalized but also the role of the state sector in the Cuban economy changes."[7] If the state sector becomes less relevant in the Cuban economy, we might look to domestic workers to understand what will happen. Their work is inextricably tied to the past, but it looks as if they already live in Cuba's future.

At once, domestic service in twenty-first century Cuba is totally different from and quite similar to the work before 1961. One definitive difference is this: Domestic service in Cuba's twenty-first century will not suffer from a dearth of documentation.[8] In the twentieth century, that dearth was no accident, and it benefited the powerful. For the association between blackness, femininity, and servitude to remain strong, no one could delve too deeply into the realities of domestic service and who performed it. The complexities would have challenged the notion of an easy intimacy between servants and employers (and therefore black and white Cubans). This book *is* that challenge. While most domestic workers might not have been African-descended women for much of the twentieth century, most working African-descended women were domestic workers. They were far from complacent, and they suffered no "false consciousness": Domestics advocated for themselves in evolving ways between the 1880s and 1950s. For too long, those who would control domestics' labor obscured their efforts and made their inner lives opaque. *Hierarchies at Home* has chipped away at this opacity to give readers a more complete and transparent view of the lives of working-class women, especially working-class women of African descent, in Cuba.

---

[7] López-Levy, "Democratizing Cuba?" *North American Congress on Latin America*, November 14, 2018, https://nacla.org/news/2018/11/14/democratizing-cuba.

[8] Hicks, "Domestic Service in a New Cuba." *North American Congress on Latin America*, 2019.

# Bibliography

ARCHIVES CONSULTED

Archivo Nacional de Cuba, Havana, Cuba (ANC)
    Audiencia de la Habana
    Consejo de Administración
    Registro de Asociaciones
Archivos Históricos Provicinciales de Camagüey, Camagüey, Cuba (AHPC)
    Escuela del Hogar de Camagüey
    Movimiento Obrero
    Registro de Asociaciones
Archivos Históricos Provinciales de Santiago de Cuba, Santiago de Cuba, Cuba
    (AHPSC)
    Gobierno Provincial
    Juzgado de Primera Instancia
    Protocolos Notariales
Cuban Heritage Collection, University of Miami, Miami, Florida (CHC)
    Burdsall Family Papers
    Diana G. Kirby Papers
    Elena Mederos Papers
    Eusebia Cosme Collection
    Lyceum y Lawn Tennis Club Collection
    Lydia Cabrera Collection
    Maria Luisa Guerrero Collection
    Patronato de Matanzas Records
Hoover Institution, Stanford University, Palo Alto, California
    Citizens' Committee for a Free Cuba
    Cuban Freedom Committee
Instituto de Historia, Havana, Cuba
National Archives of the United States of America, College Park, Maryland
    Foreign Service Post Records

General Records of the Department of State
Records of the Military Government of Cuba
Periodicals, Cuba
  *Albores: Revista Cubana Ilustrada*, Camagüey
  *Bohemia*, Havana
  *Boletín de organización: órgano official de la Federacion de Trabjadores de
    la Habana*, Havana
  *Carga. Órgano Oficial del Sindicato General de Obreros y Dependientes
    de Almacenes, sus Anexos y Similares de la Habana*, Havana
  *Diario de Cuba*, Santiago de Cuba
  *Diario de la Marina*, Havana
  *El Avance Criollo*, Santiago de Cuba
  *Granma*, Havana
  *Información*, Havana
  *Juventud Rebelde,* Havana.
  *La Higiene*, Havana
  *La Política Cómica*, Havana
  *La Voz Obrera*, Santiago de Cuba
  *Mujeres*, Havana, www.mujeres.cu/gen_art.php?MQ==
  *Noticias de Hoy*, Havana
  *Revista Económica*, Havana
  *Revista de la Asociación Feminina de Camgüey*, Camagüey
  *Revolución*, Havana
Periodicals, United States
  *The Crisis*
  *Life*
  *Miami Herald*
  *Monthly Labor Review*
  *The New York Times*
  *North American Congress on Latin America*
  *T Magazine*
Tamiment Library and Robert F. Wager Labor Archives, New York University,
  New York, New York
  New Leader Collection of Letters from Cuba
University of Illinois Urbana-Champaign, Urbana-Champaign, Illinois
  Oscar and Ruth Lewis Papers


FILMS

Weisman, Jean and Belkis Vega. "From Maids to Compañeras." City University
  of New York Caribbean Exchange Program, 1998. Videocassette (VHS)


PUBLISHED SOURCES

Alfonso, Dr. Ramón M. La prostitución en Cuba y especialmente en La Habana:
  memoria de la Comisión de Higiene Especial de la Isla de Cuba elevada al

Secretario de Gobernación cumpliendo un precepto reglamentario. Havana: Comisión de Higiene Especial, 1902.

Manumision Económica de la Mujer Cubana: necesidad y medios de obtenerla. Villaclara: Imp. Y Papelería "El Iris," 1903.

Ally, Shireen. *From Servants to Workers: South African Domestic Workers and the Democratic State.* Ithaca, NY: Cornell University Press, 2009.

Andaya, Elise. *Conceiving Cuba: Reproduction, Women, and the State in the Post-Soviet Era.* New Brunswick, NJ: Rutgers University Press, 2014.

"Reproducing the Revolution: Gender, Kinship and the State in Contemporary Cuba." Ph.D. diss., New York University. Ann Arbor, MI: UMI, 2007.

Applebaum, Nancy P., Anne S. Macpherson, and Karin Alejandra Rosenblatt, eds. *Race and Nation in Modern Latin America.* Chapel Hill: University of North Carolina Press, 2003.

Baldacci, Alexis. "Consumer Culture and Everyday Life in Revolutionary Cuba, 1971–1986." Ph.D. diss., University of Florida Press, 2018.

Barcia Zequeira, María del Carmen. *Oficios de mujer. Parteras, nodrizas y "amigas": Servicios públicos en espacios privados (siglo XVII–siglo XIX).* Santiago de Cuba: Instituto Cubano del Libro Editorial Oriente, 2015.

Barragán, Yesenia. The Free Womb Project, https://thefreewombproject.com/.

Beattie, Peter M. *The Tribute of Blood: Army, Honor, Race, and Nation in Brazil, 1864–1945.* Durham, NC: Duke University Press, 2001.

Bederman, Gail. *Manliness and Civilization: A Cultural History of Gender and Race in the United States, 1880–1917.* Chicago: University of Chicago Press, 1995.

Behar, Ruth. "Honeymoon Nightgowns that a Black Woman Saved for a White Woman: A Perilous Journey into the Cuban Historical Imagination." *American Studies* 40, no. 2/3 (Summer 2000): 287–302.

Bentancourt, Juan Rene. *El Negro: Ciudadano del futuro.* Havana: Cardenas, 1959.

Bliss, Katherine. *Compromised Positions: Prostitution, Public Health, and Gender Politics in Revolutionary Mexico City.* University Park: Pennsylvania State University Press, 2001.

Borges, Milo A. *Compilación ordenada y complete de la legislación cubana (1899–1934).* Havana: Cultural S. A., 1940.

Boris, Eileen, and Premilla Nadasen. "Introduction: Historicizing Domestic Workers' Resistance and Organizing." *International Labour and Working Class History* 88 (October 2015): 4–10.

Briggs, Laura. *How All Politics Became Reproductive Politics: From Welfare Reform to Trump.* Oakland: University of California Press, 2017.

Brimmer, Brandi C. "Black Women's Politics, Narratives of Sexual Immorality, and Pension Bureaucracy in Mary Lee's North Carolina Neighborhood." *The Journal of Southern History* 80, no. 4 (November 2014): 827–858.

Bronfman, Alejandra. *Measures of Equality: Social Science, Citizenship, and Race in Cuba, 1902–1940.* Chapel Hill: University of North Carolina Press, 2004.

Brunson, Takkara. "Constructing Afro-Cuban Womanhood: Race, Gender, and Citizenship in Republican-Era Cuba, 1902–1958." Ph.D. diss., University of Texas at Austin, 2011.

Bustamante, Michael J. "Anti-Communist Anti-Imperialism? Agrupación Abdala and the Shifting Contours of Cuban Exile Politics, 1968–1986." *Journal of American Ethnic History* 35, no. 1 (Fall 2015): 71–99.

*Cuban Memory Wars: Retrospective Politics in Revolution and Exile.* Chapel Hill: University of North Carolina Press, 2021.

Calella Sanz, Miguel G. *Derecho del Trabajo en la República de Cuba.* Havana: Ediciones de la Revista "Indice," 1946.

*La Jornada del Trabajo y los descansos.* Havana: Imprenta "El Score," 1937.

Carr, Barry. "Mill Occupations and Soviets: The Mobilisation of Sugar Workers in Cuba 1917–1933." *Journal of Latin American Studies* 28, no. 1 (February 1996): 129–158.

Casanovas, Joan. *Bread, or Bullets! Urban Labor and Spanish Colonialism in Cuba, 1850–1898.* Pittsburgh, PA: University of Pittsburgh Press, 1998.

Casey, Matthew. *Empire's Guest Workers: Haitian Migrants in Cuba during the Age of U.S. Occupation.* Cambridge: Cambridge University Press, 2017.

Castillo Bueno, María de los Reyes, and Daisy Rubiera Castillo. *Reyita: The Life of a Black Cuban Woman in the Twentieth Century.* Translated by Anne McLean. Durham, NC: Duke University Press, 2000. Originally published 1997.

Caulfield, SueAnn. "The History of Gender in the Historiography of Latin America." *Hispanic American Historical Review* 81, no. 3–4 (August 2001): 449–490.

*In Defense of Honor: Sexual Morality, Modernity, and Nation in Early-Twentieth-Century Brazil.* Durham, NC: Duke University Press, 2000.

Chaney, Elsa M., and Mary Garcia Castro, eds. *Muchachas No More: Household Workers in Latin America and the Caribbean.* Philadelphia: Temple University Press, 1989.

Chase, Michelle. *Revolution within the Revolution: Women and Gender Politics in Cuba, 1952–1962.* Chapel Hill: University of North Carolina Press, 2015.

Chira, Adriana. "Affective Debts: Manumission by Grace and the Making of Gradual Emancipation Laws in Cuba, 1817–68." *Law and History Review* 36, no. 1 (February 2018): 1–33.

*Código Civil. Hecho Extensivo a Cuba por R.D. de 31 de julio de 1889.* Tercera Edición: Jesus Montero, 1956.

Comallonga, J. y María de los A. Ortiz. *Tratado de Enseñanza Domestica y Agricola.* Havana: Impreta Montalvo y Cardenas, 1918.

Comisión Nacional Codificadora. *Proyecto del código del trabajo.* Havana: Imprenta "El Siglo XX," 1925.

Commission on Cuban Affairs. *Problems of the New Cuba.* New York: Foreign Policy Association, Inc., 1935.

Connolly, N. B. D. *A World More Concrete: Real Estate and the Remaking of Jim Crow South Florida.* Chicago: University of Chicago Press, 2014.

Cowling, Camilia. *Conceiving Freedom: Women of Color, Gender, and the Abolition of Slavery in Havana and Rio de Janeiro.* Chapel Hill: University of North Carolina Press, 2013.

Cuba. *Censo de población. Estadísticas industrial y Agrícola de Cuba–1931.* Havana: Editorial Luz-Hilo, 1939.

Davey, Richard. *Cuba Past and Present*. London: Chapman & Hall, 1898.

de la Fuente, Alejandro. *A Nation for All: Race, Inequality, and Politics in Twentieth-Century Cuba*. Chapel Hill: University of North Carolina Press, 2001.

"Two Dangers, One Solution: Immigration, Race and Labor in Working-Class Cuba, 1900–1930." *International Labor and Working-Class History* no. 51 (Spring 1997): 30–49.

Dias, Maria Odila Silva. *Power and Everyday Life: The Lives of Working Women in Nineteenth-Century Brazil*. Translated by Ann Frost. New Brunswick, NJ: Rutgers University Press, 1995.

Díaz Castañon, Maria del Pilar. *Ideología y revolución: Cuba, 1959–1962*. Havana: Editorial de Ciencias Sociales, 2001.

Dore, Elizabeth, and Maxine Molyneux. *Hidden Histories of Gender and the State in Latin America*. Durham, NC: Duke University Press, 2000.

Eire, Carlos. *Waiting for Snow in Havana: Confessions of a Cuban Boy*. New York: The Free Press, 2003.

Elena, Eduardo. *Dignifying Argentina: Peronism, Citizenship, and Mass Consumption*. Pittsburgh, PA: University of Pittsburgh Press, 2011.

Ernestina. *El ama de casa: resumen de las cualidades y conocimientos necesarios a la mujer en sus funciones practices de ama de casa*. Havana: Biblioteca del Diario de la Familia, 1906.

Farnsworth-Alvear, Ann. *Dulcinea in the Factory: Myths, Morals, Men, and Women in Colombia's Industrial Experiment, 1905–1960*. Durham, NC: Duke University Press, 2000.

Fernández-Silva, Adriana, and Patricio Uribasterra. Interview with Adriana Fernández-Silva, January 29, 2010. CHC, University of Miami Digital Collection, https://umiami.mediaspace.kaltura.com/media/Interview+with+Adriana+Fernandez-Silva/0_am84m1fs/30433711.

Ferrer, Ada. *Insurgent Cuba: Race, Nation and Revolution, 1868–1898*. Chapel Hill: University of North Carolina Press, 1999.

"Rustic Men, Civilized Nation: Race, Culture and Contention on the Eve of Cuban Independence." *Hispanic American Historical Review* 78, no. 4 (1998): 663–686.

Finch, Aisha. *Rethinking Slave Rebellion in Cuba: La Escalera and the Insurgencies of 1841–1844*. Chapel Hill: University of North Carolina Press, 2015.

Findlay, Eileen. *Imposing Decency: The Politics of Sexuality and Race in Puerto Rico, 1870–1920*. Durham, NC: Duke University Press, 1999.

François, Marie Eileen. "The Products of Consumption: Housework in Latin American Political Economies and Cultures." *History Compass* 6, no. 1 (2008): 207–242.

Franklin, Sarah L. *Women and Slavery in Nineteenth-Century Colonial Cuba*. Rochester, NY: University of Rochester Press, 2012.

French, John D., and Daniel James, eds. *The Gendered World of Latin American Women Workers: From Household and Factory to the Union Hall and Ballot Box*. Durham, NC: Duke University Press, 1997.

Fuentes, Marisa. *Dispossessed Lives: Enslaved Women, Violence, and the Archive*. Philadelphia: University of Pennsylvania Press, 2016.

Gallenga, Antonio Carlo Napoleone. *The Pearl of the Antilles*. London: Chapman and Hall, 1873.

García, Pedro, and Felipe Velasco. *Pícaros y rameras; su vida y malas costumbres*. Havana: n. p., 1913.

Gill, Lesley. *Precarious Dependencies: Gender, Class, and Domestic Service in Bolivia*. New York: Columbia University Press, 1994.

Glenn, Evelyn Nakano. "From Servitude to Service Work: Historical Continuities in the Racial Division of Paid Reproductive Labor." *Signs* 18, no. 1 (1992): 1–43.

Glymph, Thavolia. *Out of the House of Bondage: The Transformation of the Plantation Household*. Durham, NC: Duke University Press, 2011.

Gobierno General de la isla de Cuba. *Reglamento y cartilla para la organización del servicio doméstico en esta isla*. Puerto Príncipe: Imprenta "El Fomento," 1889.

Gomes da Cunha, Olivia. "Learning to Serve: Intimacy, Morality, and Violence." Translated by Micol Seigel. *Hispanic American Historical Review* 88, no. 3 (2008): 455–491.

Gotkowitz, Laura. *A Revolution for Our Rights: Indigenous Struggle for Land and Justice in Bolivia, 1880–1952*. Durham, NC: Duke University Press, 2007.

Guerra, Lillian. "Former Slum Dwellers, the Communist Youth, and the Lewis Project in Cuba, 1969–1971." *Cuban Studies* 43 (2015): 67–89.

*Heroes, Martyrs, and Political Messiahs in Revolutionary Cuba, 1946–1958*. New Haven, CT: Yale University Press, 2018.

*Visions of Power in Cuba: Revolution, Redemption, and Resistance, 1959–1971*. Chapel Hill: University of North Carolina Press, 2012.

Guerra, Wendy. *Revolution Sunday*. Translated by Achy Obejas. Brooklyn, NY: Melville House Publishing, 2018.

Guridy, Frank. *Forging Diaspora: Afro-Cubans and African-Americans in a World of Empire and Jim Crow*. Chapel Hill: University of North Carolina Press, 2010.

Guy, Donna. "Girls in Prison: The Role of the Buenos Aires Casa Correccional de Mujeres as an Institution for Child Rescue, 1890–1940." In *Crime and Punishment in Latin America: Law and Society in Late Colonial Times*, edited by Ricardo D. Salvatore, Carlos Aguirre, and Gilbert M. Joseph, 369–390. Durham, NC: Duke University Press, 2001.

Hamilton, Carrie. *Sexual Revolutions in Cuba: Passion, Politics, and Memory*. Chapel Hill: University of North Carolina Press, 2012.

Hansen, Karen Tranberg. *Distant Companions: Servants and Employers in Zambia, 1900–1985*. Ithaca, NY: Cornell University Press, 1989.

"Household Work as a Man's Job: Sex and Gender in Domestic Service in Zambia." *Anthropology Today* 2, no. 3 (June 1986): 18–23.

Hart Phillips, R. *Cuban Sideshow*. Havana: Cuban Press, 1935.

Hartman, Saidiya. *Wayward Lives, Beautiful Experiments: Intimate Histories of Riotous Black Girls, Troublesome Women, and Queer Radicals*. New York: W. W. Norton & Company, 2019.

Helg, Aline. *Our Rightful Share: The Afro-Cuban Struggle for Equality, 1886–1912*. Chapel Hill: University of North Carolina Press, 1995.

Henderson, Kaitlyn. "Black Activism in the Red Party: Black Politics and the Cuban Communist Party, 1925–1962." Ph.D. diss., Tulane University, 2018.

Hernández Guasch, Zaylin. "Las relaciones de servidumbre en el servicio doméstico habanero desde finales de los años cuarenta hasta 1959." *Perfiles de la cultura cubana* 8 (enero-junio 2012), http://www.perfiles.cult.cu/index .php?r=site/articulo&id=261.

*Religiosas de María Inmaculada al servicio de la Iglesia y la juventud en Cuba.* Havana: Religiosas de María Inmaculada, 2015.

Hevia Lanier, Oilda, ed. *Emergiendo del silencio: mujeres negras en la historia de Cuba.* Havana: Editorial de Ciencias Sociales, 2016.

Hewitt, Steven. "Republican Ideas and the Reality of Patronage: A Study of the Veterans' Movement in Cuba." Ph.D. diss., University of Wolverhampton, 2009.

Hidalgo, Sara. "The Making of a 'Simple Domestic': Domestic Workers, the Supreme Court, and the Law in Postrevolutionary Mexico." *International and Working-Class History* 94 (Fall 2018): 55–79.

Holston, James. "The Misrule of Law: Land and Usurpation in Brazil." *Comparative Studies in History and Society* 33, no. 4 (October 1991): 695–725.

Hunter, Tera. *To 'Joy My Freedom: Black Women's Lives and Labors after the Civil War.* Cambridge, MA: Harvard University Press, 1997.

Hutchison, Elizabeth Quay. "Shifting Solidarities: The Politics of Household Workers in Cold War Chile." *Hispanic American Historical Review* 91, no. 1 (2011): 129–162.

Hynson, Rachel. "'Count, Capture, and Reeducate': The Campaign to Rehabilitate Cuba's Female Sex Workers, 1959–1966." *Journal of the History of Sexuality* 24, no. 1 (2015): 125–153.

"Sex and State Making in Revolutionary Cuba, 1959–1969." Ph.D. diss., University of North Carolina at Chapel Hill, 2014.

Izquierdo, Elena Gil. "La Educación de las Domésticas: Una Agudización de la Lucha de Clases," University of Florida document, undated.

James, C. L. R. *The Black Jacobins: Toussaint L'Ouverture and the San Domingo Revolution.* New York: Vintage, 1989.

James, Daniel. *Doña María's Story: Life History, Memory, and Political Identity.* Durham, NC: Duke University Press, 2000.

Jelin, Elizabeth. "Migration and Labor Force Participation of Latin American Women: The Domestic Servants in the Cities." *Signs* 3, no. 1 (1977): 129–141.

Johnson, Lyman L., and Sonya Lipsett-Rivera, eds. *The Faces of Honor: Sex, Shame, and Violence in Colonial Latin America.* Albuquerque: University of New Mexico Press, 2001.

Johnson, Michelle A. "'Decent and Fair': Aspects of Domestic Service in Jamaica, 1920–1970." *Journal of Caribbean History* 30, no. 1/2 (1996): 83–106.

Joseph, Gilbert M., and Daniel Nugent, eds. *Everyday Forms of State Formation: Revolution and the Negotiation of Rule in Modern Mexico.* Durham, NC: Duke University Press, 1994.

Kaplan, Dana Evan. "Fleeing the Revolution: The Exodus of Cuban Jewry in the Early 1960s." *Cuban Studies* (2005): 129–154.

Kozameh, Sara. "Harvest of Revolution: Agrarian Reform and the Making of Revolutionary Cuba, 1958–1970." Ph.D. diss., New York University, 2020.

Kozol, Jonathan. *Children of the Revolution: A Yankee Teacher in the Cuban Schools*. New York: Delacourte Press, 1978.

Lafuente Salvador, Mireya. *Recuerdos*. San Diego, CA: Del Sol Publishing, 2005.

Lambe, Jennifer L. *Madhouse: Psychiatry and Politics in Cuban History*. Chapel Hill: University of North Carolina Press, 2017.

Lauderdale Graham, Sandra. *House and Street: The Domestic World of Servants and Masters in Nineteenth-Century Rio de Janeiro*. Austin: University of Texas Press, 1992.

Leiner, Marvin. *Children Are the Revolution: Daycare in Cuba*. New York: Viking Press, 1974.

Lewis, Oscar, Ruth M. Lewis, and Susan Rigdon. *Four Women Living the Revolution: An Oral History of Contemporary Cuba*. Urbana: University of Illinois Press, 1977.

Lindsey, Lisa A. "Domesticity and Difference: Male Breadwinners, Working Women, and Colonial Citizenship in the 1945 Nigerian General Strike." *American Historical Review* 104, no. 3 (June 1999): 783–812.

Lockwood, Lee. *Castro's Cuba, Cuba's Fidel*. New York: Vintage, 1969.

López, A. Ricardo, and Barbara Weinstein, eds. *The Making of the Middle Class: Towards a Transnational History*. Durham, NC: Duke University Press, 2012.

López, Kathleen. *Cubans: A Transnational History*. Chapel Hill: University of North Carolina Press, 2013.

Lucero, Bonnie A. *Revolutionary Masculinity and Racial Inequality: Gendering War and Politics in Cuba, 1895–1902*. Albuquerque: University of New Mexico Press, 2018.

Mallon, Florencia. "The Promise and Dilemma of Subaltern Studies: Perspectives from Latin American History." *American Historical Review* 99, no. 5 (1994): 1491–1515.

Marko, Tamera. "A Wet Nurse, Her Masters, a Folkhealer, a Pediatrician, and Two Babies: Negotiation of a 'Raceless' Motherhood Ideal and Cultural Legacy of Slavery in 1880 Rio de Janeiro." *CILAS Working Paper* 21 (July 2004): 49–79.

Matthews, Franklin. *The New-Born Cuba*. New York: Harper & Bros., 1899.

Masdeu, Jesús. *La Gallega*. Havana: Casa Editora El Dante, 1927.

*La raza triste*. Havana: Imprenta y Papelería Rambla y Bouza, 1924.

May, Vanessa. *Unprotected Labor: Household Workers, Politics, and Middle-Class Reform in New York, 1870–1940*. Chapel Hill: University of North Carolina Press, 2011.

McCleod, Marc Christian. "Undesirable Aliens: Haitian and British West Indian Immigrant Workers in Cuba, 1898 to 1940." Ph.D. diss., University of Texas at Austin, 2000.

McClintock, Anne. *Imperial Leather: Race, Gender, and Sexuality in the Colonial Contest*. New York: Routledge, 1995.

McElya, Micki. *Clinging to Mammy: The Faithful Slave in Twentieth-Century America*. Cambridge, MA: Harvard University Press, 2007.

McHatton-Ripley, Eliza. *From Flag to Flag: A Woman's Adventures and Experiences in the South during the War, in Mexico, and in Cuba.* UK: Dodo Press, 1888.

Méndez Capote, Reneé. *Memorias de una cubanita que nació con el siglo.* Barcelona: Arcos Vergara, 1984.

Milanesio, Natalia. "Redefining Men's Sexuality, Re-Signifying Male Bodies: The Argentine Law of Anti-venereal Prophylaxis, 1936." *Gender & History* 17, no. 2 (August 2005): 463–491.

Milanich, Nara. *Children of Fate: Childhood, Class, and the State in Chile, 1850–1930.* Durham, NC: Duke University Press, 2009.

"Women, Children, and the Social Organization of Domestic Labor in Chile." *Hispanic American Historical Review* 91, no. 1 (2011): 32.

Ministerio de Agricultura, Dirección de Enseñanza y Propoganda Agrícolas. *Homenaje a la Mujer Campesina en la exposición de trabajos de las Misiones Rurales de Superación del Bohío.* Havana: Fernández y Cía Impresores, 1952.

Mitchell, Michele. *Righteous Propagation: African Americans and the Politics of Racial Destiny after Reconstruction.* Chapel Hill: University of North Carolina Press, 2004.

Montejo, Esteban, and Miguel Barnet. *Biografía de un cimarrón.* Havana: Artex, 2014. Originally published in 1966.

Morgan, Jennifer. "'Some Could Suckle over Their Shoulder': Male Travelers, Female Bodies, and the Gendering of Racial Ideology, 1500–1770." *William and Mary Quarterly* 54, no. 1 (January 1997): 167–192.

Moya, José C. "Domestic Service in a Global Perspective: Gender, Migration, and Ethnic Niches." *Journal of Ethnic and Migration Studies* 33, no. 4 (2007): 559–579.

Nadasen, Premilla. *Household Workers Unite: The Untold Story of African American Women Who Built a Movement.* New York: Beacon Press, 2016.

Navarro Vega, Armando. *Cuba, el socialism y sus éxodos.* Bloomington, IN: Palibrio, 2013.

Nelson, Lowry. *Rural Cuba.* Minneapolis: University of Minnesota Press, 1950.

Novás Calvo, Lino. *La luna nona y otoros cuentos.* Buenos Aires: Imprenta Patagonia, 1942.

Olcott, Jocelyn. "Introduction: Researching and Rethinking the Labors of Love." *Hispanic American Historical Review* 91, no. 1 (2011): 1–27.

*Revolutionary Women in Postrevolutionary Mexico.* Durham, NC: Duke University Press, 2005.

Olmstead, Victor H., director. *Censo de la república de Cuba bajo la administración provisional de los Estados Unidos, 1907.* Washington, DC: Oficina del Censo de los Estados Unidos, 1908.

*Cuba: Population, History and Resources, 1907.* Washington, DC: United States Bureau of the Census, 1909.

Ortiz, Fernando. *Los negros esclavos.* Havana: Editorial de Ciencias Sociales, 1975. Originally published in 1916.

Otovo, Okezi T. *Progressive Mothers, Better Babies: Race, Public Health, and the State in Brazil, 1850–1945.* Austin: University of Texas Press, 2016.

Padrón Valdés, Abelardo H. *Quintín Bandera: General de Tres Guerras.* Havana: Editorial de Ciencias Sociales, 2006.

Padula, Alfred L. "The Fall of the Bourgeoisie: Cuba, 1959–1961." Ph.D. diss., University of New Mexico, 1974, 537.

Pagés, Julio César González. *En busca de un espacio: Historia de mujeres en Cuba.* Havana: Instituto Cubano del Libro, 2003.

Pappademos, Melina. *Envisioning Cuba: Black Political Activism and the Cuban Republic.* Chapel Hill: University of North Carolina Press, 2011.

Pariser, Robyn. "Masculinity and Organized Resistance in Domestic Service in Colonial Dar es Salaam, 1919–1961." *International Labor and Working-Class History* 88 (Fall 2015): 109–129.

Parker, David S. *Latin America's Middle Class: Unsettled Debates and New Histories.* New York: Lexington Books, 2012.

Parreñas, Rhacel, and Eileen Boris. *Intimate Labors: Cultures, Technologies, and the Politics of Care.* Stanford, CA: Stanford University Press, 2010.

Pérez, Louis A., Jr. *Cuba: Between Reform and Revolution.* Oxford: Oxford University Press, 2011.

*Cuba in the American Imagination: Metaphor and the Imperial Ethos.* Chapel Hill: University of North Carolina Press, 2008.

*On Becoming Cuban. Identity, Nationality, and Culture.* Chapel Hill: University of North Carolina Press, 1999.

Pérez-Firmat, Gustavo. *Next Year in Cuba: A Cubano's Coming-of-Age in America.* Houston, TX: Arte Público Press, 2006.

Pérez-Sarduy, Pedro. *The Maids of Havana.* Translated by Jonathan Curry-Machado. Bloomington, IN: AuthorHouse, 2010.

Ponte, Antonio José. "We Have No Recipes for the Food of the Future." *E-Misférica* 12, no. 1 (2015), https://hemisphericinstitute.org/en/emisferica-121-caribbean-rasanblaj/12-1-essays/e-121-essay-ponte-no-tenemos-recetas.html.

Porter, Susie S. *Working Women in Mexico City: Public Discourses and Material Conditions, 1879–1931.* Tucson: University of Arizona Press, 2003.

Premo, Bianca. "'Misunderstood Love': Children and Wet Nurses, Creoles and Kings in Lima's Enlightenment." *Colonial Latin American Review* 14, no. 2 (December 2005): 231–261.

Proctor, Frank "Trey," III. "Gender and the Manumission of Slaves in New Spain." *Hispanic American Historical Review* 86, no. 13 (2006): 309–336.

Putnam, Lara. *The Company They Kept: Migrants and the Politics of Gender in Caribbean Costa Rica, 1870–1960.* Chapel Hill: University of North Carolina Press, 2002.

Randall, Margaret. *Mujeres en la revolución.* Mexico City: Siglo XXI Editores S. A., 1972.

Ray, Raka, and Seemin Quayum. *Cultures of Servitude: Modernity, Domesticity, and Class in India.* Stanford, CA: Stanford University Press, 2009.

Red Cross (Cuba). *La Cruz Roja en Cuba.* Washington, DC, 1900.

Republic of Cuba. *Census of the Republic of Cuba, 1919.* Havana: Maza, Arroyo y Caso, 1919.

República de Cuba. *Censo de 1943.* Havana: Impresores Obispo, 1943.

Ricardo-López-Pederos, A., and Barbara Weinstein, eds. *The Making of the Middle Class: Toward a Transnational History.* Durham, NC: Duke University Press, 2012.

Rodríguez, Daniel. *The Right to Live in Health: Medical Politics in Postindependence Havana.* Chapel Hill: University of North Carolina Press, 2020.

"A Blessed Formula for Progress: The Politics of Health, Medicine and Welfare in Havana (1897–1935)." Ph.D. diss., New York University, 2013.

Romero, Mary A. *Maid in the U.S.A.* New York: Routledge Press, 1992.

Romero Almodóvar, Magela. "El Trabajo Doméstico Renumerado a Domicilio en Cuba: Un estudio de caso en Miramar." Tesis de doctorado, Universidad de la Habana. Havana: Editorial Universitario, 2017.

"Royal Decree and Instructional Circular for the Indies on the Regulation, Treatment and Work Regimen of Slaves. May 31, 1789." In *Voices of the Enslaved in Nineteenth-Century Cuba: A Documentary History,* edited by Gloria García Rodríguez, 47–54. Translated by Nancy L. Westrate. Chapel Hill: University of North Carolina Press, 2011.

Rubbo, Anna and Michael T. Taussig. "Up off Their Knees: Servanthood in Southwest Colombia." *Latin American Perspectives* 10, no. 4 (1983): 5–23.

Salvatore, Ricardo, Carlos Aguirre, and Gilbert Joseph, eds. *Crime and Punishment in Latin America: Law and Society since Late Colonial Times.* Durham, NC: Duke University Press, 2001.

Schwall, Elizabeth B. *Dancing with the Revolution: Power, Politics, and Privilege in Cuba.* Chapel Hill: University of North Carolina Press, 2021.

Scott, James. *Weapons of the Weak: Everyday Forms of Peasant Resistance.* New Haven, CT: Yale University Press, 1987.

Scott, Joan. "The 'Class' We Have Lost.'" *International and Working Class History* 57 (2000): 69–75.

"Gender: A Useful Category of Historical Analysis." *American Historical Review* 91, no. 5 (December 1986): 1053–1076.

Scott, Rebecca. "Defining the Boundaries of Freedom in the World of Cane: Cuba, Brazil, and Louisiana after Emancipation." *Hispanic American Historical Review* 99, no. 1 (February 1994): 70–102.

*Slave Emancipation in Cuba: The Transition to Free Labor, 1869–1899.* Princeton, NJ: Princeton University Press, 1985.

Scott, Rebecca, and Michael Zeuske. "Property in Writing, Property on the Ground: Pigs, Horses, Land, and Citizenship in the Aftermath of Slavery, Cuba, 1880–1909." *Comparative Studies in Society and History* 44, no. 4 (October 2002): 669–699.

Secades, Manuel. *Tesis: Leída, sostenida y aprobada el día 27 de mayo de 1902 en la Universidad de la Habana en los ejercicios del doctorado en derecho civil, y ampliada con estudios posteriores, y con las observaciones de los ilustrados catedráticos que formaban el tribunal.* Havana: Tipografía de "El Figaro," 1903.

Secretariado Económico Social de la Junta Nacional de Acción Católica Cubana. *Primer Catálogo de las obras sociales catolicas de Cuba.* Havana, 1953.

Seigel, Micol. *Uneven Encounters: Making Race and Nation in Brazil and the United States.* Durham, NC: Duke University Press, 2009.

Simkin, John. "Paul Bethel." Spartacus Educational, September 1997, https:// spartacus-educational.com/JFKbethelP.htm.

Sippial, Tiffany. *Prostitution, Modernity, and the Making of the Cuban Republic, 1840–1920.* Chapel Hill: University of North Carolina Press, 2013.

Skelly, Jack. *I Remember Cuba: Growing up Cuban-American, a Memoir of a Town Called Banes.* Morgan Hill, CA: Bookstand Publishing, 2006.

Sotelo Eastman, Alexander. "The Neglected Narratives of Cuba's Partido Independiente de Color: Civil Rights, Popular Politics, and Emancipatory Reading Practices." *The Americas* 76, no. 1 (2019), 41–76.

Spence-Benson, Devyn. *Antiracism in Cuba: The Unfinished Revolution.* Chapel Hill: University of North Carolina Press, 2016.

Steedman, Carolyn. *Labours Lost: Domestic Service and the Making of Modern England.* Cambridge: Cambridge University Press, 2009.

Stern, Steve. *Remembering Pinochet's Chile: On the Eve of London 1998.* Durham, NC: Duke University Press, 2004.

*The Secret History of Gender: Men, Women and Power in Late-Colonial Mexico.* Chapel Hill: University of North Carolina Press, 1995.

Stolcke, Verena. *Marriage, Class and Color in 19th-Century Cuba: A Study of Racial Attitudes and Sexual Values in a Slave Society.* Ann Arbor: University of Michigan Press, 1989.

Stoler, Ann Laura. *Along the Archival Grain: Epistemic Anxieties and Colonial Common Sense.* Princeton, NJ: Princeton University Press, 2009.

*Carnal Knowledge and Imperial Power: Race and the Intimate in Colonial Rule.* Berkeley: University of California Press, 2002.

Stoner, K. Lynn. *From the House to the Streets: The Cuban Women's Movement for Legal Reform, 1898–1940.* Durham, NC: Duke University Press, 1991.

"Ofelia Domínguez Navarro: The Making of a Cuban Socialist Feminist." In *The Human Tradition in Latin America: The Twentieth Century*, edited by William H. Beezley and Judith Bell, 119–140. Landham: SR Books, 1987.

Stubbs, Jean. "Social and Political Motherhood of Cuba: Mariana Grajales Cuello." In *Engendering History: Caribbean Women in Historical Perspective*, edited by Verene Shepherd, Bridget Brereton, and Barbara Bailey, 296–317. New York: St. Martin's Press, 1995.

Swanger, Joanna Beth. "Lands of Rebellion: Oriente and Escambray Encountering Cuban State Formation, 1934–1974." Ph.D. diss., University of Texas at Austin. Ann Arbor, MI: UMI, 1999.

*Rebel Lands of Cuba: The Campesino Struggles of Oriente and Escambray, 1934–1974.* Lanham, MD: Lexington Books, 2015.

Tinsman, Heidi. "The Indispensable Services of Sisters: Considering Domestic Service in the United States and Latin American Studies." *Journal of Women's History* 4, no. 1 (1992): 37–59.

*Partners in Conflict: The Politics of Gender, Sexuality, and Labor in the Chilean Agrarian Reform, 1950–1973.* Durham, NC: Duke University Press, 2002.

Trouillot, Michel-Rolph. *Silencing the Past: Power and the Production of History.* Boston: Beacon Press, 1995.

Twinam, Ann. *Public Lives, Private Secrets: Gender, Honor, Sexuality and Illegitimacy in Colonial Spanish America.* Stanford, CA: Stanford University Press, 2007.
United States Consular Reports. *Labor in America, Asia, Africa, Australia, and Polynesia.* Washington, DC: Government Printing Office, 1885.
United States War Department. *Censo de la república de Cuba bajo la administración provisional de los Estados Unidos, 1907.* Washington, DC: Oficina del censo de los Estados Unidos, 1908.
  *Report on the Census of Cuba, 1899.* Washington, DC: Government Printing Office, 1900.
Urban, Kelly. "The Sick Republic: Tuberculosis, Public Health, and Politics in Cuba, 1925–1965." Ph.D. diss., University of Pittsburgh, 2017.
Varona Socías, Jesmir. "Where Joaquín de Agüero Rests." Translated by José Carlos García Cruz. *Oficina del Historiador da la ciudad de Camagüey,* March 28, 2019, www.ohcamaguey.cu/en/where-joaquin-de-aguero-rests/.
Villaverdes, Cirilio. *Cecilia Valdés o la Loma del Angel.* Havana: Imprenta Literaria, 1839.
Wallace-Sanders, Kimberly. *Mammy: A Century of Race, Gender, and Southern Memory.* Ann Arbor: University of Michigan Press, 2008.
Weeks, Kathi. *The Problem with Work: Feminism, Marxism, Antiwork Politics, and Postwork Imaginaries.* Durham, NC: Duke University Press, 2011.
West, Emily, and R. J. Knight. "Mothers' Milk: Slavery, Wet-Nursing, and Black and White Women in the Antebellum South." *Journal of Southern History* 83, no. 1 (February 2017): 37–68.
Whitney, Robert. "The Architect of the Cuban State: Fulgencio Batista and Populism in Cuba, 1937–1940." *Journal of Latin American Studies* 32, no. 2 (May 2000): 435–459.
Zeuske, Michael. "Hidden Markers, Open Secrets: On Naming, Race-Marking, and Race-Making in Cuba." *New West Indian Guide* 76, no. 3 (2002): 211–242.

# Index